When We Dead Awaken

When We Dead Awaken

Australia, New Zealand, and the Armenian Genocide

James Robins

I.B. TAURIS
LONDON • NEW YORK • OXFORD • NEW DELHI • SYDNEY

I.B. TAURIS
Bloomsbury Publishing Plc
50 Bedford Square, London, WC1B 3DP, UK
1385 Broadway, New York, NY 10018, USA

BLOOMSBURY, I.B. TAURIS and the I.B. Tauris logo
are trademarks of Bloomsbury Publishing Plc

First published in Great Britain 2021

Copyright © James Robins, 2021

James Robins has asserted his right under the Copyright, Designs
and Patents Act, 1988, to be identified as Author of this work.

For legal purposes the Acknowledgements on p. xii constitute
an extension of this copyright page.

Cover image: Australasian Orphanage, Antelias. Courtesy of Missak Kelechian.

All rights reserved. No part of this publication may be reproduced or transmitted in
any form or by any means, electronic or mechanical, including photocopying,
recording, or any information storage or retrieval system, without prior permission in
writing from the publishers.

Bloomsbury Publishing Plc does not have any control over, or responsibility for,
any third-party websites referred to or in this book. All internet addresses given
in this book were correct at the time of going to press. The author and publisher
regret any inconvenience caused if addresses have changed or sites have
ceased to exist, but can accept no responsibility for any such changes.

A catalogue record for this book is available from the British Library.

A catalog record for this book is available from the Library of Congress.

ISBN:	HB:	978-1-8386-0749-4
	PB:	978-0-7556-0031-1
	ePDF:	978-1-8386-0750-0
	eBook:	978-1-8386-0751-7

Typeset by Integra Software Services Pvt. Ltd.
Printed and bound in Great Britain

To find out more about our authors and books visit www.bloomsbury.com
and sign up for our newsletters

For my mother.
With her, anything is possible.

Contents

List of Illustrations — viii
A note on nomenclature — xi
Acknowledgements — xii

An introduction: Long shadows — 1
1 Pro patria mori — 5
2 Common religion — 25
3 Halcyon days — 49
4 One day in April — 65
5 'Ashes within me, ashes around me' — 71
6 Ghosts — 89
7 'Of passions like our own …' — 105
8 The hush-hush brigade — 117
9 No justice, no peace — 131
10 The golden chain of mercy — 143
11 An old paper mill — 163
12 Paper Eichmanns — 179
A conclusion: Lying side by side — 195

Notes — 211
Bibliography — 244
Index — 254

List of Illustrations

1 The Ottoman Empire, circa 1919
 Credit: Photo by The Print Collector/The Print Collector/Getty Images xiii

Chapter 1

2 Istanbul
 Caption: 'A view of Beyoğlu, Istanbul in the late 19th century, through the eye of Armenian photographer M. Iranian'
 Credit: Suna and İnan Kıraç Foundation Photography Collection/Pera Müzesi 9
3 Armenian victims in Erzerum in 1895
 Caption: 'Child victims of the Hamidian Terror in Erzerum, 1895'
 Credit: William Lewis Sachtleben Collection, UCLA 20

Chapter 2

4 Talat
 Caption: 'Mehmed Talât: "within him, there is a subdued daemonic temper chained up…"'
 Credit: George Grantham Bain Collection/Library of Congress 28
5 Enver
 Caption: 'Ismail Enver, the bellicose generalissimo'
 Credit: AGBU Nubar Library, Paris 30
6 Zohrab
 Caption: '"Between truth and falsehood, choose truth": Krikor Zohrab'
 Credit: AGBU Nubar Library, Paris 32
7 Yesayan
 Caption: 'The young prodigy Zabel Yesayan'
 Credit: Yerevan Museum of Literature and Arts 38

Chapter 3

8 Anzac troopship
 Caption: 'They went like kings in a pageant to their imminent death…'
 Credit: Australian War Memorial 63

Chapter 5

9   Bodies
    Caption: 'Panos Terlemezian, *A Mother Looking for Her Son among the Corpses*, undated'
    Credit: National Gallery of Armenia (Oil on canvas, 40 x 32.5 cm)   74
10 Deportation
    Caption: '"Living martyrs, every day dying a few deaths and returning to life again."'
    Credit: Laurence MacDaniels papers, Cornell University Library   76
11 Killing Fields
    Caption: 'Killing Fields'
    Credit: Laurence MacDaniels papers, Cornell University Library   79
12 Camps
    Caption: 'The Camps'
    Credit: Armin T Wegner   86

Chapter 6

13 White and Luscombe
    Caption: 'Anzacs outside their Armenian homes in Afion: Thomas Walter White and Leslie Luscombe'
    Credit: Australian War Memorial   99
14 Edward Mousley
    Caption: 'Edward Opotiki Mousley'
    Credit: Printed in Edward Opotiki Mousley, *The Secrets of a Kuttite: An Authentic Story of Kut, Adventures in Captivity and Stamboul Intrigue*, London: John Lane, 1922   101

Chapter 8

15 Robert Nicol
    Caption: '"I've been up to the Palace": Robert Nicol'
    Credit: unknown   122
16 Stanley Savige
    Caption: '"We were forced to leave them to their fate": Stanley Savige'
    Credit: Australian War Memorial   125

Chapter 10

17 Mustafa Kemal
    Caption: 'Mustafa Kemal, hero of Gallipoli'
    Credit: Printed in Rafael de Nogales, *Four Years Beneath the Crescent*,
    New York: Charles Scribner's Sons, 1926   144
18 Loyal Lincoln Wirt
    Caption: 'Reverend Loyal Lincoln Wirt'
    Credit: Evan Wirt and Family   151
19 Australian Flour
    Caption: '"Anzac Bread!" The *Hobson's Bay* departs Princes Pier,
    Melbourne'
    Credit: Evan Wirt and Family   156
20 Charles Dobson
    Caption: 'Charles Dobson'
    Credit: Tyree Studio Collection/Nelson Provincial Museum   157
21 Izmir
    Caption: '"Just one sheet of flame…getting more terrible all the time":
    HMS *Iron Duke* in the foreground as Izmir burns'
    Credit: *London Illustrated News*/Mary Evans Picture Library   160

Chapter 11

22 Antelias
    Caption: 'The completed orphanage, as viewed from the beach'
    Credit: Missak Kelechian Collection   165
23 Lydia and Hilda
    Caption: 'Lydia Knudsen (L) and Hilda King with a young orphan'
    Credit: Missak Kelechian Collection   167
24 James Cresswell
    Caption: 'In the dorms, James Cresswell (standing) inspects donated
    blankets with (L–R) Lydia Knudsen, Hilda King, and John Knudsen'
    Credit: Missak Kelechian Collection   172

Conclusion

25 Mustafa Kemal & Şükrü Kaya
    Caption: 'Mustafa Kemal (L) with Şükrü Kaya in 1927'
    Credit: unknown   201

A note on nomenclature

Throughout this work, modern place names are used: Istanbul rather than Constantinople, İzmir instead of Smyrna, Tbilisi over Tiflis and so on. 'Eastern Anatolia' or 'the Six Provinces' are more frequently deployed than the contemporaneous 'Western Armenia'. This is not for any political purpose, and I do not wish to obscure disputes, as with the renaming of Diyarbekir to Diyarbakır. Rather the goal is to ease the burden on the reader, to not clutter up the page, or the narrative, with parentheses.

For Armenian names, I have mostly used D-K-I-B spellings over T-G-Y-P formulations. For Turkish, the below guide should be helpful to those unfamiliar with the language and its phonetics.

> C or c sounds like j as in juice, jewel, joint
> Ç or ç sounds like ch: cheek, chain, chew
> Ş and ş is a sh sound: sheep, shine, shower
> Ğ and ğ lengthens the preceding vowel, almost silent (Erdo-an for Erdoğan)
> İ with a dot is elongated, like eel
> I or ı without a dot is more abrupt, as in the first syllable of earnest
> Ö and ö as with the German umlaut, the ur sound in nurse or purse
> Ü and ü are rounded, like tube or sue
> The circumflex ^ extends a vowel sound. Talât is sounded as Talaat

Acknowledgements

Simply put, *When We Dead Awaken* would not be possible without the rigorous, groundbreaking and essential research done by Vicken Babkenian. For the framework of my argument, and for individual sources, for my constant hounding notes and questions – in short, for everything – I am forever in his debt. Maria Armoudian has been a forthright, sympathetic and incredibly supportive mentor. She first introduced me – along with Dr Panayiotis Diamadis – to this topic on a rainy Tuesday night years ago, and has been in my corner ever since. Her intelligence, insight, dedication and honesty are constantly inspiring.

Special thanks are also due to Copyright Licensing New Zealand, who through their Research Grant scheme, provided a generous sum to allow me to pursue some of the most critical archival work in this project. Furthermore, the National Association for Armenian Studies and Research and the University of Auckland/Te Whare Wānanga o Tāmaki Makaurau have been just as charitable, allowing for the equally important surveying of New Zealand and Australian newspaper records – without which this text would be significantly poorer.

For sharing Desmond Hurley's manuscript, my sincere gratefulness goes to the Hurley family. It is privilege to be airing some of his research for the first time, and I hope one day to see that bountiful manuscript in print. Similar thanks go to the Wirt and Knudsen families, for sharing their photographs and stories, as well as Missak Kelechian for providing these astounding pictures of the Australasian Orphanage.

At Bloomsbury, my thanks are due first to Tomasz Hoskins for lobbying to get this book published, and to Nayiri Kendir for having to put up with my incessant pestering. My gratitude also to Giles Herman, Gogulanathan Bactavatchalane, Viswasirasini Govindarajan, and the team at Integra.

My thanks, in no particular order of preference, also go to: Peter Stanley, Vahram Ter-Matevosyan, Taner Akçam, Bedross Der Matossian, Harutyun Marutyan, Edita Gzoyan, Peter Balakian, Auguste Okosdinossian, Tony Wright, Alex Braae, James Snell, Madeleine Farman and Oscar Featherstone, Samuel Denny, Gordon McLauchlan, Chris Reed, the Nimmo family, Ryan Holder, Russell Baillie, Pamela Stirling, Haig Kayserian, Hoory Karnik Yeldizian.

Above all, for tolerating so many lamplit late nights, for bearing my exasperation and complaints, and for such exquisite editing, my ceaseless gratitude will have to be paid out, my beloved Sophie, over a lifetime.

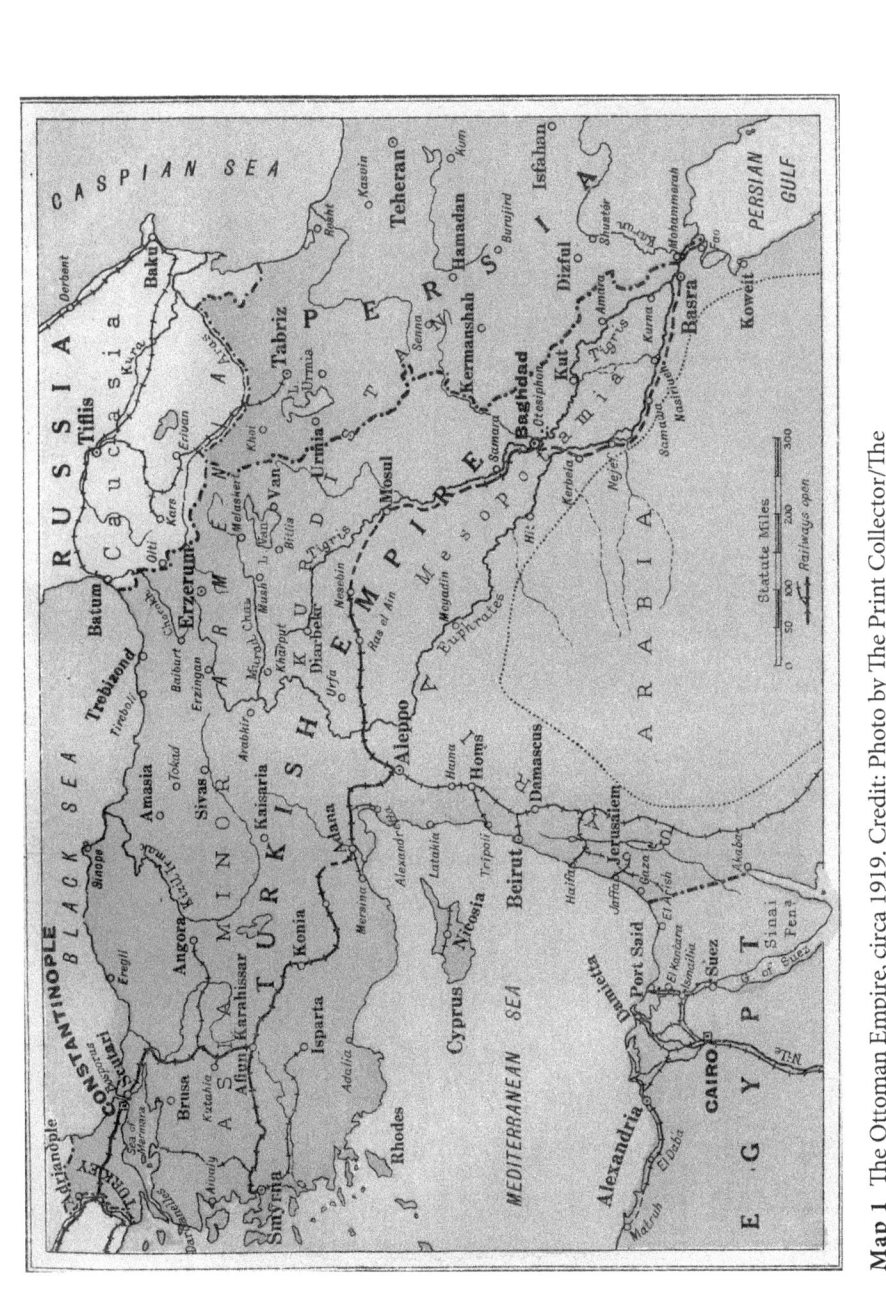

Map 1 The Ottoman Empire, circa 1919. Credit: Photo by The Print Collector/The Print Collector/Getty Images

An introduction
Long shadows

A blue dawn broke over the hush, new light disputing the cool wash of lamp glow. Amidst the gathered thousands, drowsy, uncomprehending children wiped sleep from their eyes. In chill morning's still apprehension, lapel-pinned poppies did not flutter. From the wan collage of faces, a dull glint of proud polished medallions, splinters of handed-down ribbon, the strong jutted chin and braced back of honour guards. Then, a mournful coda to stir hearts: The Last Post's bugle blasts. It's always the silence between notes which knots your throat.

All stiffen at the lamentations of remembrance, gaze cast downwards. There are fewer appeals to a high power than there once was, but this is still a congregation, a reverential scene repeated hundreds of times over – before the noble limestone Cenotaph in Auckland, in the bluster above Tarakena Bay, and in small towns where everyone knows everyone's name. On Sydney's Martin Place, eerie scenes of battles barely recalled are projected onto high-rises and office blocks. Over a calm Aegean Sea, its ripples barely visible in the gloom, pilgrims shudder themselves from sleeping bags atop Gallipoli's sharp cliffs, where a century earlier, soldiers stormed shell-strewn beaches.

They came in the small hours to remember. Some had grandparents or great-grandparents – mere ancestors now – who fought, were injured and had been dashed against the rock face. The rest were moved by obligation, paying respects to those who, as the legend goes, gave their lives defending liberty.

Princes, presidents and prime ministers read their speeches. Wreathes burdened with the named fallen were laid at Lone Pine and Chunuk Bair. Pensive columns passed a dominating granite slab inscribed with the famed Words to the Anzac Mothers, taking comfort in their tone of peace and reconciliation.

This day, this lofty processional, enshrines Australia and New Zealand's most exalted collective experience. The fitful birth of a nation's narrative: an existence forged in steel, blood and courage.

One day earlier, an equally sombre ceremony took place. Princes, presidents and prime ministers too arrived at Tsitsernakaberd, a hilltop in Yerevan, the capital of Armenia. They read their speeches. They whispered prayers. They atoned.

A ring of jagged, imposing grey-black steeles reaching for a bright Caucasian sky encage a flickering eternal flame. Dignitaries approached it hesitantly, each bearing a single yellow rose, until the centrepiece was thick with flowers. Grandchildren, great-grandchildren, formed a sentry watch, cradling in worn arms heirlooms, portraits, weathered photographs, stories and fragmented memories. Mementos to be laid on the petalled memorial bed: evidence for the world to witness what their forebears had endured. The ache of inherited loss etched like old marble into every face.

Church bells tolled throughout the country. One hundred peals for one hundred years, repeated in Los Angeles, Beirut, Moscow and Montreal. Landmarks dimmed their lights: the Eiffel Tower and Colosseum going dark. Citizens in their abridged homeland, or flung into diaspora, crossed themselves, made their quiet vow of Never Again. Their tears, shed in compassion, anger or yearning for repair, are a measure of resilience.

Every last one of these commemorations, public or private, popular or minor, was reverent of lives lost, of lineages snuffed out before their time. But inherent in these days, 24 and 25 April, critical to their rituals, are denial, falsehood and forgetting, although we do not care to admit it.

To the very hour, on the night of 24 April and the morning of 25 April 1915, as Anzac troops swayed apprehensively in their ships off the Dardanelles coast, the intellectual and political elite of Armenian society in the Ottoman Empire were hauled from their homes, imprisoned and then banished.

And while those soldiers scrapped for mere inches of Gallipoli's soil, killing squads swept swiftly through hamlets, cities and towns, hunting Armenian men. Those left behind – women, children and the elderly – were corralled south, to the desert wastes of Syria. Endless convoys. Death marches.

From the most fearsome man to the weakest child, from celebrated artists to feminist intellectuals, from the glittering capital to the most isolated village, few were spared the onslaught: a campaign by the ruling Committee of Union and Progress to transform by total cruelty and deprivation a plural, diverse empire into a homogenous and rigid nation state – to rid that land utterly of its minorities.

During the First World War and its aftermath, perhaps over a million Armenians were destroyed, along with 250,000 Assyrians. These years also saw the expulsion of more than a million ethnic Greeks.

The Polish-Jewish jurist Raphael Lemkin had to invent the term 'genocide' in 1943 to describe what had happened, had to invent a new law to prohibit it. Yet the killers and thieves of the Ottoman regime – the very foe Anzac soldiers were battling to defeat – went free and unpunished. Instead, the guilty party morphed into the first government of the Turkish Republic, led by Gallipoli veteran Mustafa Kemal, a strongman who oversaw the final clearance of non-Muslim minorities from Anatolia.

Contrary to the folklore – the mythology – that envisions him as a liberator, saviour, secularist and modernizer, Kemal ruled with an iron fist. He broke utterly with the past, hauling his new country from a deleterious collapse into a future cleaved from anything recognizable. There was no reckoning with the genocide, no repenting. Rather, the Republic engraved into its foundational principles a belief defended with adamantine strength to this day: that the Armenian Genocide never happened.

Imagine for a moment if Germany said this of the Jews and the Roma, and we can begin to see the injustice.

And yet to deny such a thing would be to deny the interweaving, the imbrication of the Anzac story with Armenian experience. Anzac soldiers captured at Gallipoli held in the Ottoman interior as prisoners of war witnessed the genocide as it took place. Other soldiers fought bitterly to protect the persecuted, and gave their lives in doing so. New Zealanders and Australians alike signed up to the Armenian relief cause, lending their succour to survivors. In tandem with an unprecedented international aid effort, funds established throughout Australasia raised money and donated food and clothing to support a people who had been whittled down to the very marrow of their being.

The attrition of memory, the slow operation of history and the deliberate obscuring of scholars have separated these facts. This book, therefore, is an attempt to piece together these apparently disparate strands, to mend what Ian Buruma once called the 'political corruption of historical memory'.

In salvaging these stories of bloodshed and terror, heroism and humanity, we must pick apart the grand mythology which has smothered and replaced them – the more palatable story that suits our yearning for reconciliation enshrined in the Anzac Special Relationship shared between Australia, New Zealand and Turkey. This myth makes us no wiser, nor does it bring us any closer to understanding the First World War and its vast, traumatic legacy. This new history explodes the myth from the inside, so that we might create something more honest and truthful in its place.

For the most part, this book is a narrative, a style chosen for its accessibility to an unknowing reader. It recounts a story – a maligned and traduced story though it is – and can give only a hint of trauma, of depravity and of unendurable experiences endured. We like to imagine that mere words can convey experience. Many have tried.

But no language, separated from feeling by distance to the past, can ever describe what it is like to have the soles of your feet worn away over seven months of walking; can never capture the sound of a knife slicing sinew and muscle; can never convey the smell of a rapist to his young victim. Nor the sound of a whimper when long-separated parents and children reunite after a decade of mourning; nor the shade of blushed cheek warmed by basic comforts; nor the sound of a town hall that resounds with passionate solidarity.

It will only ever be an approximation of feeling: An echo, or a lingering murmur. But that feeling must be imprinted no matter how vague or faint, for the sake of history and understanding, and for justice.

This book can therefore only grasp at lives, and arrest their long shadows.

1

Pro patria mori

There is a mountain called Ararat, its peak permanently tipped by ice and snow: a towering epicentre, a stone-faced sentinel and a witness to the first furtive kicks of civilization.

Three lakes and three seas encircle the mountain: to the west, the bustling Black Sea; eastwards, Urmia and Sevan mark the gateway to the Caspian; in the south, the salted shores of Van and onwards to the Mediterranean.

Guided by a dove, the common tale holds, Noah and his lifeboat ran aground on Ararat after the Flood. If this legend is to be believed, it is from the mountain's slopes that all human and animal life descended to begin again in a purged new world.

Journeys across this highland are slow, volcanic tempers having long ago rent great peaks and valleys into fertile umber. The Euphrates and Tigris Rivers find their sources between tectonic cracks, spilling out to the desert and the Persian Gulf. The Silk Road searches through its more navigable southern reaches.

From the time of antiquity to the recent past, this busy corridor between Europe, Asia and the Middle East has been governed by the whims of warlords, traders, usurpers, rival faiths; the ebb and flow of kingdoms and empires. It is here, in the fourteenth century before the Common Era, that the first whispers of an Armenian people will be heard.

Their origins are mysterious. Even the name 'Armenia' is of uncertain provenance, lost to the prehistory of humankind. The Armenian language, hardened by stiff consonants, forms a distinct branch of the Indo-European tree. Pagan gods demand their worship – deities of sun, moon and rain – later to be corrupted by Greek and Zoroastrian fables. They have heroes, too: the Babylonian exile Hayk who felled a tyrant; Vahakn, slayer of dragons.

For millennia, their homeland is invaded, conquered and plundered by Hittites, Persians, Seleucids and others. Only once will the region be united under an Armenian banner, during the era of Tigran the Great in the first century BCE, a powerful but short-lived burst of empire contending with the ailing Roman Republic.

Gregory the Illuminator brings the teachings of a Jewish Nazarene dissident to the Armenians in the early 300s, shortly before Constantine's conversion, making them arguably the first Christian people in the world. The Apostolic Church emerges as a pillar of identity, upholding a firm independence from both Catholicism and Eastern Orthodoxy. Countless churches, monasteries and cathedrals are hived from dark rock, their cupolas made to resemble Ararat's peak – redoubts in ages of war, treasure houses of sacred texts. *Khachkars*, carved stone tablets bearing intricate cruciform patterns, dot the landscape. To bring the Bible to the masses, a scholar priest named Mesrob Mashtots devises an alphabet in the fifth century: thirty-six letters, read from left to right, an elegant script.

By this potent combination of a distinct faith and a strong literary pedigree amongst the elite, Armenian life and culture endures – even as cycles of occupation roll on. Muslim Arabs arrive in the seventh century, Byzantines in the tenth and Seljuks soon after. Under this pressure, Armenians begin migrating en masse towards the Mediterranean's northeastern coast. Here, they establish a kingdom known as Cilicia, later to become a base for marauding Crusaders on their quest to control the Holy Lands.

Then, further invaders: Mongols and Mamluks who break the back of Armenian society for generations. Finally Turks, descendants of roaming tribes from Central Asia, surge through Anatolia westward.

In 1453, twenty-one-year-old Mehmed II seizes Constantinople from the Byzantines. He anoints himself Conqueror and renames the ancient city Istanbul, the third capital of the rising Ottoman Empire. Cilicia splits apart not long after. Armenians become a colonized people once more.

The Ottoman Empire is a formidable machine of conquest and permanent warfare, mobilized for expansion. At its peak, the state is gargantuan, spanning Arabia and North Africa, parts of the Caucasus, the entirety of Anatolia and a European heartland: the Balkans, Greece, parts of Ukraine and Romania, pressing as far west as Austria.

From the Red Sea to the Danube, the Sultan reigns: a supreme ruler drawn from the House of Osman, Caliph of all Muslims, defender of the pilgrimage cities of Mecca and Medina.

Armenians comprise a small patch in an elaborate, multi-ethnic and multilingual Ottoman quilt. Turks are dominant. Beneath them, Arabs, Kurds,

Jews, Assyrians, and various European peoples who will one day fragment and define themselves as Serbs, Bulgarians, Albanians, Montenegrins and Greeks.

Unlike early Christianity, Islam is built as a political force as well as a faith. The *Koran* and its accompanying *Hadith* lay out the ideal for Muslim rule, particularly for how to treat other monotheisms – People of the Book. Ottoman authority is split along religious lines into little theocracies known as *millets*, the Sultan delegating limited power to clerical figureheads. For the Armenians, a Patriarch acts as de facto leader of the community.

The *millet* system is a pact of privilege and subjugation. Armenians can practise their religion freely, operate civil courts, run schools, hospitals and businesses, but their status is second class. Churches and bell towers cannot shadow the minarets of mosques. Christians must make way for Muslims in the street. Access to Muslim courts is severely restricted. Their testimony carries little weight. They are not allowed to carry weapons.

Not separate and equal, then, but separate and protected. Compared to medieval Europe, it is an enlightened form of government and social organization. Armenians, by their willingness to keep their heads down, to make the necessary prostrations, earn the nickname 'Loyal *millet*'.

At the beginning of the nineteenth century, by far the majority of Armenians are peasants scratching out feudal lives in their ancestral lands, subdivided into the six *vilayets*, or provinces of eastern Anatolia: Van, Erzurum, Harput, Bitlis, Diyarbakır and Sivas.

For one hundred generations, Armenian women have wrung scarlet-hued clothes in the arterial ramblings of rivers and streams. They tend the silkworms, and with their husbands and sons, toil with rough-hewn tills in the grain fields, or pick pomegranates, dates, apples, tobacco and grapes. Winemaking originates here, fermented in vast pottery urns. Hillsides are indented with shepherds' tracks, the wanderings over which livestock have long been driven.

Armenian homes are simple, mud brick and tiled rooves mostly, often warren-like and fortified against fearsome itinerant tribes who survive by stealing. Armenian families are extensive and tightly bound with sincere respect given to elders, for they know the rhythm of seasons most intimately: winter's bitter chill and the warm promise of harvest. These homes smell thickly of smoke, a fire kept burning in a small pit in the living room, both for heat and for cooking. Over shredded chunks of lavash, stories, are shared around the fire, epic poems and lyrical songs of Armenian rulers and warriors past, like Saint Vartan the rebel king.

If the Armenian nation is to have a soul, it is here among the grazing herds, the apricot orchards and around the home hearth.

Because of their poverty and isolation, these peasants are tied to their neighbours. Conversations between Turkish, Greek, Armenian, Assyrian and settled Kurdish families can flit between languages, or develop a unique combined patois of their own. Customs filter across these ethnic lines, as do business partnerships, mutual aid and even friendships: the Armenian goatherd will know the Turkish tobacco farmer further down the valley, just as the Greek silk harvester will greet the Assyrian ploughman. Often, the only divisions between clans can be found on days of worship. Intermarriage is a taboo rarely breached.

Still, inequities thrive. Rural chieftains undisturbed by local authority extort protection money. Muslim landlords dominate. Common practice sees nomadic Kurds, who spend much of the year in the mountains, demanding to be quartered in Armenian homes when snow sets in – a hated tradition that leads to abuse and rape, against which no complaint can be made.

Electricity, even railways, has not yet penetrated these far-flung regions. Instead, rural roads still hum with oxen-pulled carts delivering surplus to market towns: rugged hives of blacksmiths and bakers, tailors of silk and rollers of cigars. Produce for the port cities: thriving and wealthy patchworks of schools and bazaars, jewellers, craftsmen and merchant houses lining the quayside. The Armenian *hamal* is a common sight: porters bearing heavy loads in patched wide-fitting trousers and tatty waistcoats. Because of their success in trade, Armenians come to be known in the West by a similar stereotype to the Jews of Europe: economically prosperous despite their political suppression.

And then, there is Istanbul: an imperial nerve centre sprawling over seven hills, jostling the Golden Horn, its vistas dominated by Haiga Sophia's radiant dome and the heaven-reaching spires of its rival twin, the Blue Mosque. A bridge at Galata – which both Leonardo da Vinci and Michelangelo were once invited to design – links the grubby fervour of markets to the lofty uphill European quarter of Pera. Below the second-floor overhangs of apartments, between dense stalls of cardamom, cinnamon, paprika, mastic, fig, rose and jasmine, small *kahvehane* brew bitter black drinks: coffeehouses, a space for gossip and schemes, dissent and disputation.

Part of the capital's illustrious sprawl, an Armenian elite achieve notoriety and respect as doctors, bankers, pharmacists, poets, musicians and industrialists – shipyard owners and silk mill tycoons, men who reek of iron and modernity. The Duzian family run the Imperial Mint. The Dadians guard the state arsenal. Beloved of the Sultan's court is the Balyan dynasty, a lineage of architects just as adept at churches as they are mosques. Their designs are everywhere, from the gaudy mesh of styles that adorn Dolmabahçe Palace to the imposing frontages of Taksim Barracks.[1]

But this well-to-do community is rarely allowed to ascend the loftiest levels of political influence. That privilege, for the most part, remains with Muslims, and them alone. But there is an essential interdependence. The Armenian elite need powerful patrons at court. The Ottomans, in turn, need Armenian wealth.

Orientalists of the era speak of 'Armenia', yet such a nation doesn't really exist. It is an imagined homeland. For now.

The Ottomans' engine of conquest trembles to a halt in the late seventeenth century. New pressures rise from Western Europe, bringing serious shocks to the system.

The French Revolution unleashes regicide, radicalism and twenty years of ravage. But above all, that great severance with hereditary monarchy imbues a new spirit in Europe: the rise of nationalism. No longer bound to the punitive protection of kings and aristocrats, 'subjects' begin to think of themselves as 'citizens', tied together by language, culture, ethnicity, religion and a shared history.

Figure 2 'A view of Beyoğlu, Istanbul in the late 19th century, through the eye of Armenian photographer M. Iranian'. Credit: Suna and İnan Kıraç Foundation Photography Collection/Pera Müzesi.

The first nationalist uprisings against Ottoman rule come from the West, inflamed by Napoleon's campaigns of liberation. Serbs free themselves from the Sultan in 1804 and, after a crackdown, again in 1817. The Greeks follow soon after, kick-starting an insurrection in 1821 and drawing in the Great Powers of Europe to their aid, rousing a Romantic spirit embodied by the poet Byron, who gives his life for the Hellenistic cause. The result, in 1830, is total Greek independence.

The Ottoman Empire's century of erosion has begun, a steady buckling under the weight of nationalist insurgencies within and Great Power pressures without.

To the north, the Russian Empire covetously eyes the Dardanelles Straits and Istanbul, which they longingly call Tsargrad. Justification for land-grabs is cloaked in the rhetoric of religion and antiquity. Russia sees itself as the successor state to the fallen Byzantines, upholders of Eastern Orthodoxy. Its emperors proclaim spiritual solidarity with put-upon Christians of the Ottoman domain, hoping to exploit separatist means for imperial ends. Separated only by the Black Sea, much blood will be spilled between these imperial rivals.

The British, meanwhile, fear Russian expansion. Under the guise of liberal interventionism, they too proclaim solidarity with Ottoman Christians with an eye to maintaining supremacy in the Mediterranean and securing Indian colonies. The British want the Ottoman Empire weak and malleable but still stable, a bulwark against Tsarist ambitions.

Those ambitions seem unstoppable. Russia encroaches through the Caucasus region, subsuming its imbricated peoples. By 1828, Armenians find themselves divided yet again, this time between Ottoman and Russian rule.

It is clear that the Sultan cannot maintain his moribund state in its present condition. Reform is necessary, if not vital, for survival.

Sultan Mahmud II and his successor son Abdülmecid cautiously enact a decades-long modernizing and centralizing project known as *Tanzimât*, or reorganization, which touches all areas of Ottoman life: education, banking, trade, taxation, the military and even styles of dress for the upper classes. In 1839 and 1856, two royal diktats tackle the sensitive subject of relations between Muslim and non-Muslim. *Tanzimât* will be given to them equally, and they, in turn, will be considered equal before the law.

Taken together, this incremental ideology is called Ottomanism, an attempt to harmonize and strengthen diverse peoples into a potent force. If a shining example of imperial unity can be forged, it may forestall any more nationalists ripping apart the fragile Ottoman quilt.

For Armenians, *Tanzimât* is both curse and blessing. An emerging intelligentsia in Istanbul quickly harnesses the progressive spirit of the age. From coffeehouse debates and salon meetings, journalists, poets and musicians give birth to *Zartonk*, or The Awakening, a movement to rouse Armenian patriotic consciousness from its slumber. In 1860 an Armenian National Constitution lays out new rules for governing their own *millet*. A National Assembly undermines the patriarch's authority and lay figures enter positions of limited power.

This cultural renaissance expands beyond the borders of the Empire. Young Russian Armenians, the first generation born under the Tsars' rule, take up study in St Petersburg and Moscow, or even as far as Leipzig, Paris and Berlin. Here, they encounter completely different strands of philosophy to what has been taught for centuries in church-run classrooms: German Idealism, French Republicanism, secularism, demythologized history and even the illicit socialism developed at the barricades of 1848. Those who return home loudly challenge conservative forces in Armenian life, especially the pious and traditional clergy. They develop an idea of Armenianness based on ethnicity and language rather than religion.

Peasant culture undergoes a profound transformation, too. Zealous Western missionaries, especially Protestants from the newly formed United States of America, travel to Anatolia and set up a network of schools and colleges. Because it is forbidden to convert Muslims, they focus on educating Christians. Armenians, and, to a lesser extent, Greeks and Assyrians begin to see that education can mean emancipation.[2] The prominence of women among the missionary teachers gives Armenian girls a model of aspiration, a way to see past the limits of loveless arranged marriages, unpaid household labour, and the strictures of duty and chastity.[3]

Still, for these peasants, the National Constitution means little. They barely feel its effects, if at all.[4] Rather, their burdens are doubled: a modernized tax-farming scheme leaches pennies from the poor, while Muslim immigrants ejected from the Russian Caucasus lay new roots alongside Armenians, cutting into limited land and disputing the careful commonalities built up in the countryside over centuries, setting up an ethnic rivalry.[5]

It is not Istanbul's intellectuals that tend to their growing anguish. Rather, it is a man who wears the tar-black vestments and elaborate beard of the Apostolic cleric: Mkrtich Khrimian.

Born in 1820, Khrimian joined the Armenian clergy after the death of his wife and daughter, becoming a dedicated educator. He tours the Six Provinces extensively, setting up schools open to all students regardless of faith. Witnessing the desperate conditions and dire plight of the Armenian peasantry up close, Khrimian grows disillusioned with the antipathy and disengagement of an Armenian elite who do not care for backward, provincial people. These are the leaders of the 'Loyal *millet*', after all.

From a monastery in the Edenic eastern city of Van, Khrimian publishes *Ardzvi Vaspurakan*, or the *Eagle of Vaspurakan*, a journal documenting the everyday barbarities and inequalities of rural Armenian life along with impassioned pleas for change, reform and struggle.[6]

These insurrectionary pleas are echoed by Hakob Hakobian, an inspired novelist who goes by the nom de plume Raffi. Although he enjoys the comforts of life in Tbilisi, a cultured city of the Caucasus, Raffi too journeys through Armenian ancestral lands, feels the pangs of despair and calls for a heroic fight against the oppressor. He yearns for a Golden Age of Armenian liberty, free from the moral and intellectual stagnation of servitude. In 1880, he galvanizes the populace with *Khent*, or *The Fool*.

The hero of *The Fool* is named Vartan (for the rebel king of ages past), a handsome smuggler and gun-runner, 'a lithe and fearless creature' whose cold heart is softened by the beauty of an Armenian farmer's daughter.[7] This farmer, Khacho, represents all that is docile and subservient in Armenian culture, willing to open his home to the depredations of a local Kurdish lord, a personification of the Biblical instruction 'whosoever shall smite thee on thy right cheek, turn to him the other also'.[8]

Raffi's real villain is not the Kurdish lord but an Armenian tax collector, a man of schemes and plots named Thomas Effendi who ingratiates himself with province governors and police chiefs. He is all that is debased in Armenian life under imperial rule – a collaborator. Raffi too pours scorn on the entire clergy (save for Mkrtich Khrimian) as corrupt, uncaring, decadent and more willing to let their own flock starve than part from the wealth of tithes. The author inserts himself into the tale as Levon Salman, a shambling but passionate ink-stained revolutionary who, not unlike the Narodniks in Russia, goes 'back to the people' to learn their ways and hand out radical pamphlets. This is Raffi's broadside against the detached intellectuals of Istanbul:

> He spoke the truth saying that we of Constantinople should have prepared the people. But what did we do? Nothing. We took no pains to learn the actual conditions in the interior. Present day Armenia with its frightful misery did not interest us. We were dazzled with its past glory ... But we did not know the

Armenian provinces were being stripped of Armenians … We did not know that instead of finding living Armenians we should find only skeletons walking about.[9]

But the truly stirring part of *The Fool* is its final pages, a riff on Nikolai Chernyshevsky's seminal 1863 work *What Is to Be Done?*. After joining a militia to fight the Ottomans and seeing for himself the smouldering ashes of Khacho's once-beautiful village, the hero Vartan finds the grave of his beloved. Weeping on this mound of earth, Vartan experiences a vision, a grief-stricken fever dream. Two hundred years into the future, he sees his friends still alive, the lands of *Vagharshapat*, *Bayazid*, and *Alashgert* transformed into a communal paradise of equality and emancipation. Industrial mills do away with the need for strenuous labour. Emboldened citizen-soldier Armenians dedicate their lives to education and study. Women and men happily walk the streets without regard for divisions of class and sex. A utopia, possible.[10]

> 'See this, my friend,' said Salman not releasing Vartan's hand. 'We see one another again after two hundred years, a good long interval … Now the livelihood of Armenians is safe; pleasant and peaceful on their native soil. But if you had known how we worked till we brought it to this condition – we worked hard – we passed through a thousand vicissitudes. We brought our ease with much blood and sweat.'[11]

Gradually, and by great effort, a hint of an idea of an Armenian nation emerges into being.

Ultimately, the Sultans' plans for reform fail. *Tanzimât* fails.[12] The project is too vast and ambitious to be implemented fully. Conservative Muslims grow uneasy as they see their traditional superiority undercut, as they notice the weakness of the Ottoman government, its continued capitulation to foreign powers.

Years of constant conflict, like the disastrous Crimean War, wrings the Ottoman treasury dry. The government floats loans on European markets to fund the military. But unable to keep up with interest payments, the Empire defaults on its debts and declares bankruptcy in 1875.

It could not be a worse moment to do so. Bulgarians, having undergone their own national revival by way of education and enlightenment, throw themselves into rebellion in April 1876.

Another European colony is trying to cleave from the Sultan's grasp. He unleashes regular soldiers and irregular militias on the Bulgarian population, massacring 12,000 civilians.

This mass murder provokes outrage in liberal Western society. Charles Darwin, Victor Hugo and Oscar Wilde condemn the Bulgarian horrors. British statesman William Gladstone shakes the chancelleries of Europe with blustering language, demanding the Ottomans be thrown out of Europe 'bag and baggage'. It becomes a catchphrase for a generation of diplomats and observers. The 'Turk' is sanctimoniously branded 'Unspeakable' and 'Terrible'.[13]

Amid the uproar and rancour, five months after the beginning of the Bulgarian uprising, a sensitive thirty-three-year-old princeling ascends to the Sultanate: Abdülhamid II. His immediate predecessors were unfit for office, the first found dead with slashed wrists and the second succumbing to a nervous breakdown.

Against this bloody start, Abdülhamid II's reign begins promisingly. He cultivates the gravitas of a reformer, agreeing to work with an underground group known as the Young Ottomans to introduce a parliament with elected representatives and a liberal constitution. Some minorities gain new rights. But such assuaging moves are not enough to halt Bulgarian demands for liberation. The nationalists continue to fight, supported by the Russians.

The crisis sparks another Russo-Ottoman war in 1877. Abdülhamid calls on Britain, a traditional ally. But under the force of Gladstone's criticism, Britain refuses to come fully to the Sultan's aid. Tsarist forces pincer into the Balkans and the Caucasus. With the gates of Istanbul threatened, Abdülhamid begs for an armistice.

Negotiations for a peace deal are scheduled for the summer of 1878 in Berlin. Mkrtich Khrimian, the radical priest, spots an opportunity.

Between 1860 and 1870, Armenians sent more than 500 written appeals to the Sultan against land theft, unfair taxation, unpunished murders of villagers and myriad other injustices.[14] It is the Armenians' only political weapon, and each complaint goes unanswered. If the Sultan will not listen and will not enforce the rights given to Armenians in the 1876 Constitution, Khrimian reasons, then perhaps the Great Powers can. The priest gains the blessing of the Armenian Patriarch and leads a delegation to Berlin. It is the first time that Armenian demands will be introduced to the staterooms of international diplomacy.

The Armenian Question has arrived
In good faith, Khrimian's delegation proposes that the Six Provinces be allowed a Christian governor, autonomy and self-rule, fairer courts and a mixed Armenian-Muslim police force.[15] In other words, a shift away from the centralizing trend in Ottoman politics towards a more federal system. At no point does Khrimian propose seceding from the Empire. But key

decisions have already been made behind his back. A deal is cut in the Treaty of Berlin: Russia backs down from its war footing in exchange for a clause which commits the Sultan to minor reforms – promises that will never be kept.[16]

'Alas, I had but a petition,' Khrimian will later mourn. He dedicates himself, from here until the end, to armed struggle.

In the coming years, the Armenian Question becomes shorthand for an intractable mire. No autonomous Armenian state can possibly be founded in the Six Provinces because Armenians do not comprise a demographic majority – they share the land, intermingled with Turks, Assyrians, Kurds and Pontic Greeks alike. It is a knotty conundrum that the Great Powers are utterly incapable – or perhaps unwilling – to settle.

With the Treaty of Berlin, a pattern has been set in hard stone. Christian nationalists under Ottoman rule revolt, seeking independence or autonomy. When the counterattack comes, they appeal to the Great Powers. Claiming this or that interest is at stake, the Powers intervene, often to the Ottomans' detriment. Peace plans strip land from the Empire. Berlin, for example, removes Bosnia, Herzegovina, Cyprus and Montenegro from Ottoman control, while Bulgaria receives de facto independence: almost one-third of total Ottoman territory and 20 per cent of its citizens.

Sultan Abdülhamid is watching the Ottoman domain shrink drastically before his eyes. His failure to stem the tide of irredentism wounds him deeply.

Rumours tell of weakness, illegitimacy and imminent collapse. European newspapers refer to the embattled regime as the 'Sick Man of Europe'. The phrase quickly becomes a cliché.

Barricaded inside Yıldız Palace overlooking the Bosporus, Abdülhamid's paranoia only grows in the final decade of the nineteenth century. An insomniac chain-smoker and coffee-drinker, he consults cranky mystics and hokey soothsayers. His reputation as a reformer is in tatters, like the Constitution which he tears up. He prorogues Parliament and orders the arrest of many of its MPs. Gone are the promises of equality for all.

The Sultan builds an immense security apparatus of spies and secret policemen to quash all dissent. He permits no challenge to his autocratic and increasingly belligerent rule. Newspapers are heavily censored. No one is allowed to even mention the word 'Armenia'. An overinflated military goes unpaid, provoking mutinous murmurings in the ranks.

Playing on the powerful image of the Caliphate, Abdülhamid promotes pan-Islamism in an attempt to organize the empire's Muslims into a stronger political unit, stoking ethnic and religious grievances. As part of this tactic, he expands the railway network, 'stitching the limits of the Empire together',[17] and decrees the creation of a 30,000-strong cavalry militia of unruly Kurdish tribesmen known as the *Hamidiye* in 1891. Although their ostensible role is to patrol the Caucasian border regions in case of yet another war against Russia, in reality the *Hamidiye* disrupt the already tender ethnic and religious divisions in the Six Provinces, often looting Armenian villages and homes, killing their residents with impunity.

In response to this new subjugation, this dimming of a hopeful horizon, a small number of Armenians turn away from the accommodating policies of the Apostolic Church and the National Assembly. Partly driven by the Great Powers' refusal to intervene successfully on their behalf, partly inspired by new currents of socialism and populism, looking to the Bulgarians for their immediate model, they heed the call of radical alternatives.

Autumn, 1885. The city of Van, where Mkrtich Khrimian still lives. Sitting on straw mats in a back room used for pressing grapes, nine men form the Amenakan Party. It is the first political formation of its kind, a new path for Armenian nationalism. They believe that revolution on behalf of the downtrodden peasantry is necessary, and they demand the 'right to rule over themselves'. But the Armenakans argue that the people are not yet ready for their tactics and that widespread education and careful planning are needed.[18]

The Armenakans seem like trifling moderates compared to the Social Democrats (*Hunchakian*), a gang of expatriates who band together in Geneva a year later, led by the dashing couple Avetis Nazarbekian and Mariam Vardanian. Avowed Marxists, the Social Democrats favour insurrectionary agitation and armed struggle for both Armenian liberation and socialism. Their newspaper publishes Karl Marx and Friedrich Engels's *The Communist Manifesto* in Armenian for the first time. They want no part in the Ottoman Empire at all, desiring the overthrow of both the Ottoman *and* Armenian bourgeoisie in favour of peasants and workers. They yearn for independence.[19]

Three years pass. The Social Democrats agree to join a popular front of various small groups: the Armenian Revolutionary Federation (ARF, or *Dashnaktsutyun*).[20] As with all embryonic emancipatory movements, its members quarrel amongst themselves about means and ends. Some favour more autonomy for Armenians *within* the Ottoman imperial system, or at best, autonomy under Ottoman suzerainty. Others, like the Social Democrats, argue that anything short of a *total* uprising is a treacherous compromise. They all claim to be working for the advancement of the Armenian people, but eye each other warily. Before long, the Social Democrats bail from the Federation, striking out alone.

One practical thing they can all do is protect Armenian peasants in the Six Provinces. Social Democrat and ARF activists cross the border from Russia bearing guns and knowledge. They train villagers in self-defence tactics against Kurdish raids and tax collectors. Propaganda campaigns call on Muslims and Christians to band together against Abdülhamid's despotism. Occasionally, they turn on their own, intimidating and assassinating members of the Armenian elite for being too close to the power they are trying to defeat. As a result, their work among a sincere and traditional peasant population is deeply disliked. It is the peasants, after all, who have to deal with inevitable crackdowns.

Their numbers are tiny, but in Abdülhamid's addled mind, these emboldened political activists pose a serious challenge to territorial integrity. Fresh and impassioned Armenian demands for a redress of complaints dovetail with the seemingly accelerating collapse of the empire. He does not want to lose any more Muslim land to Christians. The more Armenians protest, organize and fight back, the more wary and suspicious Abdülhamid becomes.

The Sultan weighs his options: he can accede to the moderate pleas of liberal Armenians, or let the revolutionaries run rampant and lose the entire eastern flank of Anatolia.

He chooses neither. Violence is his answer.

A small town in the district of Sason, June 1894. A local official arrives, escorted by the police. He wants the townspeople to pay their tax arrears and to give up revolutionaries wanted for arrest.

A band of Social Democrat activists walk out to meet him. We have already paid their taxes, they say, both to the government *and* to the local Kurdish lords. But our money buys us no protection. Unless the government defends us, we will not pay one *kuruş* more.

An argument breaks out. Tempers lost; insults traded. The activists lay into the official with kicks and slaps, berating him as he flees.

Reports of this trivial scuffle make their way into the corridors of power, bloated and inflated into a tale of fully fledged insurrection and revolt. Fearing another Serbia, another Greece, another Bulgaria, Abdülhamid sends the army and the ruthless *Hamidiye*.

Instead of restoring order, they crush Armenian peasants. Local police aid the troops in their grim task. 'No distinctions were made between persons or villages as to whether they were loyal and had paid their taxes or not,' an investigation into the killings later finds. 'The orders were to make a clean sweep. A priest and some leading men from one village went out to meet an officer, taking in their hands their tax receipts, declaring their loyalty and begging for mercy; but the village was surrounded, and all human beings put to the bayonet'.[21]

This is the opening phase of the Hamidian Terror, the first instance of organized murder committed against Armenians during peacetime. It will continue for another two years.

Foreign diplomats in the region witness the speed and scale of the slaughter. Their reports home provoke indignant shock and outrage in Europe, just like the Bulgarian Horrors. Suspecting harsh public opinion will oblige the Great Powers to intervene in his affairs, the Sultan backtracks. He tries to appease them by setting up an investigatory commission, but this only covers up the killing and blames Armenians for their own deaths, for being 'in revolt'. European politicians see through this sheaf of lies and set up their own inquiry, demanding the Sultan finally carry out the reforms set down in the 1878 Treaty of Berlin. Abdülhamid vacillates and stalls.

A volatile status quo remains.

Incensed by slaughter and indecision, Armenian Social Democrats plan a mass demonstration in the heart of Istanbul. The protest, held on 1 October 1895, sees thousands of Armenians march from the Patriarchate in Kumkapı to the government offices opposite Topkapı Palace. Some are armed. Entreating protest leaders carry a petition decrying the murderous events in Sason and condemning the Ottoman state for not protecting its victims. They demand fair taxation, security of life and property, equality before the law and freedom of conscience. Among the thousands marching is Marie Beylerian, a young writer, activist and rising voice of Armenian feminism.

As the protestors approach the prime minister's office, they find it ominously surrounded by mounted police. A senior officer steps forward, ordering the assembled Armenians to disperse immediately.

They refuse. Policemen charge their horses

A pogrom is soon underway, spreading through Istanbul's ornate streets, bazaars and alleyways by a mob with clubs and bricks. Even Armenians who stay away from the demonstration are hauled from their homes and butchered on the pavement. The frenzy continues for a nearly a week. The world's diplomats can only watch on shocked from high windows.

The Istanbul pogrom is a cue for greater anti-Armenian violence. Province to province, blood floods the land, beginning on 8 October 1895 in Trabzon on the Black Sea coast and reaching Urfa, near Aleppo, in December.

An 'ecology of violence' prevails during this second phase of Hamidian Terror. Even the slightest spark, the tiniest perceived provocation, gives way to obscene horror. Inevitably, victims try to defend themselves, again inciting further killing – a potent cycle spurred by local governors, the army and the police who stand aside.[22] Mass rape, abduction of children and widespread plunder of Armenian property accentuate the bitterness.

At the root of the massacres is an unresolved ethnic-religious animus and tension broiling up over the last fifty years. The pact which had governed relations for centuries is shattered. An Armenian middle class attaining wealth and influence is resented by Muslims who see them as ascending beyond their status. Armenian calls for reforms, autonomy, decentralization and even independence are devastating to the 'natural order'.

One day after savage pogroms in Diyarbakır, the city's Muslim leaders send a telegram to the Sultan, explaining their motives and justifying their bloody action:

> The effort to separate these Six Provinces from our Ottoman homeland has overwhelmed us all with sorrow and turned every Islamic house into an abode of lament … Feeling discontented with their current advantages they will surely strive passionately to acquire still more privileges and to realize other *unnecessary benefits that are contrary to Islamic law* … The intention of the Armenian traitors is to break the holy bond between Muslims in this region, people who are bravest and most loyal subjects of the State and the Grand Caliphate. We cannot tolerate such actions … We proclaim unanimously that we will spoil, with our blood, the lines and pages of the privileges, which will be given to the Armenians.[23]

An indignant German clergyman named Johannes Lepsius travels through decimated areas and writes back to Europe, informing the world of the closest estimate of the toll: 100,000 Armenians killed in 2,500 villages and towns, with over 500,000 survivors made destitute.[24]

The scale of the devastation is unlike anything seen before, paling even the Bulgarian Atrocities twenty years earlier. Governments, churches, peace activists,

Figure 3 'Child victims of the Hamidian Terror in Erzerum, 1895'. Credit: William Lewis Sachtleben Collection, UCLA.

prominent intellectuals and the Socialist International all denounce the Terror. Former British Prime Minister William Gladstone emerges from retirement to bluster once more in hawkish terms.

Sympathy for Armenians is especially strong in the United States due to the strong American missionary presence in Anatolia. Humanitarian societies spring into action, backed by prominent industrialists and philanthropists. Under the emphatic leadership of Clara Barton, a Civil War nurse-turned-social reformer, the American Red Cross debuts as an internationalized force, sending teams of workers to tend survivors of the calamity.[25]

Sensational, horrifying stories appear in the British Dominions, too. New Zealand and Australian newspapers carry frequent and graphic descriptions of killings while writers examine the Armenian Question in lengthy editorials, many of them excoriating the metropole, the motherland, for refusing to take sterner action.[26]

'The time has arrived when the great nations of Europe should intervene and by common consent dispossess the chronic "sick man" of the control of

Constantinople and appoint some nation as custodian,' the *Grey River Argus* opines in November 1894. 'It is a huge scandal that civilized and powerful nations should have to stand by apathetically and close their eyes to the barbarities of the most revolting kind. It is high time that they tired of the fatalistic and utterly unimprovable "sick man" of Europe'.[27]

The *Evening Post* is even more fervent in its view, arguing that Britain has given its 'consent to the Armenian holocaust ... The Powers will interpose with more words, but not with blows, lest they fall upon each other. Meanwhile, the Turkish mill is grinding the Armenian "exceeding small," and none can be found to shoot the miller'.[28]

At the heart of this desire for intervention is a paradoxical popular feeling, a simultaneous sense of fear and superiority towards the Ottomans: the Turk 'Terrible' and 'Unspeakable,' an Islamic infidel other, swarthy, sensual, mysterious, depraved, innately destructive and inimical to progress and to 'Christian civilization'. Laid against this hatred and condescending racism is an idealized image of the Armenians as pious innocents, the blameless martyred, although not European, at the very least among the first Christians in the world, therefore worthy of redemption.[29]

One George Hicks, veteran of the Crimean War, rabidly writes to the *South Canterbury Times* in late 1896, a crystalline example of such orientalism:

> I landed in the Crimea forty-two years ago ... I received the Crimean medal with four clasps, also the Turksh [*sic*] medal, which I have worn for forty years, but from this date, I will never again wear the Turkish medal, and, sir, I hope every officer and man will do the same. I send you the medal which you can dispose of as you think fit for the benefit of the Armenian Relief fund. Am sorry I cannot give more, but should our country take up the cause of the Armenians, I will volunteer to join my old regiment and fight in the front rank. I feel sure there are a great many of the old veterans who would volunteer to do the same; and although old, each man would be a match for ten of the dirty filthy Turks.[30]

Rather than act out some sad attempt at machismo, feminist groups like the Women's Christian Temperance Union (WCTU) in New Zealand and Australia do their best to help in a tangible way: writing, speaking and organizing relief drives to aid their co-religionists, 'roused to a sense of shame at such barbarities' and banding together 'for the protection and uplifting of other women'.[31]

Imploring the women of New Zealand, the journalist and editor Dolce Cabot calls for a 'huge wave of public opinion ... a monster petition to the British Government' on behalf of our 'tortured and outraged Armenian sisters'.

The celebrated poet and feminist champion Jessie Mackay puts pen to paper, excoriating the world for standing by:

> Sweet women, men may bear it, but we cannot.
> Cry ye out to the heavens, and be clear
> Of the vileness and the curse of acquiescence;
> Cry aloud and let the craven nations hear![32]

Still, the third phase of the Hamidian Terror is yet to come.

Radicalized by the unprecedented scale of the killing, a small cadre of ARF activists decide that only a strike at the heart of the imperial capital can bring the slaughter to an end. Paper petitions and begging appeals to the Sultan do not sew up wounds, after all. Force has to be met with force.

On 26 August 1896, two dozen party men armed with bombs and guns led by a brash revolutionary named Armen Garo storm the marbled halls of Istanbul's Ottoman Bank, the most important financial institution in the empire. Gunshots echo around the pillared atrium. They take dozens of hostages and threaten to demolish the entire edifice unless their demands are met, demands which seem to invite something terrible upon themselves. In their communique to foreign embassies they

> mourn in advance the loss of all those, whether foreigners or natives, who may be the victims of fate in the general alarm ... We shall die, we know, but the revolution which has penetrated to the marrow of the Armenian nation will continue to threaten the throne of the Sultan so long as we have not obtained our rights as men, so long as a single Armenian remains.[33]

The siege lasts twelve hours. White-turbaned students crowd the streets outside, demanding the heads of the revolutionaries. Russian and French diplomats negotiate a deal allowing the surviving raiders to escape on a yacht belonging to the bank's director. Not a single lira is taken from the bank's vaults, but the Armenians of Istanbul pay for the action in blood. Another pogrom is unleashed, lasting the rest of the day.

By their tenacious raid, the ARF emerge from the shadow of the Social Democrats as the leading militant Armenian party. But they are profoundly unpopular. Many of the citizens they claim to defend believe radicals have been the true cause of their suffering. Without their provocation, the Hamidian Terror might not have unfolded with such ferocity.

For all its trauma, loss and grief, the wider Armenian community still lives up its name as the 'Loyal *millet*'.

Beyond the scarring of a generation, the Terror disperses much of the Armenian intelligentsia far from their homes. Marie Beylerian survives the mob violence of the capital, but her association with the Social Democrats incriminates her. She absconds to Cairo and opens a new magazine for Armenian women called *Artemis* that will influence a new generation of female radicals.

A contemporary of Beylerian is Zabel Yessayan, a talented seventeen-year-old novelist. She is beautiful, yet her beauty belies an imperious and undaunted ambition. 'It is true,' she writes, 'that I am often forced to struggle against prejudices, but that struggle is spontaneous, strong, and always victorious because I have never retreated from my position.'[34] To avoid the chaos of the capital, she earns a place at the Sorbonne in Paris – the first Ottoman woman to study abroad.

Komitas is a gentle, playful man with melancholy eyes. Although an ordained, celibate priest, he lives in music: composer of choral hymns, collector of folk songs, much-admired by greats like Claude Debussy. His patron is none other than Mkrtich Khrimian who, from exile himself, urges Komitas to escape Anatolia by studying in Tbilisi.

Banished too is Krikor Zohrab, a dignified, towering, fiercely independent lawyer not yet in his forties, known for taking unwinnable cases for the sake of principle. He also writes short stories in the observant style of Émile Zola, and more than once Zohrab has his own 'J'Accuse!' moment with the regime. For calling an Ottoman official a torturer, he is disbarred. A personal reminder scrawled in his diary: 'My code of ethics: Between the real and the imaginary, choose the real; between truth and falsehood, choose truth. At all times. Everywhere.'[35]

For the next decade, the politics of Ottoman resistance will be the politics of outcasts and émigrés. Not just Armenians, but Turks, Macedonians and Arabs. From bases in Geneva, Paris, Salonika and Tbilisi, they plot the end of Abdülhamid's reign.

2

Common religion

It is February 1902. The venue is a mansion in the suburbs of Paris. Forty-seven delegates, illuminated by glimmering chandeliers, gather for the First Congress of Ottoman Opposition. There is a single question over which they fret and worry. All other problems – of politics and religion, economics and trade, minorities and nationalities – hinge on this forbiddingly complex and urgent obsession.

'*How can we save the state?*'

This is their quest, their goal, their anxious preoccupation.

The Ottoman Empire has grown anaemic, distressed and eroded by Great Powers pressure, obsolete institutions, nationalist separatism, widespread corruption and the Sultan's own pathological paranoia. In this society perforated with spies and informants, suspicion alone can earn a careless subject deportation to farthest Yemen.

It has been this way for nearly thirty years.

How can we save the state?

The Opposition, at its widest, takes many forms. Amongst the delegates are dignified constitutional reformers, disgruntled army officers, small pockets of radicals and revolutionaries, informal groups of secularists and Islamists, and ardent nationalist agitators.

Each group despairs of a waning country, and each has their own diverging answers for salvation. That Sultan Abdülhamid should be overthrown, the Constitution restored and Parliament called to order once more – these points are obvious. Beyond that, however, there is little agreement. From this motley assortment of cliques and schools, two implacable wings of anti-Hamidian dissent emerge.

On one side is the Sultan's own nephew Prince Sabaheddin, a louche liberal with European leanings. Through his tediously titled Association for Private Enterprise and Decentralization, the *Sultanzade* favours free trade and a looser system of government devolving power to the provinces. Sabaheddin is wildly in favour of foreign intervention and open revolution.[1]

Opposing the Prince is Ahmed Rıza, a charismatic young political theorist fired by the modernizing ideals of Positivism, a rejection of superstition in favour of scientific rationality and close observation of nature.[2] Rıza borrows the personal mantra of Positivism's founder Auguste Comte to name his organization: the Ottoman Society of Union and Progress (SUP). Behind the scenes and in the shadows, a clinical pair of organizers work to build the SUP's membership, men of action over theory: Bahaeddin Şakir and a mysterious figure known only as Nâzım, both doctors trained in Ottoman military hospitals.[3]

Initially wary of violent tactics and intervention by the Great Powers, Rıza instead favours a patriotic, enlightened form of Ottomanism to bind together the elaborate patchwork of the Empire's peoples under a banner of equality for all.[4]

Marooned between the Liberals and the SUP are an array of minority nationalists and ethnic interest groups, each with their own parties and committees. The Armenian Social Democrats, ever non-conforming, flatly refuse to get involved. The ARF, meanwhile, attempts two different strategies. First is co-operation with the Opposition in the hope of attaining some autonomy for the distressed peasantry *within* the imperial system.

Their back-up plan is murder.

The undulating melody of the *ezan* echoes hauntingly over Istanbul's fitful sleep.

It is 21 July 1905, a Friday, the Muslim holy day. A bearded and haggard-looking Sultan Abdülhamid, dressed in his medallioned finest despite the heat, steps up to an imperial cortege bound for obligatory midday worship at Yıldız Mosque. Cheering crowds line the route. He passes, but does not notice, a brand-new Vienna-made carriage parked in the visitor's area.

After prayers, at 12:43 in the afternoon, the Sultan emerges, hoping to be spirited quickly back to the safety of his palace. The Şeyhülislam, the second-highest ranked Muslim leader in the empire, stops him to chat.

12:44:48. A blast of intense heat, a sharp crack heard for kilometres around Istanbul. Clogging plumes of black smoke stain the mosque. Where the Viennese carriage once was, is a smouldering crater half-a-metre deep and three metres wide.[5] Amid wreckage of bent steel and scorched wood, twenty-six people are torn apart, and dozens more wounded.[6]

The Sultan survives. Had the Şeyhülislam not stopped him to talk, he would have been torn apart too.

Almost immediately, the police identify and smash the ARF commando cell responsible. Trials sentence the bombers to death.

A small cadre of junior military officers take note of the attempted assassination. As men of arms, they admire the Armenians' organizational skills, their dedicated activists, their tenacity and temerity. Although they never admit it publicly, they are impressed with the ARF's willingness to use radical violence.

Unlike the theoreticians and ideologues of the opposition who operate from the comfort of European capitals, these ambitious graduates of war colleges can be found in the barracks, garrisons and fortresses of the Balkans – the Ottoman heartland. They too despair of the parlous condition of the state and the corruption endemic in the military – bloated in size but underpaid and underfed.

Many harbour these grievances privately. Others band together.

The Ottoman Liberty Society, established in Salonika in 1906 quickly rises to become the most influential of the subterranean cadres. Among its originators, a broad-shouldered and brawny figure: Mehmed Talât.

Distinct from the upper-class affectations of his co-conspirators, Talât can trace his roots to a peasant village in Bulgaria. Even his friends call him a 'gypsy' behind his back. Rough in manners but an incessant schemer, he is well known for brushes with the authorities, known to brandish a gun if he doesn't get his way.[7] As chief clerk at the post office in Salonika, Talât is a key conduit in the whisper networks of the underground. 'At first sight this is a lucid mind,' a journalist will later write of Talât. 'But behind it, within him, there is a subdued daemonic temper chained up.'[8]

Providing muscle as point-man inside Third Army headquarters is Ismail Enver, a preening twenty-five-year-old adjutant major who peers condescendingly over an elaborately manicured moustache. Whereas Talât has no strong ideological beliefs, merely reflecting the prevailing currents around him, Enver looks to Germany for inspiration, an admirer of Prussian martial machismo.

To gain entry to the Liberty Society, officers undergo an enigmatic, cultish ritual. Gathering in passworded rooms, leaders obscure themselves with black veils. Inductees swear their oath wearing a red cape, one hand on a *Koran*, the other on a pistol that will be used against them should they betray the cause.[9]

One of the men who undergoes this 'revolutionary pantomime' is a clipped and curt artilleryman, his blue eyes slightly crossed, with the look of a 'very superior waiter'.[10] Imagining himself a dissident leader, having already tried to organize his own clandestine club while on service in Damascus, he is late and reluctant in joining the Liberty Society.[11]

Figure 4 'Mehmed Talât: "within him, there is a subdued daemonic temper chained up"'. Credit: George Grantham Bain Collection/Library of Congress.

This is Mustafa Kemal, not yet known as Atatürk, for that honorific is another life away yet.

Catching wind of the Liberty Society's success in attracting new devotees, the SUP organizer Dr Nâzım approaches them with an offer of collaboration. Thus, in September 1907, despite Ahmed Rıza's uneasiness on the question of violence, the two organizations are rolled together.

A new name for a new formation: the Committee of Progress and Union (CPU), now with a militarized vanguard.

Two months later, the Second Congress of Ottoman Opposition convenes, this time with a much more rigorous ethos. Prince Sabaheddin would seem like a natural friend to the Armenians with his emphasis on federalism and decentralization. But, respecting each other's militancy, the ARF sides with the CPU. They ink a joint platform, committing themselves to arranging the Sultan's demise by way of organizing tax and work strikes, mobilizing guerrillas and spreading propaganda. While the CPU opposes draft-dodging on patriotic grounds, these fresh comrades openly talk of terrorist methods.[12]

They all yearn for revolution, overthrow and renewal, but do not know that it is imminent.

In the end, it will not be careful planning and alliance-making that overthrows the Sultan, but far more immediate concerns: matters of honour; matters of the gut.

For years, the rank-and-file of the army – men who have nothing to do with the Liberty Society and their high-minded ideals – have been cleaving from the Sultan's authority, aggrieved at lack of pay, extended stints of service and their superiors' disdain.

March 1908: two cavalry units in Edirne, the fortress city guarding Istanbul from the west, publicly complain about conditions. Seventy officers in the artillery corps stage demonstrations, protests copied throughout the Balkans. April sees 1,500 reservists demand to be sent home. In May, 300 men in Scutari lay down their guns and occupy the post office. By June of 1908, the spree of protest is reaching critical mass, entire regiments in a half-dozen other strategically vital sites directing ire at their commander-in-chief.[13]

Momentum builds.

Russia's Nicholas II and Britain's Edward VII are meeting in nearby Revel. Rife rumours, untrue or otherwise, suggest that the monarchs will strip the province of Macedonia from Ottoman clutches. At the end of June, the CPU debates whether the time is right to stage an intervention against the Sultan in favour of Ottoman unity. There are also rumours that the party has been infiltrated by Hamidian agents.

An order goes out.

On 3 July 1908 Ahmed Niyazi, a gruff Albanian and close friend to Enver, leads a raid of 300 men on an armoury in the town of Resen, and then flees for the hills: *fedayi*, prepared to fight to the last. A spate of shootings cut down the Sultan's most loyal enforcers in the Balkans.

Demonstrations break out across the region, not just among Christians, but Muslims and Jews too. Troops sent to quell the rising only shrug and refuse to fire. Further assassinations of royal agents and loyalist commanders follow.

Abdülhamid has faced fits of rebellion before, but this situation is quickly spiralling out of control.[14]

In late July, as his coup de grâce, Enver unmasks himself and publicly threatens that if Abdülhamid does not restore the Constitution and Parliament, a rebel army will march to the capital.

In a carefully stage-managed move designed to save face, a humiliated Abdülhamid convenes his cabinet on 23 July and reveals his decision to give in to the CPU's demands.

But he does not step down.[15]

Figure 5 'Ismail Enver, the bellicose generalissimo'. Credit: AGBU Nubar Library, Paris.

The news passes quietly into the morning press. No hollering headlines. No commentary. It takes at least a day for the shockwave to ripple through the Ottoman Empire. And when it finally does, the people take their approving ecstasy to the streets. Armenians and Turks, disfigured for a generation by the Hamidian Terror, march and celebrate together alongside Greeks, Arabs, Jews and others, hoping that a greater friendship might flower. They pour into avenues, gardens and squares proclaiming the chorus of universal emancipation, an old slogan for a new age:

Liberté! Égalité! Fraternité!

In resplendent Pera, flags unfurl over packed streets, a sea of fezzes; parades in Adana; adulation in Tarsus; Bands play *La Marseillaise* in İzmir. A wary governor in Van refuses to release news of the Revolution until mid-August, but when we he does, thousands stream to churches decorated in red, black and white flags, the colours of blood, mourning and liberty. A procession pays its dues to heroes, passing Mkrtich Khrimian's old house, heads bowed in respect.

An Armenian leader in Istanbul writes to ARF headquarters: 'You cannot imagine how happy I am to be able to write you from this city without the slightest censorship or control. After thirty-two years of silence, the city is chanting "Freedom"; the crowds are drunk with joy. No matter: thirty years of silence are well worth thirty days of inebriation.'[16]

Enver is hailed as a 'champion of freedom' when he detrains at the CPU's home base of Salonika. Talât and the leadership meet him on the platform. 'Enver!' they shout. 'You are now Napoleon!'[17] A compliment that will prove prophetic.

Two weeks later, amid those delirious thirty days, clergy from every religious denomination that makes up the Ottoman tangle gather for a grand mass at the Holy Trinity Armenian Church. Even the Şeyhülislam, survivor of an Armenian bomb just three years earlier, joins the congregation.

Later in the afternoon, 50,000 people pile into Taksim Square for a victory rally. Amidst the roiling crowd, a man mounts a platform dressed in a well-cut dark suit. This is Krikor Zohrab, an outcast returned for the celebration.

The heat hangs low over the throng, anticipating.

Zohrab turns to his audience, made up of the infinite varieties of the empire, men he now calls brothers. In enthusiastic Turkish, he bellows: 'Our common religion is freedom!'[18]

The 1908 Revolution doesn't come from below and doesn't radically alter the Ottoman state. It is bestowed from above – a tactical decision by the Sultan. Yet the dawn of the Second Constitutional Era feels like a panacea, a hope that the arrival of a semblance of democracy will be a cure for all ills.[19]

Secret policemen disappear from the streets. Courts function outside royal control. Conservative elites – civil and religious – find themselves replaced by CPU party bosses in the provinces. A carnival of publishing: newspapers, pamphlets, magazines, comic strips. Exiles return. Zabel Yessayan, her first novel under her arm, embraces the burst of thought and creativity with vigour, taking up a post as the first female editor of a women's page. The gentle composer Komitas ventures back to the Anatolian wilds that he adores, embarking on a

Figure 6 '"Between truth and falsehood, choose truth": Krikor Zohrab'. Credit: AGBU Nubar Library, Paris.

vast project of ethnomusicology, collecting the folk songs of Turkish, Kurdish and Armenian peasants.

Lauded and popular though they are, the CPU does not immediately participate in the daily turbulence of government. Instead, they act outside the restored system as a kind of 'watchdog committee', waiting for the elections of November–December 1908 – the first vote in over three decades, the first attempt to do real competitive electoral politics in the Middle East.[20]

Coalitions form along the fracture-lines originally aired at the First Opposition Congress. Under Prince Sabaheddin's Liberal Union, a surprising truce between Europhiles, hesitant modernizers and conservative Muslims eager to protect the monarchy.

As committed radicals, the CPU and ARF maintain their alliance. Both parties have been trialling democracy for a while – the Armenians with their own semi-elected National Assembly since the 1860s and the CPU forging ahead by building a well-lubricated party machine. By the efforts of its chief organizers Drs Şakir and Nâzım, the CPU can boast 850,000 members in its 360 branches.[21]

Their manifestos, however, differ strikingly on critical matters. The Armenians, for all their suspicion, pledge to protect the Six Provinces as a crucial part of the Ottoman whole – justice, police and land reforms pending. The CPU on the other hand, in an early sign of a coming assertion of superiority, calls for Ottoman Turkish to become the official language of the bureaucracy and the schools.

All eyes turn hopeful to the Ottoman Parliament – its lower Chamber of Deputies and upper Senate. A result reasonably representative of the empire's peoples: of 323 MPs returned, 170 Turks, 67 Arabs, 31 Albanians, 25 Greeks, 6 Kurds, 4 Bulgarians, 4 Jews, 3 Serbs and 1 Vlach.[22]

Hoping for thirty MPs, Armenians gain only twelve. Among them are proven activists, respected intellectuals, and even old warriors. Armen Garo, leader of the Ottoman Bank raid in 1896 represents Erzerum alongside Vartkes Seringiulian, a wry and witty socialist who had seen his father beheaded during the Terror, who just weeks earlier had been serving a 101-year term as a political prisoner. From Van, a pair of debonair ARF men, Vahan Papazian and Arshak Vramian. From Istanbul, Krikor Zohrab.

As author and defender of the Revolution, the CPU dominates parliament with an enormous supermajority. Ahmed Rıza is installed as speaker, but he is increasingly becoming a mere figurehead in the party. Instead, it is Talât as a member for Edirne and deputy speaker who dictates policy.

For all this craving for a greater future, the CPU elite will soon learn that a supremacy of seats does not make power. Order does not mean control. Civility does not imply consensus. From minority parties, there are already expressions of caution and doubt. One writer in the popular Armenian daily *Buzantion* observes their delicate success:

> One should know that [bloodshed] has become a natural law and that natural laws are unavoidable. Whatever did not happen in the beginning could still happen. Whatever the revolution did not do, the counterrevolution will be able to do. There is only one way in order to prevent the occurrence of this contingency (bloodshed) and that is discretion, modesty, wisdom, and patience. New freedom is always fragile. Let us be careful.[23]

In a similar tone, in the same paper, another Armenian editorialist reminds his readers to be wary of this new revolutionary age: 'History is a witness,' he notes, for there is a 'barbarism that sleeps in each of us.'[24]

The Sultan reigns but does not rule. Where his word was once law, now there is a potent struggle: the palace, the cabinet, Parliament, the seven-man central committee of the CPU helmed by Talât, the Liberal Union agitating on the fringes and an array of minority blocs including the ARF. The public sphere has broken open, and though each of these factions commits themselves publicly to building a new, unified, patriotic Ottoman citizenry, they are each pulling in their own directions.[25]

A series of abrupt reality checks reveal the fragility of the Revolution. The weight of optimism crashes down hard.

At the end of 1908, all within two days, Austria-Hungary annexes Bosnia-Herzegovina, the Bulgarian government finally declares its total independence from Ottoman rule, and Crete joins in union with Greece.

Perhaps as a result, the CPU changes its name subtly to the Committee of Union and Progress (CUP) – not merely a semantic switch but indicative of their need to protect the empire's territory. Progress comes second.

Then, a new prime minister, Kâmil Paşa, veers from tentative support for the CUP to outright criticism. Interpreting Kâmil's appointment of friends to the cabinet as a bid for personal power in early 1909, the CUP engineers a confidence vote in Parliament. As men with revolvers stalk the lobbies outside the chamber, the prime minister goes down, 198 votes to 8.[26]

The ballot backfires, for politics is no longer the preserve of the powerful. In streets and in newspapers, polemics lash the CUP with accusations of treachery, underhand tactics and intimidation. This press battle culminates in the assassination of an anti-CUP editor in broad daylight on the Galata Bridge. His funeral on 7 April 1909 morphs into a demonstration against the former heroes of the Revolution.

A further souring. Reaction looms.

A week after the editor's funeral, at Taksim, in the barracks built by the Armenian Balyan family, just months earlier the site of an exhortation for unity and solidarity, soldiers strip and lock up their officers. They begin a march downhill to Sultanahmet – the Blue Mosque – demanding a return to Islamic rule and the extinguishing of the CUP.

These mutinous soldiers are soon joined by a coalition of Muslim theological students and supporters of the Liberal Union. Even a personal appeal by the Şeyhülislam does not divert them. From the Mosque, mobs spread out across the city.

Some head for the cabinet office, chanting for the resignation of ministers. Others ransack CUP headquarters. A column barges into Parliament, forcing MPs to flee and duck behind their desks. Undaunted is the Armenian CUP deputy Bedros Halajian who hollers back at the intruders wielding bayonets in his face. 'We have been elected by all the peoples of the Empire,' he shouts. 'A representative of the people does not have the right to let anyone tell him what to do … Go ahead, kill me, I'm on my feet.'[27]

This is no conspiracy from on high, no ploy by Abdülhamid himself, yet he takes full advantage of the crisis. The cabinet caves limply. The Sultan regains full authority, pardons the rebels and stacks the government with allies.[28]

With the CUP's central committee in shock, with leaders like Talât and Nâzım hiding out in the homes of Armenian activists, the party's Salonika branch steps in and moves quickly to battle the Counterrevolution. Working in close concert with ARF militias, an Action Army mobilizes, boarding trains bound for restive Istanbul on 17 April.[29]

Chaos prevails in the capital: skirmishes, street battles and careening semi-armoured cars. Gunshots echo over pavement. The *ancien régime* puts up a fleeting fight. Parliament, called to order outside the city while martial law is declared, votes to depose Sultan Abdülhamid II on 27 April 1909 and exile him to the CUP's birthplace of Salonika.

The Hamidian Era ends when his younger brother is installed as Mehmed V. He has little power.

In this brief nadir of reaction, a savage pogrom takes place, revealing the deep rifts in Ottoman society papered over during the euphoric rush of Revolution.

Adana. A bustling city crowded with churches and schools, twinned to the nearby port of Mersin, a cultural and spiritual hub for Armenians, and de facto capital of the unofficial province of Cilicia.

With summer harvest approaching, Adana is bloated with migrant workers. Hands that toil in fields will soon take life on a shocking scale.[30] As with the Terror fourteen years earlier, anti-Armenian violence is set off by the smallest of provocations.

A week before the Counterrevolution in the capital, a young Armenian carpenter named Hovhannes had been beaten up by a bunch of hooligans on his way home. Trusting in revolutionary promises of justice and equality before the law, Hovhannes went to the courthouse to lay charges. The magistrates rebuffed him. He bought a small handgun to defend himself.

Four days later, on the evening of Easter Monday, the same hooligans found him, looking to finish off their beating.

A knife. A slash. Sharp smell of burnt cordite. Hovhannes wounded; the gang leader killed.

The dead thug's body is paraded around Muslim suburbs. Rather than a common city mugging, the slaying is proclaimed as some kind of treachery, evidence that Adana's Armenians plan to break Cilicia away from the empire and that they plan to break Cilicia away from the empire, to demolish the old order even further.

The brandishing of that body is a catalyst, bringing to visceral reality the underlying economic and political tensions of the region.[31]

14 April, 11.00 am. Someone fires a shot somewhere in Adana.

Mobs appear in the market wielding clubs and iron bars, as if 'a flash of electricity' has 'armed all of the inhabitants of Adana at the same time'.[32] Armenians flee for the safety of their quarter, for mission compounds and churches. With their own weapons, they hold back the rampage for three days, even as guttering flames lick closer to their cramped neighbourhood.

17 April. Reservists are finally called up to guard threatened Armenians. The mobs disperse, their destructive energy curtailed. A detachment of the CUP's Action Army is coming to restore order.

Unsatisfied with the lack of threatened bloodshed, the local CUP party boss, a self-appointed renegade, commissions extraordinary attacks in the daily *Ittidal*, a newspaper distributed free through Muslim suburbs. The Armenians want 'independence', the paper scaremongers. Even after the Revolution, they have not stopped their demands. They buy guns openly in the market and by their 'dangerous inclinations' plan to commit 'various crimes in defiance of the law'.[33]

25 April. Again, someone, somewhere, fires several shots in the direction of the Action Army camp on Adana's outskirts. By dusk's fall, a second round of massacre. With their guns confiscated, the Armenians can only throw buckets of water at the flames, can only throw a hand up to the cutting blade.

A horizon turned red with flame, a rush of harried, blackened faces

> The crackling of guns mixed with the crackling of the fire, incessantly, for days and nights on end, and the hell of a city in flames; ... the wrenching appeals of a throng of people ... as their tormentors prepare to burn them alive; this frenzied, despairing population that stretches its arms out toward you and begs to be saved; the emotion that chokes you as the closer the fire comes, the more helpless you feel, delivered up to a pack of arsonists and throat-cutters ... hordes of butchers who trample corpses underfoot, stab them full of holes, smash in skulls with their gun butts, and then, the supreme insult, spit on their victims.[34]

In the aftermath, Zabel Yessayan ventures to Adana as part of a relief mission. For the immiserated living, she can offer limited bread and gaudy clothes – donations from the unknowing but well-meaning elite of Istanbul. For the 20,000 dead, she can do nothing.

Every survivor Yessayan meets is 'prey to a fit of inconsolable grief ... Even those who experienced that reality cannot give an account of it as a whole. They all stammer, sigh, weep, and recount only disconnected events'.[35] One woman sums up all that had happened by sweeping her hand over her head and repeating, mechanically: 'If you want to believe it, believe it; if you don't want to, don't. Everything is over, everything is finished.'[36]

In the yard of a makeshift orphanage, Yessayan finds two young boys talking to each other, wearing rags.

'Do you have a father?' one asks of the other.
'No.'
'A mother?'
'No.'
'I don't have a mother or father, either.'
'Did they kill them?'
'Yes.'
'They killed mine, too.'
A long anguished silence, and then:
'Do you want us to be brothers?'[37]

Figure 7 'The young prodigy Zabel Yessayan'. Credit: Yerevan Museum of Literature and Arts.

With the bones of Armenians still hot on the ground, recriminations begin.

Local authorities and CUP-aligned newspapers openly hold Adana's Armenians responsible for the chaos. Yessayan observes: 'Those who had not been massacred were blamed for surviving.'[38] A parliamentary commission sent to investigate the slaughter publicly refutes the provocation thesis that Armenians were planning to declare independence.³⁹ But such assurances do nothing to calm tempers. In parliament, Kirkor Zohrab is roughly manhandled by his fellow MPs for accusing the government of 'remaining faithful' to its 'long-standing tradition of denying the facts'.⁴⁰ Yessayan, in a similar cry for honesty, pleads: 'It is essential that all of us see our bleeding country in its true colours, that we learn to take a hard, courageous look at it. What I saw and heard [in Adana] was such as to rock the foundations of the whole state'.⁴¹

The savagery of Adana could have happened only during the window of Counterrevolution, but it represents the divisions – fathoms-deep – hewn by the Revolution itself: between Muslim and Christian, conservative and radical, between the old order and the new. Rather than unifying every Ottoman citizen into a common brotherhood, the Revolution has polarized. Irreversibly polarized.

For those concerned with that pressing question – *How can we save the state?*– they cannot, perhaps will not see that the Revolution is the first convulsion of a protracted death throe.

The empire is not yet a carcass, but a black flock of vultures circle.

Like their Serbian, Greek and Bulgarian neighbours before them, Albanians launch a wave of armed uprisings against imperial control in the early months of 1910. Sympathetic deputies lead a forty-man breakaway faction in parliament. The CUP's dominance is crumbling.

A year later, Italy invades the Ottomans' last North African colony of Libya: a thinly disguised cover for a land grab; an exemplary case of the '*reductio ad absurdum* of European imperialism'.⁴² CUP officers Ismail Enver and Mustafa Kemal board ships and head south, hoping to bleed the Italian government into a stalemate.

In the capital, the CUP use increasingly underhanded tactics to assert their influence on government, a slip towards authoritarianism that alarms their Armenian allies. Both the ARF leadership and independents like Zohrab and Vartkes are intimate comrades of Talât, Enver, Şakir and Nâzım. They can see the deterioration up close.

Promised plans for political, judicial and land reforms in the Six Provinces are falling by the wayside. At the close of their sixth World Congress in the summer of 1911, an ARF resolution notes with sorrow:

> Despite a series of hopeful initiatives, in the three years of constitutional rule, the government's policies not only haven't created an improved life for, and

reconciliation between, peoples of all religions and races ... The CUP has gradually withdrawn from constitutional and democratic principles, and failed to take steps to combat and cleanse itself of right wing elements.[43]

As if proving the ARF's criticism correct, the general election of 1912 – the 'Election of Clubs' – is dominated by bribes, ballot-stuffing and open intimidation by the CUP's paramilitary wing, a cadre of hardened political operatives under the control of Dr Bahaeddin Şakir tasked with gathering intelligence, shakedowns, beatings and assassinations of anyone 'deemed to be a threat to the security of the state.' *Teşkîlât-ı Mahsûsa*. The Special Organization.[44]

Anger grows. A collection of (Liberal Union-aligned) officers dubbing themselves 'Saviours' swear to end the CUP's influence. They stir up militias in the Balkans, threatening to march on Istanbul, demanding the elections of 1912 nullified.

The ARF, finally realizing the hopelessness of the alliance in which they had invested so much, breaks totally with the CUP.[45] Vartkes, meanwhile, condemns the Saviour Officers during a fiery speech in parliament. 'As long as strong adherents to a parliamentary regime remained,' he says, 'the country would never be ruled by a military dictatorship.'[46]

The coup ushers Ahmed Muhtar, an ageing field marshal with the venerable title *Gazi*, into the prime ministership, seeking to end the Albanian and Libyan conflagrations.

But no sooner is the peace settled, a new war beckons, sparked by the old.

Agitated by the closure of the Dardanelles, looking to seize on the discordant confusion of the Ottoman Empire, Russian diplomats corral the former Ottoman colonies of Bulgaria, Serbia, Greece and Montenegro into a coalition, convincing them to set aside petty border squabbles and turn their guns east, to push their former masters out of Europe totally and finally.

The First Balkan War erupts. It quickly becomes an utter rout.

Within a month, miserably equipped Ottoman soldiers outnumbered two-to-one retreat to their last resort line at Çatalca, a mere forty kilometres from Istanbul.[47] Edirne, the guardian city, Talât's electorate, falls. Only a desperate armistice, signed in December, saves the state.

In the wake of defeat, feelings of shame and deep sadness mingle with rage and hatred. Dr Şakir, overseeing a Red Crescent hospital in Edirne before the collapse, mourns for 'the lost pieces of the fatherland, for the army that lost its honor, for the populace trodden over by the enemy, and for our virtues that had become stained'.⁴⁸ Enver expresses the bitter, vengeful mood viscerally:

> How could a person forget the plains, the meadows, watered with the blood of our forefathers; abandon those places where Turkish raiders have stalled their steeds for a full four hundred years, with our mosques, our tombs, our lodges, our bridges and our castles, to leave them to our slaves, to be driven out of [Europe] to Anatolia: this was beyond a person's endurance. I am prepared to sacrifice gladly the remaining years of my life to take revenge.⁴⁹

According to his wife, Talât sheds tears for the first time, the 'saddest day in his life … when [Edirne] fell to the enemy'.⁵⁰ His 'lucid mind' and reserved demeanour begin to crack and cave in. That 'daemonic temper' is coming unchained.

An appalling humanitarian crisis compounds these shattering emotions. Both Balkan Wars are especially vicious and bloody, witness to 'cleansing' operations on all sides. Refugees flow across frontlines in all directions. Among the correspondents in the mud, covered in ash, is a veteran Russian revolutionary by the name of Leon Trotsky. From a December 1912 dispatch:

> The flesh is rotting, both that of the oxen and of people. Villages have transformed themselves into columns of smoke. People not 'under the age of twelve' are exterminating one another. They have all turned into savages and lost their humanity. The moment you lift even the corner of the curtain on these military exploits, the war reveals itself more than anything as an abomination.⁵¹

Muslims suffer by far the worst atrocities at the hands of Bulgarians: indiscriminate killings, rape, forced conversion and the systematic razing of villages. They flee to Istanbul and beyond in their tens of thousands bringing with them cholera, typhus and stories of grim horror. Haiga Sophia, like other mosques, becomes a charnel house.⁵²

Their plight stirs pity and recognition in Zabel Yessayan. 'They have been ousted from their own lands and turned into refugees,' she writes in 'Enough!', a stirring decrial of the war. 'What have we got in common? What makes us similar? When I see the expression of intense fear in their faces, my own pain, which had begun to recede, flames up again.'⁵³

Fraught negotiations for a settlement begin in London. Meek Ottoman diplomats (in a new cabinet after Ahmed Muhtar's embarrassed resignation) promise to hand Edirne permanently to the Bulgarians in exchange for definite peace.

The central committee of the CUP, fearing the loss of even more territory, reacts viscerally.

Ismail Enver puts a simple proposition to a frantic meeting of the party leadership on 22 January 1913: 'Do you trust the government?' The unanimous answer: no. 'In that case, let's overthrow it tomorrow.'[54]

Flushed with ruthlessness, resolve and guile, Enver and Talât rush a band of seventeen Special Organization men to the government offices at 2.00 pm the next day, during a cabinet session.

A firefight in the halls of power. Splintered chandeliers, bullets punching holes in elaborate furniture. In the cabinet room, the war minister Nazım Paşa leaps to his feet: 'Bastards! You've let me down. This is not what you promised.'[55]

One of Enver's henchmen coolly executes him.

Enver then approaches the prime minister. With a pistol pressed to his skull, he begins drafting his resignation: 'At the suggestion of the military … ' Enver forces him to add ' … and the people.'[56]

Within fifteen minutes, the government has been overthrown 'at the suggestion of the military and the people', a savage putsch that puts the CUP firmly in power for the first time.

Talât takes the powerful portfolio of interior minister. Enver, given several swift promotions, later takes over the War Ministry. Eventually Said Halim Paşa, an aristocratic CUP sympathizer, becomes prime minister.

Less than two weeks later, as rough coup repression rounds up the CUP's political enemies, the tentative Balkan armistice breaks down. Bulgaria turns on its former allies Serbia and Greece. The infighting gives Enver his chance to recover treasured Edirne, yet it is a pittance in compensation.

By the close of the Second Balkan War in August 1913, the Ottoman Empire has lost *70 per cent* of its European population and *85 per cent* of its European territory.

More than four centuries of Ottoman dominance in the Balkans ends. Salonika, the beloved birthplace and home of many CUP leaders, slips from their faltering grasp.[57]

Territory can be measured and mourned in miles and acres, but there is no weighing the traumatic cost of such a loss.

A rupture in the soul

The Balkan Wars fuel the CUP's deep and irreconcilable suspicion of non-Muslims as inherently disloyal, liable to cause the total breakup of the empire. Above all, the conflict demonstrates to CUP elites that 'cleansing' – designating entire groups as the enemy and forcibly removing them – is an acceptable, if not desirable, way to conduct politics and statecraft.

Together, these factors contribute to the explosive rise of a new ideology.

Strains of chauvinistic nationalism have always been latent in the CUP.

As early as 1907, Nâzım had confided in his comrade Şakir that 'the Turkish race proved the theory of survival of the fittest because of its superior characteristics'. After the Revolution, the doctor had been even more explicit:

> The [CUP] wants centralisation and a Turkish monopoly of power. *It wants no nationalities in Turkey*. It does not want Turkey to become a new Austria-Hungary. It wants a unitary Turkish nation state, with Turkish schools, a Turkish administration, and a Turkish legal system.[58]

At first, Nâzım had been an outlier, a radical. The *public* rallying cry was always for unity and pluralism. But as the CUP endures the post-Revolutionary years in fraught anguish – the Counterrevolution, Adana, the Libyan war, Albania and the Saviour Officers' coup attempt – they begin to turn away from the promises of the Constitution. Faced with chaos, disintegration, confusion, Talât's exasperation grows clearer in a secret speech to the party faithfuls in 1910:

> You are aware that by the terms of the Constitution equality of Mussulman and Ghiaur [non-Muslim, or infidel] was affirmed but you one and all know and feel that this is an unrealisable idea. The Sheriat [Islamic law], our whole past history and the sentiments of hundreds of thousands of Mussulmans and even the sentiments of the Ghiaurs themselves, who stubbornly resist every attempt to Ottomanize them, present an impenetrable barrier to the establishment of real equality.[59]

Or, put more simply by the British Ambassador: the CUP has 'given up any idea of Ottomanizing all the non-Turkish elements … To them, "Ottoman" evidently means "Turk" and their present policy of "Ottomanization" is one of pounding the non-Turkish elements in a Turkish mortar'.[60]

The shift from *inclusive* Ottomanists to *exclusive* Nationalists is well underway.

They throw out the unifying *Osmanlı* identity and set themselves apart by using the term *Türk*. It has been used for aeons in the West, but within the empire, it is pejorative slang for a poor provincial farmer. This is the first symbolic step in constructing a new ethnic identity. The term *millet*, denoting the boundaries of religious communities, evolves into *milliyet*, meaning 'nation'. *Vatan*, meaning 'birthplace', becomes 'homeland'.

The most prominent theoretician of this shift is a sociologist and poet, a former activist from the eastern city of Diyarbakır, member of the CUP's central committee, a portly, jowly man, eyes darkly ringed: Ziyâ Gökalp.

To Talât and Enver, Gökalp appears like a prophet, a 'holy man', a 'spiritual father' and a guiding light.[61] Over numerous late-night conversations, they fall under his spell, his vision of the future.[62]

Frustrated by the reality that the Ottoman Empire is not a homogenous nation state, Gökalp casts aside any notion of equality. Radicalized by the times, he asserts that pluralism is nothing more than an 'illusion'. There will be no more reconciliation or cooperation, only the superiority of Turkish culture. 'Turks are the "supermen" imagined by the German philosopher Nietzsche,' he writes. 'New life will be born from Turkishness.'[63]

Gökalp draws on ideas of linguistics and education to define who can belong to this ascendant Turkish culture. Race or ethnicity is not a guarantee. He doesn't (as Rudyard Kipling would have it) think with the blood. Instead, one must express the right spirit and ethos. 'A nation,' Gökalp explains:

> Is a cultural group composed of individuals who have received the same upbringing, and are united by a common language ... For example, we have many co-religionists who, although they are *racially not Turkish*, fully possess the Turkish spirit from the perspective of upbringing and culture ... Due to the upbringing they have received, they cannot live in any other society and will work for no other ideal than the Turkish one.[64]

Gökalp's theory, in fact, betrays his own status as an outsider: he is not an ethnic *Türk*, per se, but of Kurdish descent. Without the promise of malleability, he will be excluded from his own utopia.

Gökalp imagines new borders for his dream state: a vast tract of land stretching from the Dardanelles, through the rugged mountains of the Caucasus, beyond to the Chinese border, uniting the Turkic peoples of Asia. This fictional and quasi-mystical place he calls Turan – 'the entirety of all the countries in which Turks live, in which Turkish is spoken'.[65] As such, Gökalp's ideal is inherently expansionist, desiring more territory than the empire already possesses; a consolation for the loss of Europe. Naturally Enver, the bellicose generalissimo, is a keen believer in pan-Turanism.

Gökalp casts aside Marxism, with its obligation to class struggle, as well as Liberalism's stress on the individual. He comes to favour corporatism: the indivisibility of the nation, an organic body. Although Islam's mysticism and orthodoxy clash with his own personal secularism, he still identifies religion as a powerful coagulant in social life, a marker of cultural difference.[66]

In real political terms, Turkish Nationalism is forged in opposition: only through working with Christian groups like the ARF and battling other Christian (even Muslim) separatists does the CUP come to abandon unity and tolerance. It is a recoiling, a lashing out, less a constructive ideology than a reflex against loss. Resentful ethnic pride is their consolation for disgrace, impotence, the significant drop in status and prestige.[67]

The Balkan Wars and their accompanying humanitarian crises force CUP Nationalists to turn their backs on Ottoman Europe, now lost forever. Instead, they embrace Anatolia and its majority of Muslim Turks.

But it is a land about which they know nothing. An alien place. The CUP's leaders hail from conquered towns, cities and villages of the Balkans, not the interior.[68] Throughout 1912–13, the CUP imbues this unknown territory with desire, believing it to be some forgotten or future fatherland. Talât admits that 'Anatolia is a closed book to us. We first have to learn what is in it and then provide services that suit this nation'.[69]

Thus, Gökalp becomes head of a research department within Talât's Interior Ministry after the 1913 putsch and the consolidation of CUP rule in the provinces. He arranges surveys, sending research parties to analyse the ethnic and religious makeup of Anatolia – a project that will continue well into the 1940s.[70] Armenians, Pontic and Ionian Greeks, Kurds, Arabs, Assyrians. Turcomans. Lazi and Alevis, all to be marked up, counted and denominated.[71]

How can we save the state?

The study is the first phase in a demographic, ethnological, nation-building experiment. Anatolia is soon to become a 'laboratory in total domination',[72] internal colonization and Turkification.

Their goal is to radically alter the country. As Gökalp will put it in his famous poem 'Kızılelma', or Red Apple:

> He said it was important to get to know the East
> said the people are a garden and we are gardeners
> trees are not rejuvenated by grafting only
> first it is necessary to trim the tree.[73]

In the face of a cataclysm, they create their own. After witnessing a mass, forced migration, they enact one. In their mood of vengeance after the Balkan Wars and distrusting any Christians, the CUP first targets the empire's Greeks.

A CUP-produced pamphlet appears in the streets in late 1913. A prime example of early Turkish Nationalism in practice:

> Oh my God, how are we going to celebrate the day on which Turks and Muslims buy things from each only and consume the goods produced in Turkey as much as possible. Gentlemen, we are not asking for a great sacrifice from you in order to reach that day … The most important task is to consume Turkish products as much as possible … [Their] raggedness should be regarded as our honour and pride. The high price paid should be perceived as something cheap indeed and more beneficial to us.[74]

With this call for a boycott against foreigners and non-Muslims alike, the regime unleashes a campaign of terror on the last sliver of Ottoman Europe and the Aegean littoral – including Gelibolu, or as it is known in the West, Gallipoli.

A pall-like climate of fear settles over the region as the Special Organization ransacks Greek businesses and shops, intimidates local elites and clergy, and raids villages. Killing takes place by torchlight, then by the hot glow of farmhouses, homes and livelihoods burning. The Special Organization's thuggery is backed by quasi-legal measures: arbitrary taxation, seizure of property and forced conscription. Official 'population exchanges' with the government of Greece are arranged, escorting thousands of ordinary people onto transport ships.

A year later, during the height of the Gallipoli campaign, New Zealand's official war correspondent Malcolm Ross will travel to Mytilene, Lesbos. He will find thousands of ejected and dejected Greeks there, who tell him their stories. The CUP established a conscription scheme, one refugee explains, whereby Greek men thought they were being enlisted into the soldiery, but were instead arranged into rough worker battalions, made to mend roads. They could buy their freedom – £40, according to Ross – or leave the country altogether. They dare not return.[75]

Throughout the terror, the CUP denies any wrongdoing. Those departing Greeks are leaving by their own choice, they maintain. All the while, they are pioneering a new technique of deniability: the 'dual-track mechanism', in which governors are given separate sets of orders, one transparent and legal, the other secret and repressive. In April 1914, for example, Talât sends an 'extremely urgent and top secret' reminder to party men on the ground, instructing them to ensure Greek villagers board their boats 'without any indication being given that [the process] is the result of a [government] directive'.[76]

Once a district is largely cleared of its Greeks, the CUP bring in a new agency: the Directorate for the Settlement of Tribes and Immigrants (İAMM),[77] tied closely to Talât's Interior Ministry. The İAMM oversees the distribution of 'leftover' Greek property to Muslim refugees fleeing the Balkans – a bureaucratic plundering operation, embodying the regime's new goal of empire-wide transformation.

A conservative estimate: at least 100,000 Greeks deported in mere months.[78]

Despite its viciousness, cruelty and randomness, the regime's terror campaign is a symptom of weakness and desperation, a weakness only accentuated over the winter of 1913–14.

Reconciling their differences with independents and the Patriarchate, the ARF resolves to bring the Armenian Question back to the table of international diplomacy.

They return to lobbying the Great Powers – Britain, France, Russia and an invigorated Germany – to sponsor reforms in the Six Provinces, reforms that were never passed by the CUP. They are reluctant in doing so, but have no choice. Krikor Zohrab repeatedly tries to appeal to the constitutionalists and democrats still lingering in the CUP – to no avail. He concludes: 'We cannot salve our wounds through speeches from the rostrum of the Parliament.'[79]

The Powers tussle amongst themselves over rights and interests, as empires are wont to do.

In the end, crucially, unsurprisingly, Russia is the only supporter of the Reform Plan set out in the Yeniköy Accord of February 1914. The Six Provinces will be split into two administrative sections with a neutral foreign inspector appointed to oversee changes in each. Louis Constant Westenenk, former administrator of Dutch Indonesia, will manage the northeast from Erzerum. Nicolai Hoff, a major in the Norwegian Army, will handle the southeast from his office in Van.[80]

The Armenians are disappointed. The Reform Plan falls well short of the autonomy they envision and does not involve the participation of all the Powers, opening them up to the predictable charge of treason that they are conspiring with Russia.

The CUP regime loathes it outright, tries to stall, vacillate and drag its heels at every turn. Yet it is powerless to halt the Russian diktat. It induces a Pavlovian reflex, triggers their sense of siege, a snowballing of greater and greater crises – another ethnic or religious minority trying to break away from the Ottoman Empire, inviting in foreign powers to meddle in their affairs, to violate their sovereignty. As Zohrab notes in his diary with more than a hint of worry: 'The

Turks would rather die than accept interference of any kind from the powers in the Armenian question, although they know that the country would die along with them. They regard this as … a question of life and death for all of Turkey and their party'.[81] At the centre of it all are former friends, the ARF and CUP, the former transfigured in the latter's imagination into an ever-pressing internal enemy.

An ominous mood takes hold
In Istanbul, death threats against the Armenian Patriarch. Pro-CUP papers filled with inflammatory editorials against Armenians. Insulting graffiti down back alleys, and black marks painted above the doors of Armenian shops. Churches defaced.

Portentous signs of a coming apocalypse.

Under the cover of total war, the CUP will plan a final solution to the Armenian Question.

3

Halcyon days

The world sleepwalks towards war

Amid an assassination, a blank cheque, total mobilizations, the revving of an infernal engine, that waking from noisome slumber, Ottoman rulers plot.

History will cast them as cautious and conservative during the fraught torquing weeks of the July Crisis. Restrained, reluctant to take sides, unsure whether their armies, exhausted after four years of constant combat, can fight and win.

Such dogma deceives. In July of 1914, the CUP sees the coming war not as a galling aberration or a monumental folly, but as a *liberation*: a chance to right those wrongs committed against them. Representing the hard Nationalist wing of the CUP, propagandist Hüseyin Cahit Yalçin praises the war as 'a stroke of good fortune upon the Turkish people, who had been sure of their own decline'. The nation, he warns, will make an 'historical reckoning'.[1]

Rejected by the French, betrayed by the British and with the Russians unwilling to renege on their Reform Plan for the Six Provinces, the Ottomans instead choose to side with Germany and Austria-Hungary as a member of the Central Powers.

Warm relations with the Reich run deep. Kaiser Wilhelm II, during a state visit to Ottoman lands in 1898, had proclaimed himself a 'friend' of Muslims 'for all time'. Enver had spent two years in Berlin as military attaché before 1911. In 1913, Otto Liman von Sanders helmed a military mission to reform the bedraggled Ottoman army. German financiers fund the *Baghdadbahn*, a rail line scything south through Anatolia, linking Berlin to Mesopotamia and its oil.

The CUP wants arms, training, finance and protection. In return, the Kaiser desires the opening of a second front against Russia and to choke its lifeblood by shuttering the Dardanelles. Ambitious German planners also seek to wield the influence of Islam against enemies with colonies of large Muslim populations: India, Egypt and French North Africa. In November, they will secure a declaration of *jihad*, holy war, against their enemies. As Christians, the Germans are tactfully excluded from the incitement.

The two empires sign an ultra-secret eight-point treaty on 2 August 1914 – one day *after* Germany declares war on Russia. The CUP, then, know they are going to fight.

Two weeks later, Talât urgently recalls Major Hoff from Van, cancelling his mission to oversee the Armenian Reform Plan. On his return to Istanbul, the Norwegian major meets with Talât and Krikor Zohrab. The Armenian leader, deflated, writes to his diary that Hoff has come back with the conviction that 'Armenia needed reforms and that the Turks had no desire to enact' them.[2] His wry colleague Vartkes Seringiulian, meanwhile, greets Hoff with a joke: 'You have reformed Armenia, *inshallah*, and now you are back.'[3]

It is to be a bitter quip, for the Reform Plan is the last chance to save the Armenians.

The threat of war throws the Armenian leadership into a gloomy existential crisis. They are being torn between two poles, Russian and Ottoman. Their population is partitioned between these lands, both powers demanding total loyalty and devotion. Where will their sympathies rest? Ought the ARF to reorganize its self-defence units to protect the Armenian population? Should they link up with an advancing Russian army? Or do nothing?

In the capital, Zohrab calls together a meeting of the capital's elite. Discussions tense with unease. Zohrab, feeling increasingly pessimistic (and not knowing of the deal already cut with Germany) worries that 'if Turkey joins Russia's enemies, it will take its revenge out on us for these years of revolution and also for the Armenian Cause'.[4]

An impasse, an uneasy conclusion: Armenians, even revolutionary ones, must declare allegiance to the land and ruler to which they belong. For Russian Armenians, the Tsar and the Motherland. For Ottoman Armenians, the CUP and the Homeland. Even if it means they face each other on the battlefield.

On the evening of 13 August, as the first salvoes are unleashed in Europe, Zohrab boards a steam ferry to his home on the island of Kınalıada. Alongside him, devoted colleagues who have endured much in the last six years: Vartkes, Armen Garo and the fellow MP Vahan Papazian, preparing to leave for his electoral district of Van the next morning.

Seagulls screech and dive over dark water. 'You can be sure that they're going to do something to us,' Zohrab says.[5]

Before the modest, smooth grey stone parliament building in Wellington, New Zealand, a impatient hush swarms the thousands assembled for an anticipated declaration.

'War has broken out with Germany.'

A patriotic roar rents the warm evening air. A flutter of waved homburgs, flatcaps, handkerchiefs. Three cheers for the King.

Prime Minister William Massey, a stolid unceremonious man, head of the conservative Reform Party, entreats them to 'present a united front to our enemies … That we will be called upon to make sacrifices goes without saying, but I am confident that those sacrifices will be made individually and collectively, willingly, and in a manner in accord with the highest traditions of our race and the Empire to which we belong.'[6]

On Willis, Manners and Cuba Streets, the throng grows to over 15,000. Under the bluster of swishing Union Jacks, spontaneous renditions of *Rule Britannia* and *La Marseillaise*. Men form themselves into regimental lines six rows deep – an echo of compulsory military training – marching behind a corps of Territorials to thunderous exaltation.[7]

In Auckland, discarded evening editions are whipped up in a stampede along Queen Street, mingling with more frantic Union Jacks. A gang of men climb nine stories of an office block to wave the imperial colours. In one theatre showing newsreels, shots of British warships spark a five-minute ovation.[8]

In sumptuous Melbourne, on Collins Street, word has not yet broken out. Anxious tussles at the offices of *The Argus* and *The Age*, a clamour growing feverish. 'What's the news? Tell us the news.' A crowd of hundreds surge past a blockade of constables, grabbing at special issues of the paper still warm from the presses. The declaration spreads quickly, a ripple through the city, throughout Australia. In opera houses, packed fugue-filled cafés, hurrahs for the empire.[9]

Later that night, a gang of 2,000 'larrikins' clash with mounted police, threatening to 'smash up' foreigners, breaking the windows of Chinese shops and terrorizing their tenants.[10]

Australian Labor leader Andrew Fisher, soon to become prime minister, summarizes the mood: 'Turn your eyes to the European situation, and give the kindest feelings toward the Mother Country … Australians will stand beside our own, to help and defend her, to our last man and our last shilling.'[11]

The Boer War a decade earlier is still fresh memory, thought of as a faraway conflict with few casualties. Young men envision hardy challenges, adventure, courage and triumph. Aside from a few meek pacifists, few understand or protest the impending carnage. Even dissident socialists abandon their attack on the capitalist war machine. In the Dominions, the duty is to King first, Empire second, Country third. Reservists are called up; others barrage enlistment stations with requests to serve:

> From the gum fields and the timber mills, from the sheep runs and the dairy farms and the flax swamps, from mine and office and factory and school, shop hands and lawyers, labourers and university professors, mechanics and parsons, a few crooks and deadbeats, and a great crowd of decent chaps – they came pouring in. There was no troubled conscience ... The schools and the editors and the parsons had done their work too thoroughly for that.[12]

The unanimity of feeling is just as well. Despite Federation in Australia in 1901, and Dominion in New Zealand in 1907, both nations have no say in whether they will join the coming inferno. Their participation in the war is for London to decide.[13]

The foothills of the Caucasus Mountains divide Ottoman land from Russian. At this imperial intersection, wedged between the Black and Caspian Seas, a covert and surreptitious conflagration will erupt.

Under the cover of their deceitful neutrality the CUP reforms the Special Organization, fresh from their terror campaign against the Greeks. Enver's War Ministry, Talât's Interior Ministry and the Central Committee of the CUP all have a hand in the Special Organization's plans, but it is Dr Bahaeddin Şakir who directly oversees the daily operation of this embryonic *Einsatzgruppen* from his base in Erzerum.

Their goal is to upset the tender ethnic and religious balance in the far east of Anatolia. To pit Kurds and Turks against Russians and Armenians. Internecine fighting, they believe, will stall any advance of the Russian army in this vulnerable region.

The Special Organization is no longer made up of hardened political operatives alone. Each militia has a diverse membership: ordinary Turks, Kurdish tribesmen, regular soldiers and Circassian guerrillas. To bloat their numbers for this special task, Talât instructs prison wardens in the eastern provinces in mid-September:

> Those tribe members and other persons of influence who for past crimes are today confined in jails and prisons, or who have been sentenced but escaped,

and about whom it is hoped that they might be exploited for military actions, are to all receive a general pardon; armed gangs are to be then formed under their leadership that, when necessary, will attack enemy territory; *this will be convenient in the future for the purpose of saving the country.*[14]

Butchers and petty thieves, killers and rapists. Convicts. They are sent eastwards en masse into the fractious Caucasus to skirmish with enemy garrisons, inciting local Muslims to rebel against foreign intruders, preaching unity in the face of an aggressor. Wherever these Special Organization thugs venture, Armenian villages burn.

Russian agents provocateur try their own dirty tricks in exchange, agitating and inflaming the opposite side of the barricade, seeking declarations of loyalty from nomadic Kurds and Georgian Christians, actively arming Russian Armenian partisans.[15]

By October, the result of this clandestine meddling by competing empires is a cauldron of rampant sectarianism primed to burst. As with the Hamidian Terror, such tension clicks the cycle of reprisals into gear.[16]

By now the fortified stalemate of the Western Front has already been rutted deep into muddy French earth. The horrible pattern of the next four years is set.

Finally, officially, in early November, the Ottoman Empire enters the war. Under chill autumn rain, with the blistering thunder of artillery, the Caucasian Front opens with a series of bloody skirmishes against Russian troops. They beat each other back into trenches as the first tufts of snow fall.

Enver, thrilled by any whiff of combat, plans his counterattack. He and his officers envision an ambitious, sweeping strike across the valleys and mountains of the front. Their target is Sarıkamış, a town on the road between Erzerum and Kars hemmed in on all sides by towering slopes.

To achieve such a task, Enver must march his troops across these perilous peaks facing high winds and deep powder. He knows that his men are poorly equipped, many without coats to keep out the cold or boots to keep the freezing sludge at bay. He trusts instead in old qualities of heroism. Addressing the assembled armies, he blusters that 'success does not come from the appearance or kit of the soldiers, but from valour and brave hearts'.

Otto Liman von Sanders, the German army advisor, thinks Enver's plan is foolish and 'extremely difficult, if not altogether impossible'.[17] Nevertheless, the assault begins on 22 December 1914. Enver hopes to have victory by Christmas Day.

He comes close. Despite leaving frozen soldiers littered over the landscape during the advance, enough energy is mustered to occupy the barracks in Sarıkamış itself on 29 December.

Russian commanders are thrown into a panic. Cables arrive from the front warning of imminent defeat, advising the need to evacuate all forces from the Caucasus. In response, Grand Duke Nicholas, supreme head of the Russian army, summons a British military attaché on 30 December and begs him to 'compensate for Turkish victories in the Caucasus'.[18]

But Enver's achievement is quickly lost. A retreat sounds, a counteroffensive by the Russians made, and the war minister has a disaster on his hands. Within two weeks, in temperatures that never reach above −3°Celsius, 30,000 Ottoman soldiers perish, most of them lost to frostbite and hypothermia. Nearly 30,000 more are wounded or taken prisoner.

It is, in no uncertain terms, a humiliating catastrophe
Enver, having commanded the assault personally, flees back to Istanbul to stem the damage to his reputation, never again to command another force in the field.[19] He refuses to be held responsible for the defeat, for sending his men into the depths of the Caucasian winter without enough equipment and clothing and for throwing away their lives for nothing. He casts around for *something* or *someone* to blame. If Enver is not at fault, there must be intrigue.

He settles upon the Armenians as an absolving scapegoat.

Some Ottoman Armenians, it is true, desert the army during the battle, as noted by the medic Ali Rıza Eti, who bitterly observes that deserters would likely give away troop movements and plans. He reports resentment festering in the trenches: up to five Armenians shot every day 'by accident', Eti writes. 'If it goes on like that, there won't be any Armenians left in the battalions in a week.'[20] Of course, the young medic cannot know that desertions from all ranks are commonplace throughout the Ottoman army.[21]

An additional insult, fodder for conspiracy: the Russians supplement their force with four groups of Armenian volunteers (*druzhiny*), mostly Russian ARF members. These groups account for less than 3 per cent of the Russian Caucasus army and are prone to panic and retreat,[22] but Enver seizes on this perceived disloyalty, inflating it into a narrative of treachery and treason and playing directly into the CUP's worst fear of an internal enemy working to partition the empire. Propaganda is prepared in this accusatory tone of voice.[23]

As head of the Special Organization, Dr Bahaeddin Şakir sees the Sarıkamış defeat first-hand. He develops the view that it is 'necessary to be afraid of the enemy within as with those outside the borders'. The doctor compiles a sheaf of files on 'Armenian armed gangs' in the region, which he presents to Talât and the other CUP leaders during a series of meetings in Istanbul in late February 1915.[24]

The minutes of these meetings will forever remain lost to history. There is no knowing what is said, what kind of resentment rages and what revenge is demanded. Their resolution is only revealed by their actions. To begin dealing with the Armenians more forcefully. To suppress them. To crush them. Even to annihilate them.[25]

Talât has already warned the security services to 'follow and observe' the leadership of the Armenian political movements who he accuses of 'agitation and disturbance',[26] and instructed the police force and all government services in the eastern provinces purged of Armenian employees.[27]

The next step is to purge the army.

On 25 February 1915, Order Number 8682 is sent out from the War Ministry with Enver's signature attached. It is headed 'Increased Security Precautions'.

'Armenian individuals are absolutely not to be employed in armed service,' the order reads, 'either in the mobile armies or in the mobile and permanently deployed gendarmerie, nor in service of the offices of the army headquarters.'[28]

Over the following months, Armenians become military chattel, demoted into labour battalions, slugging carts of food and crates of ammunition, reduced to the indignity of digging trenches and latrines.

Some Ottoman commanders, with their own neuroses or suspicion or fear of Armenians, take Enver's humiliating order as a licence to utterly cleanse their own ranks.[29] Armenians in the 52nd Division – under Halil Paşa, Enver's uncle – are 'degraded, divested of their uniforms', then arranged into 'batches of 80–100 men … isolated, surrounded by Turkish officers and soldiers, and either stabbed to death or shot to death'. There is 'no accounting, and not a trace of criminal procedure against the murderers'.[30]

In his memoirs, Halil will proudly admit to 'working to destroy the Armenian nation to the last person'.[31]

This is how deep and profoundly felt the CUP's paranoia, its siege mentality, runs. It would rather jeopardize its own war effort, risk the ruin of its empire, than share it with Armenians. But it is precisely with a military justification that the CUP expands its anti-Armenian campaign to *civilians* for the first time.

December 1914. A quixotic incident occurs. The quaintly named HMS *Doris*, a British cruiser, lands marines ashore near İskenderun. The captain convinces the local Ottoman garrison to blow up their own rail locomotives under the threat of bombardment.

This region, at the right-angle corner of the Mediterranean, is so undefended that if a full-scale force is to land here, they could quickly advance north, cleaving Anatolia from the Arab provinces, cutting the Ottoman Empire in half and knocking it out of the war – a much better option than the heavily defended Gallipoli Peninsula.[32]

The CUP, wise to such weaknesses, accuses the Armenian residents of Dörtyol, a short drive north from İskenderun, of contriving to signal British warships off the coast. Whether or not the accusation is true matters little. Talât orders the province governor to 'act with the utmost force and despatch ... It is necessary to thoroughly suppress any incident by harsh and decisive means'.[33]

Dörtyol's Armenians are the first civilians targeted by the CUP, several hundred deported from the region on 12 March 1915. Many of the men are forced into labour battalions, their fate sealed. The rest do not retaliate, flee or fight back on the long trudge to Adana.[34]

In the hardy isolated town of Zeitun just north of Dörtyol, however, some young Armenian radicals choose to resist when gendarmes come looking for army deserters. They barricade themselves behind the red-hued brick walls of the Holy Mother of God monastery, and hold out until 26 March when nearby artillery shells the edifice.[35]

Flames lick at ancient spires. God is not on the side of the radicals.

Their hold-out is used as justification by the CUP when they expel the entire Armenian population of Zeitun to Konya, far to the west. No provision is made for them. Thousands die of hunger and disease.[36]

Still, there is no collective revolt. Even the local German consul Walter Rössler explicitly rules out any suggestion of a nationwide uprising, reporting that 'these unrests are rather fully explained by their seeds which exist locally and which stem from the deep suffering gripping Turkey'.[37]

Steaming past the Indian subcontinent, rammed by the thousands into troopships – ecosystems of monotony and tedium – the Australian and New Zealand expeditionary forces expect to turn south towards South Africa, then on to France.

But with the Ottoman Empire's entrance to the conflict, and with the British War Office taking up Grand Duke Nicholas's desperate (but mistaken) plea for 'compensation,' they are instead diverted to Egypt, disembarked to the desert.

First Lord of the Admiralty Winston Churchill and Secretary of State for War Herbert Kitchener are already envisioning a naval strike and invasion at the Dardanelles.

Fused together into a single unit – the Australia New Zealand Army Corps, or Anzac – training takes place near Cairo: a slog of rifle drills and hard route marches.

For most Dominion soldiers, it is their first time in a foreign land. Their first interaction with cultures other than their country's own (despised) indigenous people. Bargain-hunting in bazaars, their descriptions of Muslim Arabs are riddled with slurs and contempt. They feel a closer affinity with the city's sizeable Christian communities, Orthodox Greeks, Maronites, Copts and Armenians. A pre-diaspora diaspora.

For Dunedin-born Raymond Ward, this ancient land is a place of fascination rather than bemusement. He throws himself amongst its peoples, absorbing antiquity: Luxor, the Sphinx, the Pyramids, Thebes, Heliopolis, awing at Napoleon's Citadel. He attends a Greek mass and meets an 'Armenian gentleman' who promises to take him to an Apostolic service. 'Having always been interested in the matter of Oriental schismatics,' Ward tells his father, 'you will understand how pleased I am of these opportunities.'[38]

Lance Corporal Henry Lanser of Chatswood, Sydney, makes the most of a recording studio run by an enterprising Armenian, Setrag Mechian, scratching into shellac a three-minute Christmas message for his family – the last time they will ever hear his voice.[39]

Just a few months before making land at Gallipoli, Private Blair Cullen of Gore writes his brother, telling of intriguing downtime between trench-digging: tours of Cairo's cramped quarters led by an enterprising twelve-year-old Armenian boy named Vahan Michanian, and his visit to Michanian's home for an afternoon of tea, lounging and smoking. Cullen meets the family: the father an engineer, and an eighteen-year-old daughter who Cullen describes with more than a hint of passing passion as 'extremely nice'.

One can picture the captured imagination of young Vahan as Cullen tells him of the tiny farming town of Gore and that verdant land at the bottom of the world. Vahan writes his own letter to the Cullens:

> Dear Friend,
> I, the undersigned Vahan Michanian, aged 12 years, am an Armenian and am living in Cairo, near your brother's camp. I am one of the little friends of your brother, and I had the honor of having tea with him in our house yesterday. I am glad to inform you that your brother, Mr Blair Cullen, is in good health and

comfort. Your brother's camp is about 10 minutes' walk from our village and I often go to see him. The winter is warmer here than your summer, so don't trouble much. Please accept my and my family's kind regards and given them to yours. Waiting for your reply and wishing every victory for the just cause of the Allies.

I am, sincerely yours,
Vahan Michanian.[40]

Far to the east, touching the Persian border, fringing the shores of a vast salt lake, a grand city: Van. The closest thing Armenians have to a capital, the only place where they hold a demographic majority. Once an epicentre of medieval kingdoms, once Mkrtich Khrimian's home base, now Vahan Papazian's electorate.

More than 450 towns and villages are scattered over a nirvanaesque tableau of labourers and farmhands tilling the highland plain. Its cosmopolitan centre is divided into two quarters: the Old City, with its worn cobble streets and a ninety-metre-tall vertical rock formation topped with ancient battlements; affluent *Aygestan*, or The Vineyard, tree-lined avenues and modern villas, consulates and mission stations.

'Van in this world, paradise in the next,' goes the Armenian saying. Turkish residents sing of 'Van in this world, faith in the afterlife.'[41]

Both the ARF and the Social Democrats have long been active here. Even after their split with the CUP, a relatively enlightened governor named Hasan Tahsin Bey works closely with the ARF leadership in the city – including the MP Arshak Vramian and the dashing activist Aram Manukian – to maintain calm.

But with the war comes a new governor. Enver Paşa's brother-in-law. An old school friend of Vramian's. Cevdet Bey.

Reputation precedes arrival, Cevdet having been part of the CUP's plan to hassle and harry Russian army manoeuvres before war had been officially declared. Wherever Cevdet goes, Armenians are subject to harsh, even deadly treatment. It is this treatment that prompts Vahan Papazian, fearing for his life, to flee over the Persian border.

Vramian, meanwhile, stays put and begins collecting testimony from miserable refugees. Counting victims. After months of investigative work, in the early weeks of 1915, he cables a long memorandum to Talât's Interior Ministry. 'An anti-Christian policy will not help save the country,' Vramian advises:

> The government must cease to consider the Armenian elements in the Empire as enemies ... If the government is at present incapable of guaranteeing the

Armenians the exercise of their sacred rights – its life, honour, religion, and property – then it ought to authorise them to defend those rights. If it is to be presumed that low-level government officials have misinterpreted the central government's orders and understood nothing of its policies, then these officials must be punished and forcibly set back on the right path.[42]

Vramian believes that these regional depredations carried out against helpless peasants are the actions of disobedient officials. But he is wrong.

Within a fortnight of his arrival, Cevdet demands more troops and more guns; more Armenians rounded up for conscription. A Russian advance into the region is likely, and Cevdet fears the ARF in Van will help them.[43]

Pre-empting this imaginary rebellion, Cevdet orders door-to-door searches of Armenian houses in the city and villages in the countryside, looking for weapons. Such intrusion angers the Armenian leadership, now furiously trying to maintain order. Clarence D Ussher, American missionary and head of the Red Cross hospital in Van, observes that though oppression is rife, many of Van's leaders do 'all in their power to keep the peace throughout these months when the political situation was exceedingly complicated and the tension extreme'.

They know themselves, Ussher writes, 'to be living in a powder magazine where the smallest spark would cause an all-destructive explosion'.[44]

Churchill, ever arrogant, believes his fleets can waltz up the Dardanelles, blasting their way to Istanbul. Enver, equally arrogant, boasts to the American ambassador Henry Morgenthau he 'shall go down in history as the man who demonstrated the vulnerability of England and her fleet. I shall show that her navy is not invincible'.[45] Only one of them can be right.

After probing the Straits' defences throughout February, Churchill commits a mighty flotilla to breaching The Narrows on 18 March. At the spearhead of these iron leviathans is the dreadnought *Agamemnon*, a fact that no doubt appeals to classically trained officers. This is the channel by which the Greeks once came to siege Troy.

The air rumbles. Scorched smell of cordite burning, blunt blasted mortar, choking fumes. Shrieks, whizzes, armour drilled through in wrenching punches. The Allies do not know the true strength of the forts guarding The Narrows, reinforced with German-made Krupp behemoths, nor do they know of the thick layers of mines lolling below the waves.

The French battleship *Bouvet* sinks in two minutes, pummelled by shells. The *Irresistible* lists dangerously. The *Ocean*, sent to tow the *Irresistible* out from under the aim of Ottoman gunners, takes its own punishment and founders.

Even in their first wartime moment of triumph, rumours abound in Istanbul that the CUP is preparing to abandon the city, making plans to shift men and gold to inland Konya, even as far as Ankara. They know that a considerable force – the Anzacs – is assembling on the nearby island of Lemnos.

Their survival is far from assured.

In the town of Shadakh, just south of Van, an Armenian teacher (and ARF activist) is arrested without cause. Locals come out in support, protesting outside the mayor's office.

Another provocation in a string of many. Dutifully, Arshak Vramian proposes a joint negotiating party to diffuse the situation. Cevdet agrees. On the afternoon of 16 April, four Armenians and four Turks set out for the town.

That night, the Armenian party are slaughtered in their beds.

Cevdet has lit the match on that 'powder magazine'.

Early the following morning, the governor calls both Arshak Vramian and Aram Manukian to his office. Vramian consents to meet his old friend, but telephones Manukian and warns him not to come.

It will be his last act.

Seized by Cevdet's men, Vramian, a member of parliament, is taken outside the city limits and assassinated.

Later that day, 17 April, Clarence Ussher calls on Cevdet to see if anything can be done to ease the general strain. A colonel enters the room: the head of Cevdet's personal force, nicknamed *kasab tabouri*. The Butcher Regiment.

'You sent for me,' the colonel asks, presenting himself.

'Yes,' Cevdet replies. 'Go to Shadakh and wipe out its people.'

Then, turning to Ussher with a vicious look, Cevdet holds his hand just below his knee and says, 'I won't leave one, not one so high.'[46]

The Butcher Battalion sets out. A rolling wave of destruction across the countryside.

Word reaches Aram Manukian that his comrade Vramian is missing, the earlier negotiating party dead. He vanishes underground, preparing the population for the attack they all fear is coming.

Ashkhen Ohannesian, a teenager, observes the hushed planning: 'Every night, taking turns in homes, we had secret meetings to figure out when this was going to happen and how we could prepare to resist and defend ourselves. [They] came to our house many times. They would do drills to get used to the rifles'.[47]

Manukian strategizes. For pastoral Armenians outside the city, they can do nothing. Inside, they are divided between the Vineyard and the Old City. The latter is easy to defend, its ancient walls designed for such a purpose. Manukian chooses to stay inside the Vineyard, building trenches, shepherding children and women into churches and missionary compounds.

Ashkhen Ohannesian: 'Suddenly word came to us that the Turks were going to attack in three days. Everyone got ready; the men, who were the only fighters, positioned themselves in the basements and were ready with their rifles by small windows … The Protestant churches opened up their meetinghouses for the people to take cover, and waited for the outcome'.[48]

The attack begins on 20 April 1915. Van's Armenians are under siege.

Both sides are evenly matched in manpower, but where Cevdet's gendarmes use slick, powerful German rifles, the ARF can only muster a motley collection of antiquated hunting shotguns and repeating pistols shipped in by Russian comrades years earlier. The entire population bands together. Even the children

> go from house to house to gather the brass candle bars to make shells for the bullets. They even learned to make the powder … Sometimes the fighting was at very close range, from one house to the other. The Turks had all the ammunition and ours was very limited, so we had to be very, very careful to not waste any. Some of the Armenians had the ingenuity that, when a Turk was killed, they pulled him in with a long pole to get the ammunition he was carrying.[49]

By 21 April, the revolt, as it is portrayed, is already frontpage news in Istanbul.[50] The CUP can now twist and meld this desperate defence by Armenians in one city into an empire-wide conspiracy of usurpation and overthrow.

Into this hellish fray steps Rafael de Nogales, Venezuelan reactionary, opportunistic soldier of fortune, short and wiry in his trim uniform, a pre-Hitlerite toothbrush moustache masking his upper lip. His mercenary services had been turned down by the British and the French before the Ottoman army dispatched him east.

He lands in the province itching for a fight, only to find plunder and death. Outside the barricaded walls of Van, those Armenians yet to flee find themselves at the whims of killers working steadily.

At the opposite side of Lake Van to the city, de Nogales stalks through villages being raided by the 'rabble of the vicinity'. Homes broken into. Valuables stolen. The occupants murdered in the street. Wearing the stripes of a major, de Nogales protests to a local official, who replies that he has orders from Governor Cevdet 'to exterminate all Armenian males twelve years of age and over'.

The scene on the road to the city only confirms the veracity of what Cevdet's order has wrought: 'Screaming flocks of black vultures, disputing with the dogs the putrefied Armenian corpses thrown about on every side' and 'burning villages that bathed the sky in scarlet'. The miasma of charred flesh fills the Venezuelan's nostrils.

And yet de Nogales still joins the fight gleefully, commanding a sizeable force of troops, including Kurdish irregulars. 'Nobody gave quarter nor asked it.'[51]

During the blistering battle, Cevdet proffers a temporary ceasefire and appeals to the resisters to stop fighting. Far from a conciliatory gesture, the governor's letter, passed over the lines, speaks of 'insurgents', 'imbeciles' and 'insurrection'. Cevdet casts himself as a ruler with no choice but to fire back. 'Be warned,' he concludes, '[as] soon as the cannons arrive, they will be turned on the city and will fire away until it is nothing but a pile of rubble ... Please understand that you must abandon all hope of being saved.'[52]

Unsurprisingly, the Armenians do not surrender. They hold out desperately for an entire month. Only the arrival of a Russian army on 18 May 1915 forces Cevdet's troops back, and even then they don't leave without sending a barrage into the walls of Clarence Ussher's American-flagged missionary compound.

Aram Manukian has successfully led his fighters against an Ottoman force of several thousand, and survived.

But this is no victory, and it bears no relief. Defiance is bitter, not sweet. Van will be the scene of constant combat in the coming months and years, trading hands with the rest of the far-eastern front, its mud and mercilessness, its gore and distress.

An honour roll of massacre: 55,000 slaughtered. More than half the province's Armenian population.[53]

Partly by its own blunders and partly by its own contrivance, the CUP has finally reached an apogee of existential dread. The survival of the Ottoman Empire, the CUP's raison d'etat, has never been more threatened: a perceived 'rebellion' and 'revolt' at one end of the country, and a looming invasion at the other.

Enver Paşa tells Henry Morgenthau, the American ambassador: '[He] must understand that we are now fighting for our lives at the Dardanelles and that we are sacrificing thousands of men. While we are engaged in such a struggle as this, we cannot permit people in our own country to attack us in the back.'[54]

Figure 8 'They went like kings in a pageant to their imminent death'. Credit: Australian War Memorial.

Naval Minister Cemal Paşa concurs, advancing his own conspiracy theory: 'At the moment when the Dardanelles campaign was at its crisis, the Armenians were ordered by the French and English Commanders-in-Chief of the Forces in the Eastern Mediterranean to rise.'[55]

'So long as England does not attack [Gallipoli] or some other Turkish port there is nothing to fear,' the German Ambassador Hans von Wangenheim had prophesied at the outbreak of war. 'Otherwise, nothing can be guaranteed.'[56]

It is these two events, the defence of Van and the landings at Gallipoli, that will be the final triggers in the CUP's decision to enact the annihilatory plans drawn up during its February meetings.[57]

A nation that feels itself on the verge of destruction, after all, 'will not hesitate to destroy another group it holds responsible for its situation'.[58] As one of the last large minorities in the Ottoman Empire, the Armenians will pay the ultimate price for those who, seeking independence and liberation over the last hundred years, have broken off from it.[59]

23 April. Dr Şakir's Special Organization is taken out of the control of the War and Interior Ministries, and placed solely at the discretion of the CUP's central committee.[60]

The Anzacs board their transports at Lemnos, Gallipoli's shores marked on their maps. 'All that they felt,' the poet John Masefield will later write, 'was a gladness of exultation that their young courage was to be used. They went like kings in a pageant to their imminent death.'[61]

Talât, working closely with informants, draws up several lists. He places them in sealed envelopes, and hands them to the chief of Istanbul's police.

To be opened at the appointed hour.

4

One day in April

It begins on Saturday evening. The security men in dark uniforms with holstered guns fan out across Istanbul's dusk. They carry lists: lists of Armenians. They knock urgently at doors. Get out of bed, they say. Put your clothes on, they say. We're taking you. The men with guns and lists go to the grand homes of prominent men, to the seminaries where priests pray as they're seized, to the newspaper offices where editors walk out in chains. They haul Komitas from his Şişli apartment, the soft-natured composer still wearing his clerical robes and shivering with fright. The dragnet drags on through the night, as the city sleeps. The rap of knuckles on wood, the shouts and the threat of force repeated dozens of times over. Come with us.

Bunked deep in the holds of warships, the soldiers eat jam and cheese and bully beef. They play cards as the low throb of turbines churns them across the harbour from Mudros. Others walk the deck smoking,. Too restless for sleep. An armada stretches across the dull blue horizon, bound for a battlefield not yet defiled by death. They prepare kits and clean rifles. Some write final letters to be kept in breast pockets for their families. In case they don't see the next day's sun rise. In case they don't make it past the beach.[1]

The policemen and security men come for Dr Boghosian, chief psychiatrist at the Surp Pırgiç Armenian Hospital, at 2.00 am on Sunday morning. Three of them at his door. Come with us, they say. You're ill and need emergency care. The doctor protests, of course. He is in good health. But he is taken all the same by the men with guns and lists to the War Ministry, where they place him in a prison reserved for higher ranks.[2] They come for Krikoris Balakian too, a formidable and serious-minded priest trained in Germany, key negotiator for the dashed Reform Plan. They march him and eight others to an armoury. 'The night smelled of death.'[3]

Officers stride amongst their soldiers at 2.30 am. Stand-to, they order. The ship's engines cut. An eerie silence swarms their ears, their throats. Rum is handed out by the cupful, liberal amounts to gird them for the combat ahead. Sailors rush about with purpose, preparing the pinnaces and row boats which will take the first landing parties ashore, the operation done in mere whispers as the moon drifts below sharp cliffs standing tall in the navy-grey light of morning. The soldiers are leaden with bullets and bombs and enough biscuits to last three days. They drop slowly into their small crafts. Some shake hands. Go well, mate, they say.

The Armenian men – Komitas, Dr Boghosian, Krikoris Balakian among them – are driven to the central prison, and shoved into a wooden shack at the centre of the jail grounds. Under strict guard, the prisoners are forbidden to speak to each other. They sit quietly, sombre, on the bare wooden floor under the faint light of a flickering lantern.[4] Military cars approach in the dawn gloom every few hours, cutting their roaring engines. The iron gates yank open, bringing more Armenians into captivity, into that small shack. Some wear nothing but their nightclothes and slippers. They are drawn from the depth and breadth of Armenian cultural and political life: activists and leaders for the ARF and Social Democrats; members of Parliament; poets, novelists and journalists; lawyers, school principals and doctors; and even an umbrella salesman. Although they suspect, none of them know why they have been detained. The arrests are not legitimate, nor legal. No charge is laid against them.

Chugging pinnaces heave rowboats four-wide towards Gallipoli's shore. The sea barely murmurs as they surge coastwards. Soldiers deploy oars and with rhythmic grunts the boats bear them closer. Quiet prevails. Until one of the steam funnels on a pinnace catches fire, sending a red flare streaking across the sky, reflected dully in the water. A searchlight flicks on. Then another, ranging over the Aegean. Then all is still again, until a splash of shallow water announces the first Anzac soldiers on the beach. A solitary shot cracks from the cliff face. A pause hangs again in the morning air, bated.

It is around 5.30 am. The date is 25 April 1915. Krikoris Balakian calls it 'Red Sunday'. Others call it Anzac Day.

Australians make up the first wave of the Allied landers at Gallipoli. They expect a wide beach with a steady incline, but are dropped in the wrong place, at Arıburnu, an area of dense scrubland and perilous red-brown ravines. Some attempt to race up slippery paths towards the heights guarded by Ottoman defenders in entrenched lines with spitting rifles. Most dive for the cover of the precipice.

New Zealanders follow five hours later, crammed aboard their boats as sharp shell shrapnel flecks churned water. They are confronted by the sight of Australian dead and wounded splayed out along the sand. Men stride back from disorganized firing lines bloodied, mouths grimly hanging open. Cannon fire spreads hot flying metal over the injured on the beach, inflicting new wounds. Medics practically throw the blighted into lighters bound for the hospital ships behind. The beach keeps filling up.

The New Zealanders are ordered immediately into the fight, dashing under full packs, reaching the rough holdouts of their Australian comrades, treading on dead friends and enemies alike. Some soldiers can barely reach their allotted positions for the intensity of machine gun and rifle fire. They sit in their own shallow ditches, swearing to themselves as wounded men beyond cry out for water, for aid. For their mothers.

'The Turks have got the range of this place and they pepper it,' one man of the Auckland Battalion records. 'Dozens coming back wounded. Singie got shot in thigh. Lots dead … Latest news is that nearly all officers shot and extreme left wing retreating. No reinforcements and no artillery … I feel very frightened.'[5]

On the other side of the lines, the ambitious young CUP officer Mustafa Kemal gives the order to reinforce crumbling Ottoman defenders at Arıburnu. He personally leads a regiment to the heights overlooking the beach. 'I do not expect that any of us would not rather die than repeat the shameful story of the Balkan war,' Kemal's instructions read. 'But if there are such men among us, we should at once lay hands upon them and set them up in line to be shot!'[6]

The Ottomans hold the heights once the day is up. After that, only digging.

Imprisoned Armenians spend that day in quiet terror, watching as guards pace, listening to dull thunder: the Russian navy, pounding Marmara's forts in aid of the Anzacs.

There is only one woman among them: the writer and teacher Marie Beylerian. Zabel Yessayan, out visiting friends when the police came, hides in a friend's apartment, one of many intellectuals stashed in cupboards, under rafters, and in the gaps between walls and floors.

With evening's fall, the captives assemble at the main gate. A warden reads slowly from yet another list, checking that each man and woman is present. They are then searched, and all personal effects confiscated. The guards insist their belongings will be returned, but they won't.

The prisoner-intellectuals are divided into groups of twenty and prodded on to red military buses. Once those 240 or so are on board, they speed off into the night.

Some sob and whimper. 'Even the bravest were trembling,' Krikoris Balakian observes.[7]

Terrified, guiltless Komitas tries to hide his head under the hem of Balakian's overcoat, the great composer reduced to whimpers. 'He thought the trees were bandits on the attack … He begged me to say a blessing for him, in the hope that it would calm him.'[8]

They are piled into a steamship, taken across the water to the grand arches of Haydarpaşa train station, and from there onto a special train bound for the Anatolian interior.

> The lights went out, the car doors closed, and with the policemen and police soldiers around us, the train started. Slowly we left behind the places where we all had grieving and defenceless mothers, sisters, wives, children, as well as worldly goods. We moved to our graves, nameless and unknown, to be buried forever.[9]

This operation, carried out by direct orders from the central committee of the CUP, has a specific and defined purpose: to decapitate the spiritual, cultural and political leadership of Armenian society in the Ottoman Empire. Without political organizers to petition the government against oppression, without its writers in the popular journals and newspapers to criticize the CUP's actions and without legal experts to argue for the defence at inevitable show trials, the CUP renders the wider Armenian population rudderless and ever more vulnerable.

But the CUP's plans for this April day go much further than a roundup of the Armenian intelligentsia: Talât Paşa uses a telegraph machine installed in his private study to send a series of instructions which will have profound and awful consequences.

The first cable rules that 'no travel documents or permissions to go abroad whatsoever be given to those Armenians who are known by the government to be suspicious, and especially not the leaders and prominent members of planning and active committees'.[10] Further cables demand the complete dissolution of the ARF and the Social Democrat Party presence in every province, their newspapers forcibly shuttered and their leaders arrested to be tried in military tribunals. Further arrests are expected of 'those Armenians deemed by the government to be either important or injurious'. Anyone left over 'whose continued residency in their present districts would seem ill-advised' are to be 'concentrated in places that would appear suitable within the provincial district and that no possibility be given them to escape or flee'.[11]

Most critically of all, Talât changes the route of earlier deportations. No longer will Armenians be forced from their homes and sent to comparably more hospitable regions near major cities. Instead, Talât chooses to 'deport those whom it is seen as necessary to remove ... to the regions of southeastern Aleppo, Der Zor, and Urfa'.[12] The Syrian deserts. Not much more than wastelands.

They are to be sent to the desert to die.

There are some names that do not appear on the lists: The patriarch, Zaven Der Yeghiayan. Vartkes Seringiulian. Krikor Zohrab.

Once the extent of the roundup is clear, rather than lay low or flee, these men immediately petition Talât and Prime Minister Said Halim demanding 'mild and forgiving policies, rather than severe and repressive ones. This is how we ask the government to treat the Nation, at least out of respect for the memory of the thousands of Armenian soldiers who spilled their blood for the defence of the Ottoman fatherland'.[13]

Zohrab pesters and harangues the CUP leadership, biting back at their every excuse and justification. In a meeting with Talât, the incensed lawyer manages to extract a few concessions: perhaps, Talât admits, there were innocent people among the detained. But still, 'All those Armenians,' he says, 'who by their speeches, writings, or acts, have worked or may one day work towards the creation of an Armenia, have to be considered enemies of the state, and in the present circumstances, must be isolated.'[14]

For these 'enemies of the state' arrested on Red Sunday/Anzac Day, a fate worse than 'isolation' awaits. After their initial capture, they are divided into groups and sent to different places: the politicians and activists to Ayaş in the province of Ankara, and the intellectuals to Çankırı, northeast of Ankara city.[15]

Over the coming months, almost all of them will be tortured and killed.

But still Zohrab persists. He goes to see Talât once last time. Over an absurd, mock-metaphorical game of cards, their conversation devolves into epithets and accusations.

'Someday you will have to account for your misdeeds,' Zohrab roars.

'And who may I ask will demand such an accounting?' Talat replies, coolly.

'I will!' Zohrab exclaims, before storming from the room.[16]

A week later, both Zohrab and Vartkes are arrested.

The pair, both still members of parliament, face an arduous, circuitous journey through Anatolia. South to Aleppo, then north again to Urfa. During their descent into the maw, Zohrab is allowed to write home to his wife Clara. Ever the rational lawyer, he pleads with reason: 'Both law and justice would demand that if we were to face charges in Diyarbekir, we would first be interrogated here before being actually taken to Diyarbekir; and only if there were one iota of truth in the charges, or even the suggestion of truth, we would be sent to face trial'.[17]

He amends a note to his last letter: 'My love, my one and only, for us the last curtain is falling. I have no more strength. If I do not survive, my last advice to my children is this: they should ways love and cherish each other, and worship you, and not let their hearts ache too long, and remember me'.[18]

The trial never comes. It is on that road to Diyarbakır that Krikor Zohrab and Vartkes Seringiulian are nailed to the ground with iron stakes, and then beheaded.[19] Zohrab's official cause of death, scornfully released by the prime minister's office, is listed as 'heart trouble and apoplexy'.

And on 26 August 1915, somewhere outside Ankara, the internationally celebrated poet Daniel Varoujan is assassinated, alongside four others. Varoujan fights back, so the assailants dig out his eyes. His poem 'Alms', written a few years earlier, is addressed 'To the starving people', a haunting premonition of what is to come, of what looms low on the horizon:

> My love has gone out, with the flame in my fireplace.
> Ashes within me, ashes around me; oh, of what use is it
> To sow tears on ashes? ...
> Come to-morrow to the graveyard, O thou Hungry One!

5

'Ashes within me, ashes around me'

Genocide demands a structure of destruction. A schematic of atrocity. An architecture.

Talât directs the operation from above, organizing the gendarmerie, instructing province governors and party functionaries – moulding the immense Ottoman bureaucracy. As chief of the Special Organization's spies and slaughter squads, Dr Bahaeddin Şakir is Talât's dutiful enforcer. Enver unleashes the army. Under Şükrü Kaya, the Directorate for the Settlement of Tribes and Immigrants (İAMM) arranges the intimate detail of deportation, the confiscation of Armenian property and the establishment of Muslim émigrés into homes left behind. The courts host show trials. The Education Ministry is integral to the rigours of forcible assimilation.

This immense apparatus of power and ruin becomes, in the words of one observer, a 'shadow, or a parallel government'.[1]

Even before the suppression of the Armenian intelligentsia, Talât had secured an early recess for the Ottoman Parliament. He can rule by decree. There will be no protest, no dissent against the coming whirlwind of steel and fire.

23 May 1915: Talât sends out a circular announcing the CUP's intention to remove Armenians from every corner of the empire.[2] The very next day, the governments of Britain, France and Russia collaborate on a joint declaration, alarmed by the speed and scale of the unfolding carnage. Together, they address the Ottoman leadership directly:

> In view of those new crimes of Turkey against humanity and civilization, the Allied governments announce publicly to the Sublime Porte that they will hold personally responsible for these crimes all members of the Ottoman government and those of their agents who are implicated in such massacres.[3]

It is the first time that one government has accused another of 'crimes against humanity'. Talât, usually so belligerent in action, panics. To give himself legal cover, he begs the Cabinet to rubber-stamp the deportation order. His Interior

Ministry drafts a petition to Prime Minister Said Halim two days later justifying the extraordinary measure. The memo warns of 'pressure' and 'foreign influence' leading to the 'dividing and partition of the Ottoman homeland', and above all, the urgent need for 'eliminating this trouble ... in a manner that is both comprehensive and absolute'.[4]

The Temporary Law of Deportation passes before the week is out.

The telegraph network and the railways – modern technologies meant to emancipate – accelerate the slaughter. The Interior Ministry expects regular reports and detailed statistics, monitoring places of origin, junctions and stopping points. Bodies are to be studiously counted.[5]

The mode of Armenian erasure: a 'dual mechanism' like that so effectively trialled on Greeks in 1913–14, a system of open, legal decrees and covert, deniable instructions. In plain view, the Interior Ministry dispatches an official order to the provinces. Simultaneously, hidden from the press, the public and foreign diplomats is a separate, secret killing order issued from the CUP's Central Committee and hand-delivered by party devotees or by Dr Şakir himself, verbally or on paper to be burned once read.[6] On the ground, however, there is really little difference between the two. 'Deportation', in CUP parlance, is merely code for 'liquidation'.[7]

The heavily Armenian eastern provinces are depopulated in the summer. August and September see the removal of central and western Anatolia's Armenians. One by one, the villages, towns and cities of the Ottoman Empire are emptied. Only Istanbul's Armenians survive in numbers, protected by a web of diplomatic officialdom.[8]

In districts closest to the Caucasian front, killing extends from males over twelve to all Armenians regardless of age or gender. Very few survive in these desiccated regions.[9] At the feet of the Special Organization, the task of murder is placed. Lurid thrusts and hacks by the riverside. In concealed mountain gorges, gravity does the work of murder. By farmyard axe, heirloom knife, standard-issue bayonet and rifle.

Soft patter of blood splashing. A shriek, a cry, arrested in a gashed throat.

Air, gasped. Mothers, begged for. God, entreated. Mercy, unseen.

From his consulate office, the American diplomat Leslie Davis watches as Harput's Armenian population, some 124,000 people, are corralled and deported. Amidst it all, he feels as if 'the world were coming to an end'.[10]

Harput is circled by Sivas, Aleppo, Diyarbakır and Erzerum. It is an epicentre of death. Or, as Davis will later call it, a Slaughterhouse Province. He watches as the famished and nearly naked dregs of neighbouring regions filter through on their way to the desert.[11]

In September, Davis ventures out to the countryside to see what has been wrought. He finds bodies. Piles of them. Some half-buried, others left rotting in the open. Burnt-out wrecks of villages, their residents all gone, their property pillaged. At Bozmashen, formerly home to 300 families, Davis finds only 'a few hungry looking cats prowling around … Everywhere it was a scene of desolation and destruction'.[12]

On horseback, he ventures still further. To a lake on the road to Diyarbakır. Visiting missionaries used to swelter on the beach here in summer months. Now it is a mass grave. A picturesque scene defiled.

Davis used to be a journalist before joining the diplomatic service, and he records with crystalline detachment the array of methods:

> One of the first corpses that we saw was that of an old man with a white beard, whose skull had been crushed in by a large stone which still remained in it. A little farther along we saw the ashes of six or eight persons, only a few fragments of bones and clothing remained unburned. One red fez was conspicuous. There were also some skull bones, as they are the strongest and are always the last to be destroyed. These ashes were about twenty feet from a tree under which there was a large red spot. This upon closer examination proved to be blood, which appeared to have been there for two or three weeks. The tree had a number of bullet holes in it, indicating that the men whose ashes we saw had probably been stood up against it and shot.[13]

Further along, greater horrors. Twenty heads sticking out of the sand along the lake's edge. Another twenty bodies sitting upright under a row of trees. In the ravines that mark the topography of this land, thousands more bodies rest in broken, contorted states. The smell of rancid flesh permeates this once-peaceful spot. No matter where he rides, Davis cannot escape the miasma.

Clinical though he may be in his writing, Davis chooses not to describe in detail what has been done to women. He notes only that nearly of them lie 'flat on their back and showed signs of barbarous mutilation by the bayonets of the gendarmes … wounds having been inflicted in many cases probably after the women were dead'.

Needing to document, needing to witness against atrocity, Davis returns to the lake a few weeks later, surveying another beach where naked forms pile atop each other, and a gorge of mutilated corpses. Small babies, long dead, among the mounds. In a nearby valley, Davis finds the strewn remains of 'not less than two thousand' Armenians. Picking up an abandoned passport, he reads that its owner had been from Erzerum, further east.[14]

Figure 9 'Panos Terlemezian, *A Mother Looking for Her Son among the Corpses*, undated'. Credit: National Gallery of Armenia (Oil on canvas, 40 x 32.5 cm).

Davis estimates some 10,000 Armenian bodies at the lake and in the crags, hillsides and canyons. This place is evidently a designated killing zone. No attempt was made to bury those who died there. They are cast off and forgotten. Not even a handful of earth for them.[15]

The governor of Diyarbakır, ruler of its black basalt walls, is Dr Mehmed Reşid, perhaps the genocidaire with the bloodiest hands.[16] As a founding member of the CUP, he is one of the party's most zealous devotees. He inflicts a 'perfect reign of terror'.[17]

In June, Reşid receives two sets of instructions – the dual mechanism. Both are from Talât. The first orders Armenians deported. The second, secret instruction, carries only three words: *Yak. Vur. Öldür.* Burn. Demolish. Kill.[18]

Every corner of Reşid's domain is rinsed of non-Muslim life. A bishop is dragged through the city's streets, coated in fuel in front of a crowd and burned to within an inch of death.[19] Others have their nails pulled out with pincers, or are flayed alive.

Not content with butchering his own people, Reşid further targets Armenians arriving in Diyarbakır from surrounding regions.[20]

Aurora Mardiganian, fourteen-year-old daughter of a prosperous family from Harput, briefly stops here on her trek south. She watches as a group of 2,000 women are huddled together by Special Organization units and marched off. 'All night long we heard the screams,' Aurora will later recall. 'There would be piercing shrieks and then only the sound of hoofbeats growing fainter ... We could not sleep that night. Sometimes even now I cannot sleep, although I am safe forever. Those screams come to me in the night time, and even with my friends all about me I cannot shut them out of my ears.'[21]

Only 300 Armenians from that column survive to morning. The Jews of the city are then escorted by gendarmes into the fields to act as grave-diggers and body-collectors, bringing 'carts and donkeys with bags swung across their backs. Into the carts and bags they piled the corpses and took them to the banks of the Tigris, where the Turks made them throw their burdens into the water.'[22]

The flood of bloated bodies carried down both the Tigris and the Euphrates cause so much pollution that populations living downstream are forbidden to drink or wash in the rivers.[23]

When other governors and foreign diplomats begin complaining of the stench drifting from his open-air morgue, Talât has to explicitly instruct Reşid to bury or cremate his victims.[24]

'My Turkishness triumphed over my identity as a doctor,' Reşid will later boast. 'The Armenian bandits were a load of harmful microbes that had afflicted the body of the fatherland. Was it not the duty of the doctor to kill the microbes?'[25]

When weighed as an instrument of cruelty, the forced march has no equal. Instantly massacred Armenians, no matter how brutal their fate, are the more fortunate.

Krikoris Balakian observes this of the deprived caravans stumbling through Anatolia: 'We were living through days of such unheard-of horror, it was impossible for the mind to fully comprehend. Those of us still alive envied those

Figure 10 'Killing Fields'. Credit: Laurence MacDaniels papers, Cornell University Library.

who had already paid their inevitable dues of bloody torture and death. We survivors became living martyrs, every day dying a few deaths and returning to life again.'[26]

The deported, these 'living martyrs', almost always women and their children, are resurrected each morning on the march. The dead awake and are made to walk once again.

Very rarely are they escorted along the most direct route. Instead, they travel across scrubland and plains, through valleys and feudal villages, over mountains. On all sides the threat of theft, rape, kidnap, or simply giving up under the weight of exhaustion, or the weight of an emaciated grandparent that has to be carried. Always going. Talât specifically orders that any resisters or escapees from the convoys be killed.[27] Always going. Towards the mirage-like writhing hell of the Syrian desert where the camps wait. Towards the dust and chaos. Towards oblivion.

Deportees are forced not only to walk, but to make incomprehensible moral choices. Pleading mercy of a gendarme might earn a gunshot to the gut. Asking a villager for bread might provoke a blow to the head. To walk more slowly than the rest of the family means being left behind, left to die, but to stay with them and offer a pinch of comfort too means death. To pluck a clump of grass by the roadside is to make a choice: Eat it yourself and last another half-day, maybe? Or give it to the child reduced to a whimpering bundle of bones rag-bound in your arms? Even suicide carries a choice: be selfish and go alone over the edge, or be selfless and take a child too?

Aghavni Mazmanian faces these same immiserations and is forced to make the same impossible decisions. Her story is emblematic, representative of what hundreds of thousands of other women endure, marked eternally by arbitrary cruelty, desperation, fear, and then finally despair.

Her story is distinct in only one way: she survives.

Aghavni's life had nearly ended before it started: born in Sivas, a northeastern province home to some 200,000 Armenians, in 1895, during the years of the Hamidian Terror. Her family had been spared death by the whim – or the mercy – of an Ottoman soldier, who kissed Aghavni's cheek as her mother cradled her. 'We give your lives to this baby girl,' the soldier said. Aghavni's father did not survive the pogroms.

She is barely into womanhood when the First World War breaks out. Like so many other Armenian men, her husband Bedros is conscripted into the army and later murdered, leaving Aghavni with two children: an infant boy, and a girl, three.

She watches as Sivas's political leaders are rounded up under the pretext of hiding weapons or plotting treason. She notes the hangings: sixty on the first day, thirty on the next, another twenty-five the day after. Several thousand of the city's Armenian elite, from teachers to pharmacists, are crammed into the central prison and the cellars of religious schools and tortured regularly.

The deportation order is given on 30 June 1915. Within two weeks, the city is emptied of Armenians, street by street, neighbourhood by neighbourhood: Aghavni, her two children, their relatives and 5,800 other families. She hires a donkey to carry the children and whatever meagre belongings were grabbed on the way out. The animal lasts three days on the road.

Ahmed Muammer Bey is the governor of Sivas, and conveniently, also head of the local Special Organization unit. He positions its squads just outside the city. In an elaborately staged intervention, they halt the deportation columns, and instruct the Armenians to hand over anything valuable. If they disobey, they will be shot on the spot.

On the border between Sivas and Harput province, the Special Organization hands the column over to new guards: Kurds. Every male over the age of ten is wrenched from their families, taken to a nearby ravine, tied together in pairs, then hacked to bits, their remains thrown into the gorge below.

The rest press on, now certain of what fate awaits them.

Aghavni walks for seven months. Always going. With her mother-in-law, she alternates carrying her daughter on her back and her son in arms. She wrings scarce water into the baby's mouth from a damp cloth. 'Can you forget that?' she will later ask. 'Every day that I drink water that image comes before my eyes.' Seven months of walking. Never from town to town or by the roads, but over hillsides and mountains. She wraps her infant boy in her apron and holds the free end between her teeth. This is how Aghavni climbs.

Along the route her mother, who had been spared in 1895, falls behind. A gendarme shoots her without decorum. Aghavni sees the murder from a distance. She rushes towards her mother's bleeding body but is held back by the killer, who threatens to shoot her too. Her mother is the first to die. Her grandmother goes next – drowned by gendarmes. Her brother flees, never to be seen again. Her uncle's throat is cut.

Nearing the Syrian desert, Aghavni and the dwindling deportees glance down into the Euphrates. The river carries a multitude of corpses downstream. In her despair, Aghavni tries to join them, abandoning the children she had fought to feed, carry and protect. She throws herself under the bloody flow and loses consciousness. A gendarme dives in and pulls her from the water and slaps her awake. He is not saving her life so much as postponing death. He gives her three gold pieces on the promise that she won't attempt suicide again. Kurds loot those gold pieces from her the next day.

Soon enough, her children die too.

Only Aghavni and her mother-in-law are what's left of the family by the time they reach Der Zor. Then she is alone. Completely alone. Aghavni has nothing left but life. Bare life.

Exhausted, and with no more fight left, she lays down naked by the river bank, ready to follow those gone before.

Two elderly Turks approach. One pokes Aghavni with a stick. Her eyes flicker open.

They take her to their home, bath and clothe her. She will be sent to live with a servant and his wife. Years later, she will remarry, and have two sons; the first named Bedros in memory of her husband, and the second named for her missing brother.

'You know,' Aghavni Mazmanian will say in old age, 'even when you're dead, you still don't want to die.'[28]

Aghavni's rescuers are good people. Indeed, a few Turkish or Kurdish citizens choose not to rob the deportees or fulfil whatever sadistic desire they harbour.

Figure 11 "Living martyrs, every day dying a few deaths and returning to life again." Credit: Laurence MacDaniels papers, Cornell University Library.

Throughout the black days of the genocide there are stories of altruism, kindness and a palpable sense of injustice.

An Armenian woman, about to be deported, falls at the feet of her Turkish neighbour. Tears fill him up. 'Get up my daughter,' he says. 'Whoever has caused this, let both eyes be blinded.' That man saves a life. Another Turkish man finds a small boy with no family wandering his village. He feeds the boy, and protects him. Yet another man digs a hole near his house for a family to hide in as the town-crier passes by promising punishment for anyone harbouring the condemned.

And throughout, the overwhelming need for the rituals of burial and the veneer of closure such an act might bring. Consider the case of a twelve-year-old girl kidnapped, abused terribly by a queue of gendarmes, *returned* to her mother, and only then dying. There is little succour in a mere hole in the ground but the girl is laid down in shallow soil somewhere near Diyarbakır.

Above, on a wall, they write 'Shushawn buried here.' *A handful of earth for her.*

Or perhaps consider the young boys who find eight infant bodies on the shore of the Euphrates. They dig holes nearby, face east, cross themselves and draw another small cross in the sand next to each grave. Eight times, the ritual repeated. *A handful of earth for the little ones.*

The Victorians, prudish in their way, used a codeword for rape and sexual violence: 'Outrage'. An apt euphemism. These 'outrages' become routine on the deportation marches. As pervasive as murder, as common as starvation.

But sexual violence does not destroy in the same manner. It is a dehumanizing weapon designed to humiliate and degrade its victims, rendering them as less than chattel. An Armenian woman from Muş sees pre-adolescent girls raped by convoy guards in front of the deportees, then shot – not out of pity, but because they are too grotesquely injured to be raped again.

Violence of this kind is a display of total domination over women and children in a conservative and pious society in which communal honour depends on virginity, fidelity and subservience. Rape inflicts emotional and physical damage on the family too.[29]

Such cruelties aren't merely the product of a pitiless environment, or a moral collapse. They are institutionalized. Local authorities set up temporary camps along the main deportation arteries, sometimes outside government buildings: markets for lives.

Women and girls considered desirable, either as sex slaves or servants, or both, are examined by doctors for diseases before being sold on. If any woman refuses, she faces imprisonment until she gives in.[30] In Damascus, Armenian women and girls are advertised naked and auctioned for barely a handful of coins. At other places, they are flogged 'like pieces of old furniture at low prices, varying from one to ten liras, or from one to five sheep'.[31]

In the minds of the genocidaires, pregnant women carry Armenian 'traitors', and not a second thought is given to doing away with both mother and unborn baby. Gendarmes escorting a deportation column from Konya pick out a pregnant woman from the crowd. 'They would look at each other and say "boy or girl"', one survivor testifies, 'and pierce her belly with a sword.'[32] Other witnesses recall pregnant women's bellies cut raggedly open, the foetus removed and both killed on the spot.

Thus, Talât Paşa: 'We have been reproached for making no distinction between innocent Armenians and the guilty, but that was utterly impossible, in view of the fact that *those who are innocent today might be guilty tomorrow*.'[33]

At first, Armenians converting from Christianity to Islam are spared. Talât issues orders to this effect.[34] Many thousands willingly give up their faith in exchange for life: 'Save us!' a group of deportees from Erzincan entreat. 'We will become Muslims! We will become Germans! We will become anything you want, just save us! They are taking us to the Kemah Pass to cut our throats!'[35]

Shocked that so many will convert, Talât amends his order within a month. Conversion, forced or otherwise, will be no protection,[36] thus demonstrating that for the CUP ethnicity is the principal driver of atrocity – not religion.

'The decisive motivation in the forcible conversions of the Armenians' religions is not religious fanaticism,' the German Ambassador Paul Wolff Metternich observes, 'but the blending of the Armenians with the Muslim people of the Empire.'[37] Or as the former British Ambassador Gerald Lowther had seemingly prophesied a half-decade earlier: 'Pounding the non-Turkish elements in a Turkish mortar.'

To ensure their 'solution' to the 'Armenian Question' is indeed 'comprehensive and absolute', the CUP ensures that any Armenian not killed or expelled will have their identity obliterated using the cultural and ethnological theories of Ziya Gökalp. Turkishness can be imprinted. Children can be re-programmed.[38] It is a policy of assimilation at gunpoint.[39]

Two principal methods for such a process: by the suborning of 'abandoned' children to Turkish homes, and by their imprisonment in state-run orphanages.

For the first: Talât instructs that any child found alone, in towns or villages, by the roadside, are to be distributed amongst Turkish households so that they may be 'educated and assimilated according to local customs'. Poorer families are encouraged to take children with a small monthly cash payment from the government, or with a promise that the child's inheritance will pass to the adopting family.[40] In this way, unassuming, ordinary people are bribed into complicity.

For the second, a method of psychic degloving: Armenian children found in these dark places are stripped of their names, compelled by the cane to speak Turkish, indoctrinated into the dominant fold.

The CUP desires not just the destruction of Armenian bodies, but any trace of what is left behind: homes, bazaar stalls, warehouses, cattle, stores of fine fabric and jewellery, crops and machinery. Decrees like the transparently titled

Temporary Law of Expropriation and Confiscation codify what is to be done with plundered Armenian property – the fruits of annihilation.[41]

Prior to deportation, instructions are given to Armenians by governors, hollered by town criers, or as in the central Anatolian town of Kayseri, printed and pinned to buildings. 'Leave all your belongings,' the note reads:

> Your furniture, your beddings, your artefacts. Close your shops and businesses with everything inside. Your doors will be sealed with special stamps. On your return, you will get everything you left behind. Do not sell property or any expensive item. Buyers and sellers alike will be liable for legal action. Put your money in a bank in the same name of a relative who is out of the country. Make a list of everything you own, including livestock, and give it to the specified official so that all your things can be returned to you later. You have ten days to comply with this ultimatum.[42]

But nothing is ever returned. There are no trusts, no special stamps. Private bank accounts are no protection against the whims of a dictatorial state. If any Armenians survive, no legal action can be taken to reclaim their lost livelihoods and treasures. No provision is ever made for them to be reunited with their belongings.[43]

Instead, 'abandoned goods' are either thrown to non-Armenian locals in fire-sale public auctions or taxed by Şükrü Kaya's IAMM to redistribute back to Muslim refugees. Sometimes, the proceeds are funnelled back into the army, the Interior Ministry and the IAMM to finance the deportation process. Armenians unwillingly pay for their own demise.

The mass transfer of wealth is nothing more than state-ordered looting. And yet the CUP, as in all other areas, lays out rules, punishing officials who profit personally from Armenian spoils. Plunder serves a further purpose, similar to assimilation. If regular people will not wield a rifle or a bayonet against their former neighbours, they are expected to profit from their disappearance.

The treasure houses of Armenian cultural and social life are systematically pillaged and destroyed, too. Of the 2,538 Armenian churches, 1,996 schools and 451 monasteries that litter Anatolia and provide so much of its ancient character and aura, almost all are either appropriated for the needs of the army or smashed altogether.

Churches are defiant symbols of a distinct intellectual and religious identity, bound to the land for centuries, the locus and centre of Armenian community life. They embody the continuity of Armenian civilization, repositories of vital records and vast libraries of sacred manuscripts.

When combined with the liquidation of the Armenian clergy and other secular intellectuals, this vandalism tears asunder the 'spiritual cohesion' of a people.[44]

All roads lead to the desert. To the concentration camps. The nadir of Armenian existence.

The camps are not fine-tuned or deliberate in their cruelties. They are barely organized at all, designed to kill by chaos and destitution. There are no razor-tipped fences, nor Kapos or Kommandants or starred uniforms. Just the course of starvation, thirst, disease, coarse sunlight which blisters scalps and shoulders, and by the summer of 1916, the clubs and bayonets of the Special Organization.

In the earliest days of the CUP's campaign, the chain of concentration camps stretching across Syria were merely temporary stations where Armenians waited to be dispersed across the wilderness. They began near villages and towns 'at least five hours distant from one another' but in 'no place or condition that would allow for self-rule or defense'.[45] Aid committees, relief centres and orphanages could be set up.[46] Even in Der Zor, soon to become a packed maelstrom, expelled Armenians can eke out a meagre existence, taking jobs in local crafts, ruled by a reasonably benevolent governor.[47]

But as the genocide reaches its fevered pitch after April 1915, a great swell of destitute humanity pours like an ocean into the desert – the sum total of Anatolia's deported Armenian population.

Through the summer and autumn of 1915 some 800,000 Armenians arrive. Most are funnelled into a series of miserable transit camps north and east of Aleppo. One by one the camps fill up. No food, water or medical care is ever supplied to them by the authorities. Typhus alone takes thousands.

When the first camp overflows, survivors are compelled to walk on to the second. When that fills up with dead, the dying are shifted on again to the third camp and so on. Officials in charge of vacating their camps are ruthlessly efficient, needing little more than a week to clear out tens of thousands of people at a time.

After the final concentration camp is cleared, deportees fall upon the city of Aleppo itself, crowding the avenues and alleys with bones.

Dr Martin Niepage, a German teacher, visits some of these barely surviving groups. He tries to give them some succour. He finds that 'If one takes them food, it appears that they have forgotten how to eat. Their stomachs, weakened by months of hunger, can no longer bear food. If one gives them bread, they put it aside, indifferently; they lie there, quietly, waiting for death'.

Such sights produce an inevitable conclusion in Niepage's mind. From witnessing the state of these Armenians alone, he surmises the CUP's goal:

> What will become of the unfortunates, now just women and children, who are being hunted down throughout the city and its environs and driven into the desert by the thousands? They are pushed from place to place until the thousands are reduced to hundreds, and the hundreds to a little group, and this group is still driven elsewhere, until *nothing at all is left of it*. With that, the purpose of the journey has been attained.[48]

For months, American diplomat Jesse B Jackson watches as corpses are wheeled past his consulate in Aleppo, '10 or 12 in each cart, and the procession of 7 or 8 carts would proceed to the nearby cemetery with their gruesome loads … dangling from the sides and ends'. The bodies are dumped in trenches.[49]

At Ras Ul Ain, further east, the last stop on the rail line to Baghdad, the situation is just as desperate. Armin T. Wegner, a German medic-soldier serving nearby, disobeys orders to survey the camps. He finds:

> Hunger, death, disease, desperation on all sides. You would smell the odour of feces and decay … But all of this is nothing compared to the frightful sight of the swarms of orphans which increase daily. At the sides of the camp, a row of holes in the ground covered with rags, had been prepared for them. Girls and boys of all ages were sitting in these holes, heads together, abandoned and reduced to animals, starved without food or bread, deprived of the most basic human aid, packed tightly one against the other and trembling from the night cold, holding pieces of still smoldering wood to try to get warm.[50]

These visceral scenes are plentiful across northern Syria. Conditions are chaotic, uncontrollable. The region is so tainted that diseases spread to surrounding Arab villages, and even to the Ottoman army.[51]

The CUP decides to restore their grip on order. They shut down small teams of locals and foreigners working to provide relief. Any Ottoman official who turns a blind eye to charity will be 'severely punished'.[52] In late 1915, a decision is taken to be rid of the remaining Armenian deportees. They create a new government department under the IAMM and Talât's Interior Ministry: the Sub-Directorate for Deportees (*Sevkiyat*). It is, in essence, another branch of the Special Organization.[53]

In the desert, more deportations. Armenians are forcibly filtered through a series of new camps roughly following the curve and flow of the Euphrates: Meskene, Dibsi, Raqqa, Sabkhah. Always going. Like before, when one camp fills up, its internees are marched on to make room for the thousands yet to come.

On the slow treks through the winter of 1915–16 some 300,000 Armenians die in pestilent conditions. Jesse Jackson sends Auguste Bernau, a German businessman, on a fact-finding mission through the camps. 'As on the gates of "Hell" of Dante,' Bernau writes, 'the following should be written at the entrance of these accursed encampments: "You who enter, leave all hopes."'[54]

The worst of these infernos is Der Zor, a place that always be known as the Armenian Auschwitz.

By July 1916 Der Zor's population is 200,000 souls. Tents – not much more than stitched rags held up by sticks – cram tightly together, surrounding the town on two sides. At least 200 Armenians die *every day*.[55]

To be fed even a meagre ration, some deportees beg to be employed as gravediggers. Every morning they labour from tent to tent collecting bodies and, as Hrach Papazian tells:

> Tossed them into carts pell-mell, the dead and the dying together, so as not to waste time. At night, the living blanketed themselves with the dead to keep warm. For a mother, the best thing that could happen was for a Bedouin to come and take her child, that it might escape the mass grave. Dysentery made the air unbreathable. With their muzzles the dogs rummaged in the burst bellies of the dead.[56]

Soon, a grimmer task. Liquidation. Zeki Bey arrives at Der Zor in the summer of 1916, a man described by Auguste Bernau as remarkable only for his 'inhumanity and cruelty'.[57] Zeki is joined by an 'inspector general' from the Sub-Directorate for Deportees and a collection of Special Organization militiamen.[58]

Any surviving Armenian men are rooted out and killed in small groups – against the wishes of the military which wants to exploit their labour. Children and women are sorted, broken up into groups of up to 5,000, and force-marched south to where the Khabur tributary meets the Euphrates. Here, Zeki's militias and local Bedouins carry out their rhythmic, systematic slaughter for six months.[59]

A toll: 192,750 Armenians exterminated between July and December 1916.[60] Some 2,000 orphaned children are taken in carts and blown up with dynamite, or laid out in the desert, covered in kerosene, and burned alive.

Figure 12 'The Camps'. Credit: Armin T Wegner.

Almost no survivor accounts exist of these scarlet seasons because, by January 1919, when occupying British forces arrive in Der Zor, only 980 Armenians remain alive.[61]

Against this utter defilement, against this debasement of all humanity, against the will of a regime which desires a numberless multitude dead, defiance remains. The instinctive will to survive cannot be crushed or snuffed out.

Consider the mothers who rub ashes and sand on their daughters' faces to make them seem less pretty, less appealing to the rapist guard, or the nomad in need of a servant. *Ashes within me, ashes around me.* Consider the boy who steals grapes and suffers a beating for doing so, wolfing the fruit down as the blows land. As Celal Bey, once the governor of Aleppo, notes: 'Each human has the right to live. A kicked wolf will bite. The Armenians will defend themselves.'[62]

And defend themselves they do. At Urfa, close to the desert, a few hundred fighters hold out against the authorities for twenty-five days in the Armenian Quarter. Their leader, proud to the end, kills himself instead of facing capture. At Şabinkarahisar, in the northeast, the population resists throughout June and July. They too succumb in the end. Perhaps most famously, Armenians in Musa

Dağ fight Ottoman troops from July to September 1915 until they are rescued from the coast by the French navy.[63]

Resistance comes from within the government, too. It is little, but it does come. Some province governors and other officials openly defy the killing orders from the top, such as Celal Bey, Tahsin Bey in Erzerum, Rahmi Evranos Bey in İzmir and Nabi Bey in Malatya. Their actions merely stall slaughter. Some are sacked for insubordination. Others still are murdered for being refusing to be party to a crime.[64] In Armenian: *Meds Yeghern*. The Great Crime.

Whether by resistance or refusal, determination or unknowable will, those rescued, those who avert death, will survive with unbearable mental scarring, their conscious world fractured and sundered, never to be restored again, left only with maddening memories, and a memory of madness.

Of this, imagine your neighbour – a survivor too – 'sitting on the floor, crying and crying, pulling her hair,' telling her story over and over: 'I killed two of them. I killed two of them,' she repeats. She had been walking, always going, holding one child's hand with the other in her arms. If she stopped, the gendarme would beat them. She let one child go, and walked on. Always going, until the other child died too. This baby she buried. But still she would sit crying, pulling her hair.

'What happened to the one who was still alive?' she begs. 'The wolves ate him. The wolves ate him. One died, I know. The other one the wolves ate.'[65]

6

Ghosts

As Armenians are being disappeared, Anzacs at Gallipoli dig in.

A teeming township colonizes the tiny bay, shovelled into cliff sides. Trench life assails all senses: the smell of the unburied insulting the air, the taste of rusty water shipped in by an armada, the relentless itch of lice and the unyielding iron grasp of dysentery which thins out all ranks.

Soldiers pass time with rats, and with fear.

Ottoman defenders have beaten back every advance inland. Two empires grinding against each other like tectonic plates on this 'tongue of hilly land … suave yet austere'.[1] Men minced to pieces between them.

After one month of fighting, such disputed earth grows too thick with bloated bodies. On 24 May 1915 a temporary truce is called. A solemn procession of blurry figures emerge from trenches: nurses, chaplains, gravediggers, stretcher-bearers. Among them is Bedros Kerkyasharian, one of thirty Armenians in a sanitary company, survivor of the early battles and of Enver's order to purge ranks. Because Bedros speaks both Turkish and English, he is made to mediate between the two foes mingling in pockmarked no-man's land. When Anzacs and Ottomans alike are startled by inexperienced men dropping loaded rifles, Bedros cools their tensions.[2]

But this is not the first encounter between Australians, New Zealanders and Armenians on Gallipoli's battlefield.

At Anzac headquarters, several Armenians lend their services and knowledge. Aram Okosdinossian, a thirty-nine-year-old from Istanbul, chucks in a job making shoes for King Fuad I of Egypt to work as a translator. In late 1915, Aram poses for a photograph: moustache and goatee immaculate, cigarette between his fingers, in khaki tie and thick army greatcoat, rugged up against encroaching winter.[3]

Ley Pope, a map-maker from the Dunedin suburb of St Clair, finds himself working long nights alongside an Armenian draughtsman, marking hills and gullies: 'A first-class hand,' Pope writes of him, 'able to read and write Turkish

[and] speak French, Italian, English, Arabic, and Armenian. He started to learn English only three months before coming here, and is now probably the best of the foreigners.'[4]

Not all Armenians in the Anzacs' employ turn out to be trustworthy, however. Raymond Ward reports in a letter home that one of their Armenian interpreters had been 'caught one evening by some Australians coming from the Turkish lines, where evidently he had left behind some valuable information … Naturally he ceased to be an interpreter'.[5]

By the very nature of fighting at Gallipoli – close-quarters, attritional – taking prisoners is a rare occurrence. Maiming or killing is more common. But when it does happen, Anzacs express shock that the 'enemy' harbours secret sympathies. An anonymous colonel writes a Sydney colleague, claiming to have seen Ottoman officers driving 'Greeks and Armenian Christian conscripts up to the firing line. We frequently had wounded prisoners of this class'.[6]

Chaplain-Major John Luxford observes one of these prisoners being marched through camp, blindfolded but 'carrying his head with a pride that seemed to say "I am glad to be out of this dirty job"'. Luxford notes his lapels – a non-commissioned officer – and speaks to him in English, learning that he had spent some time in London. 'We liked this fellow because of his bearing … an absence of swagger, a natural, pleasant manner, and a freedom from anything craven.'[7]

Both Charles Bean and Malcolm Ross, official war correspondents for Australia and New Zealand, interview two Armenian prisoners of war (PoWs). They write long despatches home, widely reprinted in Australasian papers detailing their stories. One soldier had begun the war on the Caucasus front before marching to Gallipoli, a witness to 'the wholesale imprisonment and ill-treatment of the Armenian communities'.

Government censors omit this Armenian's name, but he tells Ross of seeing the bishop of Sivas's feet shod with iron and nails. Like a horse. 'He is an old man, and the head of the Armenians of this district,' the province governor reportedly said. 'Out of respect for his old age, we must see to it that he does not go barefooted.'

Of his hometown of Zile, the Armenian details to Ross and Bean a checklist of genocidal process. Massacre after massacre, the perpetrators boasting of their action. The victims' property 'commandeered by the Government'. Women deported from the town in ox-carts, left out in the cold and implored to convert to Islam to save their lives. Children stolen from them; the boys taken to madrassahs; the girls sold at auction. 'Day after day,' Ross translates, 'the unhappy girls were there like so many sheep for sale in the market.'

Ross omits many specifics of the story: 'Too horrible to put on paper'.[8]

To break Gallipoli's deadlock, Allied commanders envisage a sweeping assault on the highest point of the Sari Bair Ridge: the August Offensive.

Plans drawn up by Sir Ian Hamilton prove too complex, too dependent on exact timekeeping to succeed. An Australian strike at The Nek on 7 August sets the tone for the onslaught – a poorly conceived advance and a callous waste of life, the first wave of Australians mown down within seconds by Ottoman machine gunners. Mercilessly, commanders send two more waves over the top. Most are cut to pieces on a small patch of land. The defenders suffer no casualties at all.

The New Zealanders push forward with more success. On 8 August the Wellington Battalion, reinforced by the Aucklanders, force their way through shingle and outcrop under a curtain of fire to the crest of Chunuk Bair. They have barely slept and are desperately low on water, facing constant ranging by artillery – including their own. Bodies of comrades steadily pile up in scattered foxholes. One soldier plunged into the maelstrom records men flung into the air by explosions, silhouetted limbs spread across the sky:

> Poor old Hughie Pringle was killed, his throat ripped by a piece and presently there came groping past us Clutha McKenzie blinded. Young Mell Bull his jaw smashed and another unrecognisable. As they passed us their faces were covered in blood and seemed to hang in tatters … Physical fear is a strange thing. While all are more or less affected by it in a tight corner, most manage to contain it, but in some cases it causes them to lose all control over themselves.[9]

This is the scene at the pinnacle of the Anzac campaign.

Among this desperate number are Privates Reginald Davie, a shepherd from Manawatu, William Surgenor, a baker from Taranaki, and Albert Shoebridge, a carpenter from Fielding. They fight together in shallow trenches near the peak of Chunuk Bair.

At the blistering height of a counterattack, it seems like Davie is the only uninjured man. Surgenor, lying beside him reloading rifles, bleeds vigorously from a wound to his face. Guns run hot and 'practically every bullet found its mark'.[10] Davie too is eventually hit, a projectile shattering his right elbow and knocking him back into the trench. Surgenor binds up the wound with a makeshift bandage ripped from his own tunic.

They cannot hold out. Their position is overrun by Ottoman troops, some led by Mustafa Kemal. One of them bayonets Davie through his good arm. Only an officer's intervention saves him from being shot. The officer motions again for Davie and Surgenor to get out of the trench, and it is only then that they see a thick spread of bodies lying just beyond them – their day's work. Further along the line, the pair spot Private George Monk, a twenty-five-year-old farmer from Whanganui.

They have all become prisoners of war.[11]

Albert Shoebridge escapes Ottoman clutches, scrabbling from the trench with one arm smashed apart. He tries to work his way back to the beach to find a medic but gets lost and is eventually captured by two snipers. Escorted behind enemy lines, Shoebridge faces interrogation before being dropped at a dressing station. He is tended by an Armenian doctor who applies fresh bandages and a splint to his ruined limb.[12]

Of the hundreds of New Zealanders who take and defend Chunuk Bair between 8 and 10 August, just twenty-two become PoWs. Others will be captured in Sinai, or on various other fronts in the service of other armies. During the length of the Gallipoli campaign, sixty-seven Australians find themselves in Ottoman hands, and fifty during the August offensive.

Ten New Zealanders and at least twenty-four Australians will never return home. Often, they are buried in Christian cemeteries; Anzacs and Armenians sharing graveyards.[13]

Those who survive another three years in captivity will either witness what is being done to the Armenians of the empire, or feel the leaden weight of their absence. They will become a ghostly presence in the lives of these Anzac soldiers.

From Gallipoli, prisoners are steamed to Istanbul. 'I don't suppose any of us had in the least imagined the sight that awaited us,' reports the Australian Reginald Francis Lushington, a former Sri Lankan tea plantation manager captured on Red Sunday. 'It was all far beyond our expectations.'[14]

Across the city, different places of internment: The Taşkışla barracks near Taksim infamous for atrocious conditions, or in army hospitals like Gülhane. They make accommodation with the lice and cockroaches that infest cramped quarters.

Lushington calls his 'barrack-looking' prison a 'hell – and a hell which got worse each day we stayed there. The walls were covered with the names of unfortunate Greeks and Armenians who had been imprisoned there, and besides these names the walls were smeared with blood, human blood'.[15]

Some Anzac prisoners come face-to-face with the empire's rulers. Lushington meets the German Otto Liman von Sanders.[16] Reginald Davie, recovering from his bayonet wound, is present when Enver Paşa tours his hospital. 'He didn't take much notice of the shower of complaints hurled at him,' Davie notes.[17] Lieutenant Leslie Luscombe of Melbourne (who just weeks before the war had been holidaying in New Zealand) finds himself taken from the War Ministry to Talât's office, where the genocidaire blusters through an interpreter about treatment of Turkish PoWs. One of the party, a British captain, retorts: 'You tell Talaat Pasha that he is a bloody liar. His story is a lie.'[18]

After a stay of some weeks, the prisoners (Anzac, British, Indian, French and Russian) are transported out of the capital to various sites, to the farthest corners of Anatolia.

Several hundred, including Lushington and thirty-seven-year-old George Gunn, a tattooed driver from the central Otago town of Clyde, go to the sleepy hamlet of Ankara.[19] They are then marched, seemingly for the hell of it, from Ankara to Çankırı and back again – a distance of over 100 kilometres.

Gunn reports following 'the trail of Armenian massacres', seeing 'women's hair sticking out of the ground, and limbs and other portions of human remains revealed everywhere', and spending time in a church, its walls 'dripping with blood'.[20]

The roundtrip march takes the life of Northland carpenter Jeffrey Harney. Gunn watches him die. 'On the last day,' Lushington notes:

> Some men were too exhausted to go any further and dropped down in their tracks letting the main column go on without them. A feeling of desperation and bitter anger and utter hopelessness made these men just lie out in the snow … [A]t 4 p.m. the main column sighted the mosque and minarets of [Ankara]. What a sight we must have presented to the populace, though I dare say they had seen many Armenians in a similar plight.[21]

Leslie Luscombe stays in Ankara for a season, his first accommodation an Armenian monastery conspicuously devoid of any clergy. No hymns sung, no liturgy or incense. 'At a later date,' Luscombe reports, 'we learned that prior to arrival the monks who inhabited the [monastery] had been taken out and massacred by the Turks.'[22]

As winter arrives, prisoners find themselves without warm clothes or comforts. Luscombe is still wearing the khaki shorts he was captured in. They protest to a Red Crescent official, who promptly arranges for supplies to be brought from an Armenian warehouse overstocked with goods. 'The original owners had doubtless been liquidated,' Luscombe records with resignation.

Bed sheets, soap, razors, cutlery, hairbrushes and countless other luxury items delivered to the officers. One wonders whether Anzac captives think of the faces these razors used to shave. Whose heads used to rest on these linen pillows.

Ottoman treatment of Allied prisoners varies drastically, especially between officers and enlisted men. The former stay in convalescent camps, are paid well and enjoy a reasonable degree of liberty. Lower ranks not debilitated by war wounds or infectious illnesses are put to work in industry: building roads, churning grit in cement factories, constructing railways. Most notoriously of all, that ambitious German dream: the *Baghdadbahn*.

When war breaks out, sections spanning the Taurus and Amanus mountains dividing Anatolia from Syria are yet to be built. All arms and men must be shipped by wagon and donkey over perilous pathways reaching a height of 3,000 metres. Work is redoubled when German planners realized how valuable a direct supply line for the Sinai and Iraq campaigns will be. Engineers face the logistical nightmare of blasting three dozen tunnels through the mountains.[23]

An early Anzac prisoner at the work camps observes the scenery in a covert diary:

> For short intervals between tunnels a traveller can see the line clinging precariously to the sides of the towering Taurus mountains. These intervals disclose glimpses of majestic, inaccessible peaks, and frowning gorges. Very little timber is seen and the peaks are almost as bare as Mount Owen on the west coast of Tasmania, whilst the scenery is just as wild.[24]

The engineers, mostly Germans, are the elite, marking the circuitous route and overseeing gangs of Turks, Greeks and Armenians burdened with real toil: pick-axing, nailing and digging their way through.

But even in performing such a vital function for the Ottoman war effort, Armenian workers are not immune from first, harassment, then deportation. Some are forced to resign when their wives and families are expelled from their homes. Others have their property stolen to force them to leave.

German managers and financiers, to their credit, protest vigorously to regional governors, out of both economic interest and genuine humanitarian concern. The governors plead innocence – their orders come direct from Talât Paşa. Even a face-to-face intervention from the company's deputy director cannot persuade Talât to leave the Armenian railway labourers alone. The meeting achieves nothing, and the interior minister orders their deportation in early July 1915. The *Baghdadbahn*'s overseers are forced to steal skilled workers from the carriages trundling daily past their office windows.[25]

Allied PoWs fill the gaps. Hundreds of British, Indian, French, Russian, Australian and New Zealand soldiers shipped in.

The majority of able-bodied Anzacs spend time at various camps along the blasted paths of construction: Belemedik, Bozanti, 'Hadjikiri' and other minor stations.

George Kerr from Victoria, captured during the August offensive, records in his diary the day he arrives in Bozanti. Interned in a two-story building, he catches glimpses of a huddled group on the floor below: 'About sixty miserable creatures who, we afterwards discovered, were Greeks and Armenians employed on the tunnel. They were crouched about the fires made in old mess dishes and in that dull light, looked the lowest human beings I had ever set eyes on'.

The fires 'gave forth horrible smoke and poisoned the air with their fumes'.[26]

Anzacs and surviving Armenians live in close quarters and labour together, carving great holes through dense rock, hauling, measuring and laying sleepers.

The railway line also has another, more sinister end: a speedy way of delivering the condemned en masse to the desert. Leslie Luscombe testifies to the methodical way in which Armenians deported from western Anatolia are herded from cattle car to cattle car, cramped cages expediting them further and further away from their homes. At Eskişehir, a major junction on the western deportation route, Luscombe surveys a 'sad and depressing sight':

> On the opposite side of the platform another train was standing. It was composed of a number of empty two-tier steel sheep trucks. On the platform a considerable number of Armenian women and children were huddled together. As our train pulled into the platform, Turkish soldiers armed with whips were driving the women and children into the sheep trucks. It was evidently intended to transport them to some distant concentration camp.[27]

During those long years of toil, the disturbing dual purpose of the *Baghdadbahn* can't be far from Anzac PoWs' minds. They are enabling, by no choice of their own, the potential killing of their comrades on the Mesopotamian and Palestine fronts, and quickening the pace of the genocide.

Aboard clattering trains borne to the desert, Anzac PoWs and condemned Armenians alike are struck by a remarkable sight emerging from the heat haze:

something like a vast skyscraper reaching towards the heavens – a perpendicular column of dark rock over 200 metres tall.

Racing closer, they make out the sand-coloured citadel crowning the edifice, a fortress dating back to Hittite days. From its pinnacle, Anzac soldiers will discover the surrounding plains rich with white, purple and red flowering poppies – the very symbol of Anzac Day.

This is the next major rail junction south from Eskişehir, an ancient town the Romans used to call Akronium: Afionkarahissar, or Afion for short. The name literally translates as 'Opium Black Castle'.

At least nineteen New Zealanders and twenty Australians will spend time in Afion during the First World War. It hosts one of many PoW camps.

The first Allied internees in Afion – sailors who abandoned their submarines attempting to force the Dardanelles – are witnesses to the roundup, murder and eviction of the Armenian population. They number just under 7,500, living in a collage of small, traditional houses of whitewashed mud and wood and laid tiles crowding the base of the upright rock. Wide cobbled streets worn down by centuries of rural labour intersect bazaars and schools. Most of them speak Turkish and are poppy farmers or small tradesmen. From 15 August 1915 onwards, all but a few hundred are deported in actions overseen by the local CUP secretary.[28]

John Harrison Wheat, a dairy farmer from Gippsland, Victoria, had served aboard the Australian submersible *AE2*. He and half its crew arrive in Afion on 6 May 1915, first kept in a religious school, and then put to work on nearby roads alongside Russian and French sailors. Two days after the expulsion, Wheat makes a terse entry in his diary:

> All the Armenians are driven from the town. The principal cause of this is the Armenians are Christians and all the business of the town is carried on by them. There is a very strong feeling against the Christians in this Country. At this time thousands of Armenians were turned out of these big towns to starve and thousands were massacred.[29]

Armenian houses, shops and religious institutions are cleared out. And as many PoWs note in diaries and later accounts, the local authorities use these vacated lots and 'abandoned goods' for the shelter and internment of captured men.[30] The grand Sourp Asdvadzadzin Church at the foot of Afion's monolith, for example, becomes a holding station and a punishment building for PoWs. Certainly every officer, and some rank and file men, will spend at least some time in that Armenian church.

A church like so many others: defiled, desecrated.

Far from Afion, in the deserts of Iraq, the British army advances.

Having occupied the port of Basra early in the war, they hope to push on to Baghdad, rob the Ottoman Empire of a significant swathe of territory and seize the vast reservoirs of oil bubbling below the sand.

Part of General Charles Townshend's force in the region is a small, makeshift squadron of pilots and mechanics known as the Mesopotamian Half-Flight, piloting rickety Farman Shorthorn biplanes – 'a queer sort of bus like an assemblage of birdcages'. The crewmen map and photograph Ottoman positions, operating well beyond the safety of their own lines. Many of these airmen will be taken prisoner.

Captain Thomas Walter White is captured first. Melbourne-born, White has been a soldier from early age, training with the Australian Flying Corps when war breaks out. His mission in mid-November 1915 is to blow up telegraph wires not far from Baghdad. While rigging the explosives on the ground, they are captured by a gang of local Arabs, and handed over to the Ottoman army. Major Hugh Reilly – bald-headed, Hawkes Bay-born, Sandhurst-educated – is captured exactly a week later when his plane is forced down by shell shrapnel.

The Australian and the New Zealander are taken separately to Baghdad before they reunite in Mosul. They, and their observers, are officers, so are presented with the luxury of a wagon when they set out for Aleppo on 20 February 1916 under armed guard.

A strange meeting takes place on this trek. Both White and Reilly shake hands with Rafael de Nogales, the Venezuelan mercenary who had gleefully taken part in the siege of Van nearly a year earlier. Nogales tells White that Van's Armenians were 'done to death, the women carried off or reduced to untold misery, many of them being marched to [Ankara] or to Mosul, with nothing but the chance of charity to keep them.'

White suspects Nogales of being involved in some of the horrors. 'The awfulness of it all appealed to him more,' White says with more than a hint of disgust.[31]

They soon discover that what had been done to Van's Armenians on the eve of Gallipoli was being done to Armenians throughout the empire. At Nusaybin, White and Reilly camp in a Christian church being used as a storehouse for a massive collection of clothes and mattresses. White assumes they once belonged to the town's Armenians. He notes: 'Except for an Armenian woman or two, one would never have known that until recently they comprised almost the greater portion of the population of the town.'[32]

An eerie pattern: every village rest stop a picture of rubble and desolation. In one forsaken town, only a handful of children and women remain. One young girl makes the sign of the cross at the group of pilot-prisoners. White nods at her. As the girl approaches, he lights a cigarette with a match, places a coin in the box, and throws it to her. 'She picked it up highly delighted,' White writes in his diary.

Outside the village, they find '36 new graves, evidently of the male Christian population.'[33]

Two days later, the convoy reaches the railhead at Ras ul-Ain, site of another concentration camp. White and Reilly pass swiftly through and do not stop. White believes the camp's occupants are only 'refugees'.[34]

After a trek over the Taurus Mountains, passing the railroad workers, White, Reilly and the others, arrive in Afion on 23 March 1916 to find a commotion: three sailors escaped; the commandant in a rage.

As punishment, all high-ranking prisoners – Anzacs as well as Frenchmen and Russians – are rounded up from their quarters and taken to Surp Asdvadzadzin. White, Reilly and Leslie Luscombe are among that number. Chunuk Bair captives Reginald Davie and George Monk tag along as orderlies for the officers. As they arrive, Luscombe sees 'a number of Armenian women and children ... being driven out of the building. They had evidently been moved out to make way for us.'[35]

They pass several weeks of close confinement in that Armenian church. On their release, they are taken to new lodgings: a terrace of four two-storey Armenian houses sharing a large walled courtyard, fronting the road between the town and the railway station, 'the former occupants of which,' Reginald Davie observes, had 'gone the way of thousands and thousands of their compatriots had gone before them.'[36]

Davie's duties as an orderly involve buying food, scarce at it is, for his superiors at the bazaar. The daily task brings him in close contact to the few surviving Armenians in Afion. He is forbidden to speak to them, but dodges the prohibition. He gets his own servant, a twelve-year-old Armenian boy named Yorgi. Davie supposes this is 'Armenian for "Georgie"'. The boy's mother, father and several other relations were either killed or deported in August 1915. Only he and his sister survive.

'He used to tell me gruesome stories of Turkish atrocities that were so bad they were hard to believe,' Davie will note later in life, 'yet I always found that, whatever faults Yorgi had, lying was not one of them.'[37]

Thomas White and Leslie Luscombe share a room and become fast friends, even as they frequently come to blows over politics. White vigorously defends 'White Australia', which appals Luscombe, a dedicated socialist.

On 27 August 1916, they both meet Second Lieutenant Frank Allsopp, a farmer from Papatoetoe in Auckland, a Gallipoli veteran captured during the Battle of Romani in Suez.[38] Allsopp has the unfortunate honour of being the first New Zealand officer captured by the Ottomans, and is lucky to have survived the march across the Sinai Desert to Jerusalem, then on to Damascus, Aleppo, and through the Taurus Mountains – again past the shells of Armenian villages and toiling railroad workers.

Two days after Allsopp's arrival in Afion, a fire breaks out. Thomas White records it in his diary. From his quarters, he can see the blaze and hear the crack of rifles. A pogrom underway.

'Evidently some more Armenians were being despatched,' he writes. 'These unfortunate people except for women & children were very few in this [town], but evidently some pretext had been made to murder a few more.'

The next morning, White finds bedding and household furniture piled in nearby streets. Although he can't be sure they are Armenian belongings, he notes: 'This has been the fate of hundreds of Armenian families; that the men and sometimes women & children are despatched & their effects sold by

Figure 13 'Anzacs outside their Armenian homes in Afion: Thomas Walter White and Leslie Luscombe'. Credit: Australian War Memorial.

auction. The numbers disposed of in this way must amount to some hundreds of thousands, for in almost every town in the empire have they been massacred'.[39]

Gallipoli is silently and ignominiously evacuated in late December 1915. A consummate Allied loss. The foothold is a graveyard abandoned.

Just three months later, another disaster.

The British advance through Iraq has been unexpectedly swift. Perhaps too easy. Enver Paşa, fearing the fall of Baghdad, throws Ottoman reinforcements into the field and finally halts the onslaught with a bitter stalemate near the ancient ruins of Ctesiphon in late November 1915.

General Townshend, an unshakeably ambitious man, overstretches his mixed British and Indian force. They fall back to Kut el-Amara, a prosperous trading town nestled into a bend of the Tigris river. Hoping to recuperate, they are instead encircled: around 15,000 fighting men and 7,000 local Arabs hemmed in without chance of relief.

Townshend believes the siege will last for only a few weeks. It lasts four months. Food is rationed down to scraps. Soldiers begin to show signs of malnutrition. Indian men bear the brunt, refusing for religious reasons to eat any meat, even though leaders back home grant dispensation.

Among that number is Captain Edward Opotiki Mousley. Born in the northern New Zealand town of his middle name, he had read law at Victoria University and taught at Auckland's prestigious King's College where he saved enough money to further his studies at Emmanuel College, Cambridge. He joined the war as part of the Royal Field Artillery.[40] The hunger in Kut reduces him to writing yearning doggerel:

> So the months went by, and we ate husks,
> Chupatties, and mule, and weeds.
> We'd Divisional Orders for breakfast,
> And ribs of the silent steeds.

After much bargaining Townshend, too proud to the end, finally gives his surrender on 29 April 1916. The man who claims the waved white flag is none other than Halil Bey: uncle to Enver Paşa, famed for the slaughter of Armenians under his command, later to proclaim of 'working to destroy the Armenian nation to the last person.'[41]

Mousley is caught in the chaos as victorious Ottoman soldiers enter Kut and immediately begin looting, taking off with everything from ceremonial swords to boots. Defeated men are corralled into the main square and divided between officers and enlisted men. A division to mark their fate.

Officers take a boat upstream to Baghdad and are given donkeys for the journey ahead. Townshend will spend the rest of the war in louche luxury on the island of Büyükada, near Istanbul. His men, however, will walk.

They follow the same route traced by Thomas White and Hugh Reilly earlier in the year: Mosul, Nusaybin, Ras ul-Ain, then over the Taurus and Amanus Mountains, trudging in columns ranging from a few dozen to hundreds at a time in oven-like temperatures. The food is pathetic; the water undrinkable.

Figure 14 'Edward Opotiki Mousley'. Credit: Printed in Edward Opotiki Mousley, *The Secrets of a Kuttite: An Authentic Story of Kut, Adventures in Captivity and Stamboul Intrigue*, London: John Lane, 1922.

There is no treatment for rife and raging cases of dysentery and typhus. For an already emaciated army, this proves too much. Around 70 per cent of British Kut captives and 50 per cent of Indian prisoners die for want of basic needs.[42]

As an officer, Mousley is comparatively well treated, though he still endures the seemingly endless trek while nursing several injuries. 'I knew two seasons only,' he will later reflect, 'when we walked and when we did not.' His party feeds on meagre provisions. A handful of raisins and baked black rye bread. He spares nothing in describing comrades:

> I saw some human forms which no eye but one acquainted with the phenomenon of the trek could possibly recognise as British soldiery. They were wasted to wreathes of skin hanging upon a bone frame. For the most part they were stark naked except for a rag around their loins, their garments having been sold to buy food, bread, milk, and medicine. Their eyes were white with the death hue. Their sunken cheeks were covered with the unshaven growth of weeks … One saw the bee-hive phenomenon of flies which swarmed by the million going in and out of living men's open mouths.[43]

Fatefully, Kut soldiers march in the opposite direction to deported Armenians. The two groups often cross paths. Krikoris Balakian, the priest arrested on Red Sunday/Anzac Day, a 'living martyr' in the wilderness, encounters a group of Kut prisoners in the mountains:

> They wore short pants that came down to their knees; their legs were covered in wounds and sores; they were dirty and desiccated … their cheekbones were protruding, their eyes withdrawn deep into the sockets. The Indians were practically naked, some with just a few rags on their heads, according to custom; in the darkness an illusion of moving ghosts. 'Are there any Armenians among you? … Give us a piece of bread … We haven't had anything to eat for days.' We were dumbfounded that they spoke English … that they were British … distant friends sharing our fate, asking us for bread … What an irony indeed.[44]

Perhaps as a result of his experience, Mousley's diary of his time at Kut and as a PoW is an ebullient and jingoistic text, full or hurrahs for empire and patronizing racism towards his captors. 'The Turk is an interesting stud,' Mousley contemptuously observes. 'He is half child and half savage … [T]he country is rotten, the habits rotten, and so many wretched corrupt Turks are in authority, that one feels inclined to sweep them all away.'[45]

Nor does Mousley have any love for Armenians, describing them as 'mongrel Armenians'[46] and with disdain, 'the Jew of Turkey'.[47] Despite his attitudes, he cannot deny the reality evidenced at almost every junction of his journey.

Like White and Reilly before him, Mousley passes through Nusaybin where deserted homes dot the plain. A Turkish guard tells him they are Armenian villages, 'and that the people had all been killed earlier in the war. We passed *a great many* of these awful testimonies to the barbarity of Turkish politics'.[48] Over the Taurus Mountains, Mousley winces at the string of hamlets with 'Armenian homes smashed in and corpses half-covered with soil or flung down a hollow, where the Turk had passed'. At a brief stop in another place, he finds 'all the houses were closed with shutters. We learned that their Armenian tenants had been butchered *à la Turque*'.[49]

Further along, he is confronted with the sight of a deportation march guarded by gendarmes:

> [A] great crowd of Armenian and Greek peasants with old men and old grey-haired women and children carrying small bundles or articles of cooking, all herded together *en route* for somewhere ... In this way they are moved from place to place, their number dwindling until all have gone.[50]

From observation alone Mousley can deduce what the point of the deportations truly is.

At Bozanti, he finds British and Anzac soldiers, 'mostly from the Dardanelles', at work on the railway.[51] Many Kut prisoners end up here, put to work in an emaciated, exhausted condition.

From Bozanti, Mousley is taken to Konya, boards a train to Afion, Ankara, Çankırı and an officer's camp in the prettier surrounds of Kastamonu, near the Black Sea. There, he stays in relative comfort. But even in convalescence, Mousley is alert to the landscape around him, to what has been done on that soil.

Passing through Ankara one day, he observes Armenian houses where prisoners had once been able to buy milk and fruit 'now deserted. Weeds grew above the walls and in the burned floors. Here and there a vine or vegetable told of the swift and terrible change'.[52]

Fed up with the arduous labour of railway building, Reginald Lushington resolves to escape the camp with several comrades. A duck-and-dive flight down to the coast, towards Adana.

A patrol of gendarmes turns them in.

Adana's prisons are rife with stories of cruelty. 'We could all speak a certain amount of Turkish,' Lushington notes, 'and the tales we heard are impossible to write down, more especially so in the case of the Armenians ... '

I remember one night when sleep was impossible, a man in an Arab head dress crawled across to me, and making a sign of silence with his finger whispered in French 'I am a Christian,' and made the sign of the cross. He told me many things which are too horrible to repeat; on asking him why he dressed as an Arab, he replied that if they ever they [sic] found out he was an Armenian his life would not be worth a para. He had been rounded up with a lot of destitute Arabs. What a story his life would make.[53]

In this way, almost every Anzac PoW held in the Ottoman Empire testifies to what is being done to Armenians.[54] Many diaries contain first-hand accounts, while others record the rumours and hearsay passed between men with little else to do.[55]

To write about the Armenian Genocide in captivity, however, is a risk. Reginald Davie is present one day in Afion when the PoWs' houses are raided because the commandant suspects, correctly, that prisoners are communicating in code in letters back home.

'All writings of any kind were bundled into bags by the Turks and placed in a small guard room in the yard,' Davie notes: 'Among the confiscated papers were vivid descriptions of Armenian massacres, plans for escape, and many diaries of prisoners who hadn't minced matters when describing the "Terrible Turk" ... It was possible that some of the writers might have been shot for what they had written. It is certain that they would have been punished severely'.[56]

Rumours and stories travel far in the empire, even to its remotest redoubts. Working on the *Baghdadban* deep in the mountains, Private Daniel Creedon from Maryborough, Queensland, will die in captivity, but his diary survives thanks to the efforts of his good friend Jonas Havard from Fielding. Contained within that notebook is an abrupt but remarkable figure, jotted down on 2 February 1916.

'The people say that the Turks killed 1 ¼ million Armenians.'[57]

How can he know? Maybe he hears this from new arrivals to the railway camps; maybe from German soldiers passing through; from Armenians themselves.

The number he gives is chillingly accurate. More than a million members of an ancient people, all gone. Their last moments recorded in the scribblings, stories and memories of Anzac soldiers.

7

'Of passions like our own ...'

Thrumming cables of iron and rubber, sunk to the depths, knit together nations. The telegraph, like the railway, is an extraordinary phenomenon of the modern world. Along these pulsing tendrils, word of the Armenians' extermination reaches the farthest flung parts of the British Empire in a flurry of throb and dash.

At first, in the early months of 1915, news comes to the home front in a diffuse, uncontexted trickle: a few paragraphs for massacre; some column inches for a burning village. The war is already taking on monolithic scale, shattering all norms: within six weeks in April and May, Germany uses poison gas on the battlefield for the first time, bombs London from the air and sinks the *Lusitania*.[1]

Such events are unprecedented and capture the horrified imaginations of readers. But greater, even more unprecedented horrors are still to come.

It is James Bryce who directs the world's attention in July. Perched in the House of Lords as a viscount, he is an extraordinary conduit, tapped into a network of missionaries, consuls, travellers and journalists desperate to smuggle word out of the Ottoman Empire. From these testimonies, Bryce makes an intervention in the Lords, raising the prospect not just of widespread massacre, but of systematic deportation 'under the guise of enforced evacuations of villages' as the principal method of destruction.[2]

As a widely respected historian, jurist, former ambassador to the United States – and long-standing friend of the Armenian people – Bryce lends substantial imprimatur, allowing Australasian editors, struck by the ever-increasing rapidity of foreign reports but anxious about their sensational details, to drastically expand their coverage of the genocide.

From July onwards, readers daily encounter the foreign cable: a few terse sentences datelined Petrograd, Athens, Rome, Tbilisi or even Istanbul itself. Cables soon are supplemented with longer reports cleaved from the British and American dailies, or their own commentaries, editorials and missives.

Such a deluge of information is inescapable to any literate person, inked into every newspaper imaginable. From the largest metropolitan dailies – the *Sydney Morning Herald*, Melbourne's *The Age* and *The Argus*, the *Auckland Star*, Wellington's *Dominion* – to the smallest digging town rag or port gazette, like the *Northern Miner* or *Dunstan Times*.

Often, stories about Armenians are placed directly opposite – or even right next to – dispatches from Gallipoli. One cannot read about one without the other. Just as Anzacs and Armenians share graveyards, they share broadsheet space too.

HORRORS OF ARMENIA –
PLAIN STREWN WITH CORPSES –
FEARFUL TREATMENT OF WOMEN
Argus, April 1915

TURKISH ATROCITIES –
SYSTEMATIC SLAUGHTER OF ARMENIANS
The Mercury, September 1915

PREVIOUS ARMENIAN HORRORS ECLIPSED –
EIGHT HUNDRED THOUSAND ARMENIANS DEPORTED
New Zealand Herald, September 1915

MURDERING A PEOPLE
Adelaide Register, February 1916

Over the course of the First World War, these papers will print tens of thousands of stories on the genocide: in New Zealand, more than 13,000; in Australia, over 27,000.[3] Aside from the war itself, what is being done to Armenians is *the* major story of the age.

Towards year's end leader writers tasked with passing judgement on world events are beginning to comprehend the unprecedented nature of the crime. From the *Dominion*: 'It is believed the official intention of the campaign is extermination involving the murder of a million persons.'[4] From the Christchurch *Star*: 'the Turks took advantage of their opportunity to completely destroy the Armenian nation.'[5]

By September, the *Waikato Times*' editorialists feel sufficiently informed to conclude that 'it is not the people, not even the mob, who are responsible for this great crime. It was deliberately committed by the [Ottoman] Government'.[6] The Adelaide *Advertiser* agrees: 'a thoroughly systematised attempt, favoured by circumstances, to exterminate an entire people'.[7]

By November, the *Evening Post* is reprinting commentary from the *Manchester Guardian* claiming: '[It] may be asserted without fear of exaggerating that the Turkish outrages in Armenia are without a parallel in History ... Never has there been so resolute an attempt to exterminate a whole race, never one which promised to be so successful.'[8]

Among the hundreds of these editorials, it is perhaps the Dunedin *Evening Star*'s view given in early December that breaks one's heart the most. Titled 'The Martyrdom of a Nation', it is an urgent call for reflection and empathy – not in the language of militarism or religion – but with basic human solidarity:

> Can our readers imagine what such a holocaust means? Think for a moment of such an atrocity committed on the entire population of Dunedin, Christchurch, Wellington, and Auckland. It would almost drive us mad to contemplate it. And yet, while we are sleeping in our comfortable beds, enjoying the glories of spring, sitting in our picture theatres, and crowding our racecourses and places of amusement, these hellish doings have been happening to ... men, women, and children of passions like our own.[9]

From visceral reports passing over his embassy desk in Istanbul – like those of Leslie Davis in Harput – American Ambassador Henry Morgenthau understands the scale of what is unfolding more intimately than most. He cables home a critical message: 'Destruction of the Armenian race in Turkey is progressing rapidly.' He calls for immediate relief, funds raised in America to be funnelled to consuls and volunteers, hoping to save lives.[10]

Morgenthau's cable slips through the CUP's web of surveillance and reaches James L Barton, head of the American Board of Commissioners for Foreign Missions, the agency in charge of many schools, stations and orphanages in the Ottoman Empire since the early 1800s. As a Quaker and the former president of Euphrates College, Barton understands the urgency Morgenthau's shattering message demands. He fires off a letter to Cleveland Dodge, a well-connected magnate and philanthropist, and within days, a collection of professors, ministers, tycoons and diplomats gather into Dodge's Madison Avenue office. Barton tells them that they can 'save a remnant of a whole race'.

The Committee on Armenian Atrocities is formed on the spot with an offer of $50,000 for its immediate operation. The Rockefeller Foundation soon signs on as a prominent patron.

Weeks later, the Committee hosts its first public event at the Century Theatre in New York and adopts something of a statement of principle – a resolution declaring 'that the slaughter of noncombatant men, the tortures, mutilations, and outrages committed upon women and children wherever committed have given to the fairest places upon the earth the semblance of hell ... We call upon the nations at war to cease these crimes against civilization and morality'.[11]

These are the frantic opening moments of what will grow to become one of the world's largest ever aid organizations: Near East Relief, a new form of private, non-governmental humanitarianism.[12]

In London, too, James Bryce joins with religious figureheads (including the archbishop of Canterbury) and leading lights of the feminist movement to establish the Armenian Refugees Fund, quickly taken up by Mansion House, becoming the Lord Mayor's Fund.

As the United States has not yet entered the War, Near East Relief's appeals – backed up by detailed and extensive coverage – move and motivate Americans to donate vast sums and immense amounts of goods to the cause of Armenian relief.[13] From factory workers to bankers, sympathy pours forth. In mid-October, barely a month after its founding, the Committee cables its first US$100,00 to Morgenthau to be spent on food and medical supplies.

Rapid expansion follows. A network of fundraisers and benefactors built. Pamphlets printed for public education. Representatives tour east coast cities setting up local committees. Churches, synagogues, Rotary Clubs, women's organizations and Sunday schools enlist to help.[14] The phrase 'Starving Armenians', common parlance during the Hamidian Terror, is revived in American vernacular as shorthand – a warning to children to finish their dinner. Woodrow Wilson issues a presidential proclamation in October 1916 imploring citizens to fundraise.

By the end of that year, US$20 million has been sent to Anatolia, then on to the bleak deserts of Syria.[15]

A letter to the editor appears in *The Argus*, December 1915: 'Never has language seemed more utterly bankrupt of the power of adequate expression of human anguish than in the cyclone of destruction and misery that is deluging so many lands with blood.'

The impassioned author of this letter is one Edith Searle, resident of Victoria, prominent in the local church movement. Apparently on her own initiative and without any licence from the London Fund, she announces the founding of her own Armenian Relief Fund with an office on Malvern Road in Prahran. Searle begs Victorians, indeed all Australians, take up the 'long-smothered cry' of the

Armenians. 'Shall we follow America's example, and ... spare something for these most pitiful of all?'[16]

Her plea is met instead with pitiful near silence. In the first six months of operation, a small stream of donations amounts to around £300 – not an inconsiderable effort for a tiny clutch of volunteers, but a paltry sum when laid against the millions donated to Belgian, Serbian and Polish funds, to socks and cakes and scarves and cigarettes for the troops.[17]

Six months later, Searle writes again, the indignation and bitterness palpable in her voice. 'Though the daily papers have given enough news of the terrible atrocities ... brave Armenians who have flocked from all over the world to fight for the "righteous cause" have been sadly overlooked in Australia.'[18]

So it is too in New Zealand, where almost no one takes up the 'long-smothered cry'. There are few enterprising and self-sacrificing volunteers like Edith Searle. The war effort, after all, bites harder in Aotearoa, where rampant inflation and exorbitant costs of living strain pocketbooks.[19] The Christchurch *Press*, surveying the international situation, admits: '[The} mind is really incapable of grasping the vast amount of suffering caused by this war ... To-day we have harrowing accounts of massacre and destitution in Armenia, which in ordinary times would arouse indignation and practical sympathy. The struggle is so vast and affects us so closely that the sufferings of peoples far away, in whom we have no direct interest, are regarded as incidents.'[20]

By October 1916, without any committee at all, a meagre £15 is collected from the alms baskets of churches.[21] And even a direct appeal from the Lord Mayor's Fund to Wellington Mayor JP Luke – 'in the confident hope that the desperate condition of these unfortunate people will move you to give them all the help in your power' – barely makes an impact.[22]

A year later, the total is only at £20 (plus fifteen shillings and five pence).[23]

There are, however, moral-minded pioneers: for speech day at Diocesan Girls High School in Auckland – a school that will later educate the part-Armenian future Chief Justice Sian Elias – pupils forgo prize money in favour of donating their winnings to the Armenian Fund.[24]

And it is the great suffragette Jessie Mackay who, with typical classical aplomb, turns her pen once more to the plight of Armenians, just as she had done during the Hamidian Terror. 'Were the horrors of the war in Europe less stupefying than they are,' she notes, 'we would turn more often in spirit to the most hopeless and broken land on earth – Armenia.'

Mackay, ever invested in women proving their worth against men, heaps praise on American relief workers, often women themselves, still holding on at their stations, desperately trying to give aid. But, Mackay says, 'Let no one imagine that relief has ever been approximately equal to the decimated, exiled, tortured, martyr people, the deliberate dispossession and partial extermination of which stands as one of the monumental crimes of all history.'

Her sense of that history, of irony, of injustice is still just as acute as it had been twenty years earlier. Ultimate blame for the genocide, she insists, lies at the door of the Great Powers for their hypocritical failure to solve the Armenian Question. 'Were our Imperial conscience as tender as our imperial pride is great, for every penny that trickles into the Armenian Relief Fund a thousand pounds would gladly be given to still the memory of what we promised at the Berlin Congress of 1878, and failed to perform.'[25]

However much Edith Searle and Jessie MacKay despair, Armenians have not really been 'sadly overlooked'. Sympathetic sentiment exists. What the relief movement really needs is manpower.

December 1916 sees the creation of the Victorian Friends of Armenia (VFA), a collection of civil and religious leaders determined to expand fundraising and relief efforts. Subsuming Searle's Armenian Relief Fund, its leadership committee expands from one to nineteen people.

Two months later, on Tuesday 20 February 1917, in the gothic revival Assembly Hall on the corner of Collins and Russell Streets, the VFA holds its first public meeting, chaired by a member of the Legislative Council. Among the string of speakers, one man gives his stirring oratory with a hint of an eastern accent. A rare sight to any Australian: an Armenian, in person: forty-seven-year-old Haroutiun Balakian, brother of the 'living martyr' Krikoris Balakian who had been arrested on Red Sunday.

Haroutiun bears the scars of cruel treatment, having been tortured during the Hamidian Terror, accused of being the leader of an underground revolutionary cell in his birthplace of Tokat. Now, a resident of Melbourne for twenty years as a textile merchant, frequently travelling to New Zealand to pitch his wares, he is something of a self-appointed leader to the handful of Armenians who live in Australasia.[26] Even as he believes his brother dead, Haroutiun lends his voice to the beginning of a new stage in the Armenian relief movement.

'We are convinced,' the meeting's motion reads, 'that [Armenian] claims for help are so strong that the whole civilised world should co-operate forthwith to save them.'[27]

Heeding this call for co-operation, Melbourne's mayor convenes a meeting of the Council of Churches, which agrees to an 'Armenian Sunday' to be held on 22

April – two days before Anzac Day, the first true grassroots drive for Armenian relief in the country.

Instantly, collections rise: in a single day, the VFA nets more than £2000.[28]

Sydney and Adelaide forge their own committees.[29] With approval from the Commonwealth Button Fund – a quaint fundraising agency – a 'Suffering Nations' day is hosted in December 1917.

Melbourne becomes a city of pageantry: balloons and cake stalls, ladies bedecked in Sunday whites and lavish hats hawking adornments. Of the options available, for a single shilling, pedestrians and passers-by can obtain a tin button with a twee oriental image of camels, palms, minarets, sand, with 'SERVIA – SYRIA – ARMENIA' emblazoned in red lettering. Or, the pricier, more esteemed version: 'FOR THE SUFFERING NATIONS' surrounding Victoria's state emblem, available in brass (10s/6d) and silver (£1).[30]

In Sydney, the committee goes further than simply collecting funds. They appeal for 'new or second-hand garments, or material or anything that may help in sending succours forward', goods to be sent to the YWCA depot on Castlereagh Street, carried free of freight charges on rail lines.[31]

The movement rapidly multiplies, not just in ability and moral authority – adapting the methods of patriotic war work, building church and civil coalitions – but in imagination too.

Throughout the British Empire, there is total uniformity of feeling towards their German enemy: the 'Hun'; the rampaging 'Barbarian'; Kaiser Bill spreading his 'Kultur' over the globe.

Stoked by the War Propaganda Bureau at Wellington House, London, there is no act too obscene for which the Second Reich is given blame. Rumours of German complicity, organization, or participation in the Armenian Genocide are frequently boosted by the press and by politicians.

Thus, a common refrain enters the vernacular of the war years: BELGIUM. SERBIA. POLAND. ARMENIA. A quartet of bloodthirstiness for which Germans are incessantly held responsible, a formula incredibly useful as a rhetorical device for justifying the perpetuation of the war, in forcing through unpopular conscription bills.

In early 1916, the Canterbury Women's Institute, a long-standing feminist intellectual club, addresses an open letter to New Zealand Prime Minister William Massey arguing against a proposed bill of forced military service.[32] Massey's bluff response, widely reprinted, hinges on his portrayal of the war 'which Germany has forced upon the British Empire', a war that threatens not only 'national existence' and the 'safety of the Empire' but also 'the world's free democracies'. New Zealand, Massey insists, is partaking in the war in the 'best interests of humanity', against crimes committed in Belgium, Poland, Serbia, and

> the even greater enormity committed by Germany's ally in Armenia, where the Turks either massacred or drove to their death in the desert large numbers of Armenians, whose greatest crime was that they were a thrifty, industrious, law-abiding and Christian people. With a word, Germany could have stayed the hand of the Turks, but although presentations were made to her on the subject, she refused to raise her voice on behalf of the Armenians. The fate that has befallen Belgium, Poland, Servia, and Armenia might very well be ours if Germany gained the day in Europe. Our brave New Zealanders who are at the front are, therefore, as truly engaged in the defence of their country as they would be here, repelling the onslaughts of an invader.[33]

At a recruiting drive on Martin Place on Trafalgar Day 1915 Sir Joseph Carruthers, co-founder of the Australian Liberal Party and former premier of NSW, gives a soaring oratory punctuated with shouts of 'hear, hear!' and choruses of cheers. 'The spirit of our race is the same to-day as it was in Nelson's time,' Carruthers hollers, 'and if it can be aroused it will triumph as it did then, when it saved Europe and the world from military domination.'

> If Germany [wins] we shall be made to feel the concentrated hate of the Huns and the Turks. Remember Belgium, remember Poland, and remember the Armenians. The blood-stained fields of the countries where murder, lust, and rapine have held sway for the last [eleven] months will be repeated in British territories. You don't realise that; nor did the peaceful inhabitants of Belgium, Poland or Armenia realise it until too late.[34]

In a comparable tone of voice, Robert Alexander Wright, Reform MP for Wellington Suburbs and Country, addresses a recruiting rally at the Lower Hutt Town Hall in March 1916. The *New Zealand Times* reports Wright presenting the war as 'a war of defence – defence not merely of the Empire but of civilisation itself against the brutal oppression and domination of the modern Huns'. Wright then insists that Germany 'allowed the Turks to murder practically the whole Armenian nation, when a word from her would have stopped the frightful slaughter.' Any man who says he has nothing to fight for, Wright declares, is not a man at all.[35]

Wright's appeal to masculinity is met with such fervour and applause from his audience that he deploys the same device again a week later at another meeting in

Khandallah, referring 'in some detail to the Armenian massacres', attributing 'to German craft and callousness the torture and murder of the 800,000 Armenians who had died miserably at the hands of the Turks'.[36]

The Liberal MP Thomas Mason Wilford, member of the New Zealand wartime unity cabinet as Minister of Justice, again echoes this refrain during a parliamentary debate on the Military Service Act of 1916. 'Carrying the war to a successful and a proper conclusion' is the 'antidote for unpreparedness,' Wilford claims. 'Unpreparedness is answerable to-day, and has been paid for by the women of Belgium, [Serbia], Armenia, and northern France.'[37]

Taking up this theme of suffering Armenian women, William Earnshaw (MLC) argues that conscription is essential to avoid the slaughter of the weak. 'Are not [the] women in [Serbia], in Armenia, in Belgium, and in France suffering these barbarities? And are not [those] women our women in this war? Most surely they are. What frightfulness has been committed by the Germans in this war!'[38]

Are they not our women? Earnshaw asks. For him, and dozens of other legislators in Australia and New Zealand, such an appeal remains entirely cynical, bound up in the noble cause of the war. They do not offer out of their own pockets for the relief committees, as so many other citizens do.

But there is one politician who does take it upon himself to visit those women and bring their plight greater attention.

Richard McCallum, MP for Wairau and long-standing advocate for education, is dispatched to Egypt by Defence Minister James Allen in early 1916 to tour the Allied training grounds. While there, McCallum visits Port Said and finds 4,000 Armenians living in a tent camp outside the city – survivors and resisters, many of them children and women. For nearly two months these Armenians held out on the mountain Musa Dağ battling the troops sent to deport them, until a French cruiser came to their rescue.

On his return home, McCallum tells the *New Zealand Times*, 'It is understood that at the present time husbands and brothers of some of the women in camp are unwillingly bearing arms against the Allies.'[39] And in parliament, McCallum asks James Allen to consider whether 'assistance should be given to the unfortunate Armenians and Jews in Egypt'.[40] McCallum notes the Musa Dağ Armenians are being tended by a £2000-per-month grant from the British government which supplies only the bare essentials. It would be, McCallum says, a 'graceful and proper thing on the part of [the New Zealand] Government to forward some contribution, no matter how small'.[41]

In reply, James Allen parries and evades. Contributions have already been made to *other* victims of the war, but perhaps he will put the matter before the Cabinet.

Notwithstanding McCallum's earnest attempts to help, and whether or not Allen is being honest, whether he ever will put the matter before the Cabinet, it does not stop him from a deploying a ruthless insincerity.

Two years later, in a ceremony at Nelson's Church Steps, Allen marks the fourth year of war as acting prime minister, in uniform. The *Nelson Evening Mail* paraphrases his speech:

> It was difficult to realise while enjoying that day's beautiful sunshine that for four years a devastating war had been going on – that hell had been let loose upon the earth. That was not too strong a thing to say, as every Commandment had been broken. Thou shalt not murder! There were the murders of Capt. Fryatt, Nurse Cavell, and the wholesale slaughter of Armenians ... It was the business of the Allies to remove this hell upon earth. *It was our duty and privilege to assist.*[42]

If the language of politicians to describe the Germans is full of bluster, brimstone, curses and condemnations, the language of soldiers themselves in describing the Ottomans carries a more nervous tone. There is never any doubt as to the inherent evil of Germans, but as regards 'the Turks', or 'Mehmet' or 'Abdul', there is a sense of irony and paradox.

From the trenches of Gallipoli comes a grudging respect for the common Ottoman soldier whom Anzacs face across no man's land. 'Johnny Turk,' they call him. A motif emerges in letters and in the dispatches of correspondents, that of the 'clean fighter' and 'gentleman' in combat. This view clashes with what they read in the press, what their governments tells them, what they know from school, what they hear from captured Armenians at the front – the 'terrible' and 'unspeakable' Turk of old.

In a letter home reporting his brother missing and commenting on captured Anzacs, Trooper Gee Spooner of the South Island harbour town of Akaroa admits that 'in spite of the Armenian massacres, I am sure prisoners of war will be well treated by the Turks. They have fought a fair fight with us, so we must speak fair by them.'[43]

Some diggers remain unmoved by their experience against the Ottomans, however. Taking the other side of the opinion is Chaplain Captain JR Sullivan, just recently returned from Gallipoli. Speaking at the YMCA in Wellington on 18

November 1915, Sullivan tells his audience that they should 'effectively dispose of the idea' that the Turk is 'a civilized being and not a fiend as the Armenian horrors have proved him to be over and over again'.[44]

In the press, a vigorous debate takes up this paradox, this sense of schizophrenia. The *Free Lance*, a boisterous conservative illustrated weekly, uses the metaphor of Dr Jekyll and Mr Hyde to compare what is happening at Gallipoli, and beyond its battlefield:

> The Turk of to-day is proving himself what he always has been, *a dual personality*, on one side a villainously evil ruffian, on the other quite a decent chap ... Our boys at the Dardanelles praise him as a fair as well as a brave fighter ... But what about the Turk and his conduct towards the unhappy Armenians? ... At Gallipoli the Turkish Dr. Jekyll can be quite a benevolent fellow, hitting the Unbeliever as hard as he can, but, after having hit him, picking up and tending his wounds with genuine care and kindness. In Asia Minor, the Turkish Mr. Hyde murders, ravishes, and commits all the same old horrors which earned for him the title of the 'The Unspeakable Turk'.[45]

The Press, too, makes note of this *dual personality*: 'On the Gallipoli Peninsula, against the British, they are clean fighters, much cleaner than the Germans, but in Armenia they have committed the most appalling massacres and outrages. Is it that they are chivalrous in the Peninsula because they respect their foes as good fighters, and are barbarians in Armenia because they despise the Armenians as a conquered race?'[46]

Some writers find no contradiction whatever. No paradox worth considering. The *Pelorus Guardian* of Havelock North, citing an Australian paper, claims in early 1916:

> It is a rather remarkable fact ... that English soldiers in Gallipoli have been giving the Turk a certificate as a soldier and a gentleman, while English statesmen and journalists at home have been painting him as a devil. Common sense seems to say that both pictures cannot be true. And yet the evidence makes it clear enough that both pictures, as a matter of fact, are true. *There is nothing contradictory of human nature as we know it in the suggestion that a man may be a gentleman in dealing with those whom he regards as his equals, and a devil in dealing with those whom he regards as his inferiors.* The same man may be a gentleman in Gallipoli and a devil in Armenia.[47]

Rather than square such a circle, *The Evening Post* finds the whole question of a 'dual personality' strongly distasteful. 'There has been a tendency,' it notes:

To regard the Turk as not so black as he has been painted, to think of the Turkish soldier as a clean fighter, and of the Turkish Government as rather entitled to compassion as the reluctant tool and victim of German ambition than to loathing and hatred for its own sins. This inevitable result of the obsession of our imagination by the diabolical wickedness of our supreme enemy is entirely fallacious. The methods of the [Ottoman Government] are as corrupt, as oppressive, and as murderous as they were when 'Abdul the Damned' was the execration of the civilised world [48]

For some, however, the potent image of the clean and gentlemanly Ottoman soldier is so powerful as to dissolve all moral qualms and still uneasy consciences. To have faced Australians and New Zealanders in combat and not been found wanting – such a feat outweighs any other consideration. Among the believers of such a thesis: Charles Bean, official correspondent at Gallipoli now on the Western Front, soon to become a household name in Australia. He includes a small verse in his wildly popular *Anzac Book*, a compendium of quips, communiqués, cartoons and letters from the trenches:

For though your name be black as ink
For murder and rapine
Carried out in happy concert
With your Christians from the Rhine,
We will judge you, Mr Abdul,
By the test by which *we* can –
That with all your breath, in life, in death,
You've played the gentleman.[49]

8

The hush-hush brigade

The war sows rage and desperation in the earth, and manures it with men.

For those who live through it, images of apocalypse and judgement are never far from mind. The war savages and rents societies, indebts empires, wrecks trade and collapses families. It takes on a grim life of its own, seemingly escaping the grasp of powerful men who think they can control barbarism.

France, where the Anzacs end up, is an abattoir of mud and blood, deforested fields and grieving widows. Reserves run thin. Explosives churn the ground to mush.

After earning a reprieve at Gallipoli, the Ottomans are routed in Sinai, then Palestine by the Allies under General Allenby. On the Caucasus front, Russian soldiers move swiftly through fortresses, any opposition simply melting away. Behind these lines, Armenians returnees commit desultory murders on Turks and Kurds alike, people already labouring under famine conditions.

It is not the gas attacks, civilian bombings, sinking of merchant ships or indeed the genocide which brings the United States into the conflagration on the side of the Allies, but a bungle by German diplomats who invite Mexico to invade their northern neighbour. President Woodrow Wilson asks Congress for a declaration, which they give him on 6 April 1917 – only against Germany and Austria-Hungary, not the Ottoman Empire.

Bullish former President Theodore Roosevelt is enraged by the failure to combat the perpetrators of the genocide. He writes incisive polemics against American non-involvement:

> I feel that we are guilty of a peculiarly odious form of hypocrisy when we profess friendship for Armenia and the downtrodden races of Turkey, but don't go to war with Turkey ... [F]ailure to act against Turkey is to condone it; because the failure to deal radically with the Turkish horror means that all talk of guaranteeing the future peace of the world is mischievous nonsense; and because when we now refuse war with Turkey we show that our announcement that we meant to 'make the world safe for democracy' was insincere claptrap.[1]

Democracy does survive, though, as a rebellion against the global cataclysm.

In February 1917, a broad coalition of Russian workers, peasants, soldiers and the bourgeoisie force the hated Tsar Nicholas II to abdicate. Dual power replaces him: an ineffectual Provisional Government under the blustering Alexander Kerensky, and the antagonistic Soviet. Vladimir Ilyich Lenin returns to the Finland Station from exile promising peace, bread and land. Inspired, French soldiers threaten, and then carry out their own mutiny in April, demanding they be cannon fodder no longer. In October, Lenin's Bolsheviks seize total power in Russia.

The bread and land never arrive, but a kind of peace does.

Soviet Russia opens negotiations for a settlement with the Central Powers in December 1917, and the Treaty of Brest-Litovsk is agreed in March 1918, redrawing the borders of the Caucasus back to their pre-war position. Talât Paşa, now prime minister, is one of the signatories. The men of the Red Army, occupying Anatolia as far west as Erzincan, sensing an end to a reviled war, simply drop their guns and walk home.

The sudden collapse of Imperial Russia is an unbelievable and irresistible opportunity for the Ottoman Empire, so sure of its imminent defeat. Free of resistance to the east, Enver Paşa's immediate goal is the re-conquest of lost territory: the industrial belt of Kars, Ardahan and Batum. In the back of the generalissimo's mind is a revived vision of a pan-Turkic empire stretching to the very borders of China.

As an ideology, pan-Turkism desires not only vast land and resources, but also the extirpation of the ancient Christian populations of the region. Now, as before, it demands an empire for Muslims and Muslims alone.[2]

Invigorated Ottoman armies are cobbled together from the Caucasus defence. CUP devotee and Gallipoli veteran Kâzım Karabekir is made a brigadier general, tasked with pushing eastwards towards Yerevan and Gyumri – places where genocide survivors cower in their thousands. For a thrust into Iran, Enver anoints proven zealots and fanatics, not least Enver's uncle Halil – the emphatic genocidaire who takes the honorific 'Kut' after his conquest of that city. In charge of the Sixth Army is Ali İhsan Sâbis, a man who professes great 'pride in telling German officers that he killed Armenians with his own hands'.[3] Nuri Paşa, Enver's half-brother, heads a so-called 'Army of Islam'.

Otto von Lossow, a German general, summarizes their war aims in May 1918:

> The unlimited Turkish demands towards those regions which are purely Armenian ... are intended to achieve a border further than the Brest Treaty, to monopolise the economic exploitation of the Armenians of Transcaucasia ...

The aim of Turkish policy ... is to attain the Armenian regions and to annihilate the Armenians ... All of the utterances of Talat and Enver to the contrary are lies ... There will be no place left for Armenians to live.[4]

Kâzım Karabekir's swift eastwards advance through Erzincan and Erzerum, towards Kars, sets the Caucasus in a panic. In the place of empire and military order, provincial soviets tussle for power with a Caucasus Committee made up of Armenians, Georgians and Azeris still loyal to a provisional government that no longer exists.

At the point of Karabekir's sword, fearing impending conquest, the Committee votes for a purely symbolic independence: the Transcaucasian Federation, an eleventh-hour attempt to unite the region's imbricated nationalities, an organization that will last less than a week.

With Ottoman troops pressing towards Yerevan's dusty and decrepit streets, as Aram Manukian attempts to mount a desperate resistance (as he had done at Van in 1915), Georgian delegates break off, declaring their independence. The Azeris quickly follow. The Armenian National Council, an ARF-dominated body, has no choice but to declare the founding of their own state as well.

Thus, on 30 May 1918, the First Republic of Armenia is born.[5]

But what a paltry declaration it is. Weighed against the dreams of generations of Armenian utopians who yearn for liberty, autonomy and self-determination, the Republic cannot be more pitiful. Its population of 700,000 are mostly displaced peoples, crowding a threatened capital without any functioning institutions, riven with blight and diseased air.

It is, as one Armenian leader describes it, the 'untimely birth' of a 'sick child'.[6]

A reprieve from the mountainous furrows of the border between Ottoman and Iranian lands: a vast salt lake, one of the largest in the world, and a city which nestles its banks.

Urmia. A paradise of avenues and courtyards plane tree-lined. Buildings of deep red sun-dried bricks with large white-framed windows trace the flow of snow to the shore. A place where time is measured in millennia, home to a diverse population of Shia Muslims, Armenians, Jews and a large minority of Assyrians, sometimes called Syrians, or falsely, Nestorians for their unique church dating back to the earliest years of Christianity, speakers of Aramaic, tracers of their lineage to the bygone Assyrian Empire of antiquity.

Urmia is the site of one of the earliest American missions in the land, a Presbyterian station established in 1835, now run by Dr William Shedd, an enlightened Princeton graduate with a trim grey-flecked beard, and his California-born wife Mary Lewis Shedd. The couple act as de facto leaders in an isolated and sometimes lawless part of the world.

Urmia's Christians escape the worst of the CUP's annihilation campaign due to the loose and intermittent protection of Russian soldiers. But as armed authority dissolves into the mountains, they have their turn.

By April 1918, Ottoman armies retake Van. Its defenders, or those still surviving, finally abandon their home. They hold Ottoman forces at bay near Dilman and Salmas, allowing some 35,000 Armenian refugees, bearing their livelihoods on their backs, to trek southeast to the safety of Urmia. Mary Shedd goes out to care for this incoming torrent of misery:

> Men, women, and children, in one night, rushed pell-mell over the pass into Urmia, or tried to ... Those who came last were caught in the jam on the pass and were robbed and killed ... The most of them reached Urmia and scattered about in the villages or camped around the city.[7]

The Ottomans, led by Ali Ihsan Sâbis and ably assisted by Kurdish irregulars, follow the escapees, quickly spreading out around the outer limits of the city. By July at least 80,000 Christians, Armenian and Assyrian alike, camp in and around Urmia.

With gates barricaded, Urmia's defence is down to men and boys with hunting rifles or Russian guns picked up from where their former owners dropped them. Mary Shedd observes the Ottomans 'pressing from both passes', defenders 'fighting for their existence' in these 'weeks of anxious fear with the battle line but a few miles away'.[8]

The British War Office takes note of this fresh Ottoman aggression. At stake are the oil-rich regions around Baku, a cityscape scarred by towering drills and pumpjacks.

In the hope of securing the oilfields, General Lionel Dunsterville is appointed head of a small commando army: a 'Hush-Hush Brigade' comprised of the elite of British and Dominion soldiers. Fifteen hundred, all counted, including eleven officers and twenty-three NCOs of the New Zealand Division, and several dozen other Australians.[9] They are all volunteers, decorated and proven, many of them signing up to escape the mires of France.

On a chilly morning in January 1918, the Dunsterforce, as it comes to be called, assembles on the parade ground of the Tower of London.

Among that number is Captain Robert Kenneth Nicol.

Born to Eva Nicol and her husband William in 1893, Nicol had grown up a bright and fit kid in the suburb of Lower Hutt, playing football, earning a scholarship to Petone District High School. He joined his father's business at eighteen, painting houses perched on Wellington's steep hills.

Then war came, and he signed up almost immediately, drilling at Trentham Camp in his stiff khakis and wrapped puttees – shoulders back, heels together. Trained as a mortar man, he had been sent to Gallipoli and its shell-strafed valleys, taking part in the assault on Chunuk Bair, escaping capture, escaping with his life unlike so many others.[10] Then, a year later, amid the wretched bogs of Passchendaele near La Basse-Ville, Nicol won himself a Military Cross.

Amid the chaos of an advance, heavy shelling had killed all his commanding officers. He took initiative and ten men with him, rushing a position of fifty Germans, shouting as he went. According to his medal citation, Nicol stabbed six of them to death. 'Conspicuous gallantry', it reads. 'Utmost fearlessness'. In war, this is what 'devotion to duty' demands.[11]

For his prize, Nicol brushes up for a visit to Buckingham Palace where King George V pinned honours to his breast. A picture taken after the ceremony shows Nicol in his uniformed finery, adamantine jaw and immense paintbrush black eyebrows under lemon-squeezer hat. He writes home to his parents, nonchalantly: 'I've been up to the Palace to meet George, and he shook my dook.'[12]

His Dunsterforce mission remains a secret, even after he's signed up to it and standing – shoulders back, heels together – on that freezing parade ground. The only orders he has received are to buy both full winter and summer kits (including some undignified pleated shorts) and undergo a thorough medical exam.

General William Robertson addresses Nicol and his fellow officers in oblique terms:

> Gentleman, I am indeed pleased to see you for I recognise that before me I see gathered from the Imperial Army and the troops of the various Dominions, the cream of the British Army, and in whatever you undertake, I wish you good luck and God speed.[13]

They depart London on 29 January, still in the dark, passing through France, Italy, Suez and Basra. It isn't until they are deep into Iraq, aboard a flotilla up the Tigris, that they discover the plan. Seize the oilfields at Baku. Train local irregulars. Hold the line. They venture over the Persian border on foot, marching eastwards over 560 kilometres to Hamedan.[14]

Encamped, word reaches Dunsterforce commanders of the siege crisis unfolding in Urmia.

Dunsterville reasons that a delaying action will help them reach Baku quicker. At his request, a Royal Air Force biplane makes the precarious round trip from Baghdad to the lakeside city, offering soldiers and arms for defence. Local Armenian and Assyrian militias under the control of Agha Petros eagerly accept.

Dunsterville then arranges a small detachment of twenty-three officers and a cavalry squadron. At its head, he appoints Stanley Savige, a captain from Victoria,

Figure 15 '"I've been up to the Palace": Robert Nicol'. Credit: unknown.

like Robert Nicol a Gallipoli veteran and Military Cross winner. Joining him are Sergeants Frank Brophy from Parnell, Henry Tollan from Timaru, Bernard Murphy from Australia, Raymond Barrell of Tararua, a former farmer from Mosgiel named Alexander Nimmo and Nicol himself.[15]

On the morning of 19 July this small column, laden with twelve Lewis machine guns weighing thirteen kilograms each, 100,000 rounds of ammunition, and £45,000 in silver, shake hands with the remaining comrades and bid farewell, tramping out under a sulphurous Persian sun. They are to wait at a town called Sain Kala for Agha Petros, a talented linguist turned by the war from a teacher to a militia leader. Petros is tasked with breaking through the Ottoman lines south, meeting up with the Dunsterforce squad, and escorting them back to the city in the hope it can be held.

The rendezvous date is four days later, 23 July.

It passes with no arrival. No sign of horses kicking dust on the horizon.

Savige and his men fall back to Takab, occupying themselves by training a local police force, waiting as the days pass quietly over broken foothills and steep gorges.

In Urmia, Ottoman soldiers push ever closer to the city and its trapped inhabitants. Any safety awarded by Petros' militias and the foreign missionaries, including Dr Shedd and his wife Mary, is fast giving out.

On 31 July, a long-dreaded disaster arrives.

Panic surges through the countryside. Tens of thousands of Armenian and Assyrian refugees claw up meagre belongings, strapping them to cattle or their own well-worn backs. Dr Shedd rushes out to stop them, hoping they will hold out until the promised British arrive, hoping he can save his flock from destruction. But the exodus is underway. Shedd accepts the inevitable.

Mounting his horse early next morning wearing a luminous, incongruous cream safari suit, he turns to Mary. 'Well,' he says drily, 'we're going to have some more experiences together.'[16]

A scramble. At least 60,000 Armenians and Assyrians evacuating, following the shore of Lake Urmia south. Mary Shedd surveys the desperate jumble:

> The first day there were numerous little bridges made of sticks and earth, over which quilts were thrown to make them passable for carts. The jam at the bridges was indescribable confusion; every kind of vehicle, ox-carts, buffalo-wagons, troikas or springless wagons, furgans like prairie schooners, hay wagons, phaetons, and Red Cross carts, remnants of the Russian Hospital[17]

As soon as the convoy gets going, the Ottoman army and its Kurdish accessories rush forward, attacking and plundering sickly stragglers who cannot keep up. 'Frequently we heard of attacks on the rear,' Mary recalls. 'Some were killed, others taken captive and we heard no more about them. The fugitives were kept in a state of nervous fear and were ready to run and leave their loads of food and bedding at the first alarm.'[18]

On the banks of a river, Mary sees one of her students unable to carry both of her children across the water:

> She held one child over her head and waded through the river. Looking back she saw that it was too late to return for the other one and he was left sitting there on the opposite bank. The memory of her deserted baby haunted her day and night.[19]

Twenty-five-year-old Miriam Yohannan, an Assyrian daughter of a prominent family, married to a generous doctor named David, flees Urmia with the bulk of the refugees. She is wealthy enough to afford a horse-drawn carriage on which they pile belongings and children. She too witnesses the plight of mothers on the march who, like so many victims of the genocide's earliest phases, endure the worst cruelty.

'From the first day we left home, we met exhausted people on the roads,' Miriam will later write. 'We saw an apparently sick mother reclining on a stone, nursing her child; on close inspection we found her dead and the poor tot still nursing. There were hundreds of similar cases.'[20]

The convoy stretches dozens of kilometres along a thinly sketched road. The fittest manage to stay an hour's ride ahead of the attackers behind. Dr Shedd, conspicuous in his suit and helmet, tries to raise a gang of horsemen to protect the slowest, the most vulnerable.

Thinking themselves safe one night, Miriam Yohannan and her family camp by the bank of a stream. In the morning, they wake to find cavalry advancing through the fierce sunrise, their swords gleaming. In a rush, she collects her children, boards their carriage and sets off at full speed with David at the reigns. 'His only thought was to put as much distance between us and the enemy as he possibly could.'

In his desperation, he forgets the rough roads. The carriage lurches, tumbling over heavily. Miriam is pinned underneath. 'All around us the frightened refugees were running as fast as they could but not one gave us a thought. Again and again we begged them to help us but urgent pleading fell on deaf ears.' They manage to wrench free. The soldiers bear closer. They right the carriage, leaving most of their belongings scattered in the dust.[21]

Figure 16 '"We were forced to leave them to their fate": Stanley Savige'. Credit: Australian War Memorial.

Word reaches Stanley Savige's Dunsterforce detachment: Agha Petros is on his way.

The soldiers gallop back to Sain Kala. On 3 August, they finally meet, the Assyrian horsemen carrying a banner of white silk fringed with gold.

Petros inform Savige what is unfolding just behind them. The soldiers soon see the calamity themselves, emerging from their tents to find 'thousands in the valley, and along the road they were still streaming in thousands more ... Terror and despair was written deeply on their faces.'[22]

Urmia is lost. Savige knows that aside from the cavalry assailing the most fatigued refugees there is an Ottoman force of 500 further north. Impossible odds. There is no tactical advantage to be gained in pressing on, in protecting these foreigners. No orders insist they have to.

Savige addresses his two-dozen men. He asks for volunteers to act as a rearguard. Nine soldiers raise their hands, including Robert Nicol and Alexander Nimmo.

Shouldering their machine guns, they go down into the shadowed valley.

They march north, passing villages where the refugees have murdered locals. 'The crops,' Savige notes, 'which had been harvested and stacked on the outskirts, were all set afire by the Christians in retaliation for what they had endured.' He describes it as 'the outcome of pure fanaticism', and yet is quick to point out the corollary: 'Bad as the conduct of these Christians was, one has to bear in mind their awful treatment at the hands of the Turks.'[23]

Mary Shedd too notices the same acts of desperate ruthlessness, pointing out that some Iranians joined in the attacks on Armenians and Assyrians after the refugees 'plundered the shops and houses and in other ways aroused the enmity of the villagers'.[24]

Savige sees that little can be done. They press on.

In the late afternoon of 5 August, Savige's volunteer squad meets Mary Shedd on the road. To borrow Nicol's phrase, they shook each other's dooks.

Taking up positions at the rear of the exodus, Savige, Nicol, Nimmo and the other skirmish with Ottoman cavalry in the evening, sending them back under cover and away from their prey.

A camp is set up in a nearby village.[25] The troops bunk down amongst exhausted refugees. One soldier finds a sheep for supper, skewered over a fire. As last meals go, Nicol could do worse. Wrapped in his coat on a bed of straw, in hostile country, surrounded by the heaving night of empires at the extremes of mortality, Nicol will spend his final night on earth.

6 August 1918.

Some men stir before the first streak of dawn flashes over grey skies.[26] Stretching, yawning, they set about preparing breakfast, but are quickly interrupted: 150 horsemen in the valley nearby, closing quickly.

Nicol, swearing as he goes, checks his guns and mounts up. The last refugees are already on their way out, racing for the path to Sain Kala. Nicol's task is forward.

Savige orders him to collect a few armed locals and cover the left flank of the village with his Lewis gun. Savige takes the opposite position, by a low mud wall in a poplar grove. He bides until the enemy is within the pinprick circle of his sights, and lets fly. Nicol joins in.

A steady chug of fire fills the valley. Ottoman rifles crack back, aiming for the mules carrying the squad's ammunition.

Seeing their transports tumbling over, Nicol hands off his gun to a comrade. He ducks forward, finding Alexander Nimmo and ordering him to collect the magazines strewn across the ground.[27]

These will be Nicol's last words. Last words spoken by one New Zealander to another in the heat of battle in the wilds of Iran. So far from home, from Lower Hutt. Last words spoken defending some 60,000 Armenian and Assyrian refugees from annihilation.

Nicol advances into the open.

He is hit once. Falls.

Savige sees him go down. He yells at three other soldiers, telling them to reach Nicol on horseback. Each of them has their mounts shot out from under them, but the riders escape.

Nicol lies motionless in the dirt.

Any further attempts are futile. The rearguard's flanks are being pushed hard. With reluctance, and ammunition running low, Savige decides on a running, retreating fight.

'We knew that, so long as we continued fighting,' Savige recalls, 'the Turkish Commander would concentrate his efforts on wiping us out, before turning the energies of his men on looting the unfortunate people.'[28]

The squad catches up to the refugee column's main body seven hours later, without rest, without food. Without Robert Nicol.

Savige helps to bury Dr William Shedd, who had succumbed to cholera on the last flight. Nicol's body weighs heavily on Savige, too. He hopes, against all reason, that the young lad is only wounded and feigning death until he can bolt for shelter at the first chance. He cannot bear to leave him to the whims of Ottoman soldiers. When a group of British cavalry appear, Savige asks them to go back and find Nicol's body. They too have to retreat under heavy fire.

Savige's mind turns dark. He and his men are without food and water, as are the refugees before them. Little can be done. Some troops let children and women ride their horses while they walk alongside – a mere gesture. Too many are falling behind.

'It would have been absolute folly,' Savige reflects, miserably, 'for a mere handful of us to remain behind in the attempt to save a few.'

> With heavy hearts and big lumps in our throats, we were forced to turn a deaf ear to the pleadings of these poor unfortunates, who called upon us to save them. To have drawn our revolvers and shot them would have been more humane, knowing full well how cruelly they would be treated by the foe behind, but to shoot the old, the cripples and the infants in cold blood was little beyond any Britisher. Thus with aching hearts, we were forced to leave them to their fate.[29]

By contrast, Miriam Yohannan meets the remainder of the Dunsterforce party at Sain Kala. 'They were very sympathetic and did their utmost to help us,' she remembers. 'The nearness to us of the stalwart and very polite Tommies gave us courage.'[30]

Safety beckons at Bijar, another long walk out of hell. The ranks of refugees gradually thin out, scattered across desolate country. Old men and women succumb. Children cry in the night by their hundreds. Dysentery, cholera, typhus, diphtheria and malnutrition set in. Maggots gnaw the bullet wounds of young girls. A 'bedraggled mass of humanity … crawling along wearily', according to Lieutenant Sawyer, a Gisbornite. By his estimation, 'about 7000 people died during the first 100 miles of the march'.[31]

A Royal Army Film Unit is on hand to record the exodus towards Iraq, capturing the endless stream of beasts and people. Children cling to the waists of their parents. Deeply tanned faces stare into the camera's lens as they pass, faces expressionless as the desert. Always going.[32]

Even the well-to-do cannot escape the punishment of eviction. Miriam Yohannan's husband David dies in Bijar, victim first of cholera then a number of botched semi-barbaric surgeries which poison his blood.

Major Fred Starnes, in his previous life a farmer from Nelson, does his best to organize a meagre relief, sending out men into the villages along the path. These grow into 'rescue squads', travelling parched land by motorcar in the hope of bringing Van and Urmia's residents back to security.

The British decide to build a vast, sprawling camp at Baqubah, just outside Baghdad. The refugees must travel a further 500 kilometres to find succour. By early September 1918, there are 45,000 people in this tent city. Around 10,000 of them are Armenians who have endured since Van – where the disaster began a full four years earlier.[33]

Those Armenians and Assyrians that remain behind in Urmia and its surrounding villages, however, suffer a fate far worse.

Two weeks after taking the city and killing most of its Christian remnants, Ali Ihsan Sâbis enters Tabriz on the opposite side of the lake, demanding its Armenian leaders as hostages. He is met by a delegation. He addresses them:

> I thank you for having come out to greet me, but listen to what I am going to tell you ... We killed the Armenians of Khoy, and I gave the order to massacre the Armenians of Maku. If you wish to be well treated, honour the promises that you have just made. If you do not, I cannot offer you any guarantees.[34]

A few days later, Ali Ihsan meets the city's Armenian archbishop. 'I have had half a million of your co-religionists massacred,' he quips. 'I can offer you a cup of tea if you like.'[35]

Similar treatment is dealt out when General Dunsterville and the bulk of the Hush-Hush Brigade evacuate Baku after holding it for a few weeks.[36] One witness to the frenzied bloodletting of the city's Christians describes children's throats cut, 'slaughtered like lambs'.[37]

The Urmia exodus and all its attendant horrors form the central pillar of what Assyrians will come to call *Seyfo*, or The Sword, an equivalent term to *Meds Yeghern*. But such an experience will be hidden or obscured in history. Testimony of great crimes will be recorded by survivors, but will remain untranslated from native tongues. The Assyrian Genocide will become just another mass killing on the mere periphery of the past.[38]

To believe the propaganda, Captain Robert Nicol of Lower Hutt dies protecting the British Empire against the evil influence of Prussian militarism. But there are no Prussians here, let alone Germans. Or perhaps he gives his life for the nebulous ideal of liberal democracy, or for the still more esoteric idea of New Zealand? The noble verse of King and cabinet insists he sacrificed his life. But for whom? To answer this question is to rethink the very concepts of wartime sacrifice and heroism.

Robert Nicol was not *ordered* to fall in with the rearguard on that bright August day. He volunteered. No doubt he did not wish to die. But his death, his sacrifice, and the efforts of his comrades, allowed tens of thousands of others to live. He may have earned himself a Military Cross for honour and bravery in battle, but his true heroism is in defending the vulnerable from the blackest fate of all.

A year later, Mary Shedd returns to the valley and looks for that New Zealander who sacrificed himself, but will find nothing. When he falls, he is twenty-four years old. His parents believe for a long while that he is merely 'Missing in Action'. Until Stanley Savige, decorated with a Distinguished Service Order for his rescue, tells Eva Nicol how her son was killed.

Nicol's name adorns the central column of the Commonwealth War Graves Commission memorial in Tehran, and in April 2010, a plaque will be laid at Trentham Memorial Chapel, that same camp where he trained – shoulders back, heels together – as a bright and fit young boy just under a century earlier. The plaque will be laid by Wellington's small Assyrian community, aided by a delegation of more diaspora Assyrians from Australia. A quarter guard drills on the parade ground, and the 'Last Post' plays.

Hearts swells in those moments, in pride and in mourning.

The memorial carries a dedication:

For gallantry and sacrifice … From this day you will be remembered by Assyria and New Zealand and your heroic deed never forgotten.

9

No justice, no peace

Aboard the great grey hulk of the *Agamemnon*, battle-scarred from its punishment during the Dardanelles campaign, the Ottoman Empire surrenders.

The British have taken Jerusalem, Baghdad and Damascus. Bulgaria gives up, cutting off supply lines to Germany. With nothing left to bargain, Rauf Bey signs the armistice aboard the battleship moored at Mudros, from whence the Anzacs had departed for Gallipoli, shadowed by immense deck guns, on 30 October 1918.

Two days later, under cover of darkness, ringleaders of the CUP abscond Istanbul, stealing aboard a disguised German torpedo-boat bound for Berlin and comfortable exile. The guilty party includes Prime Minister Talât, disgraced War Minister Enver, Special Organization chiefs Şakir and Nâzım, Der Zor's butcher Zeki and a handful of others.

Genocidaires all. Rats amid the sinking.

Tramcars halt in Wellington's streets for a roaring procession making its way to the Town Hall. Against white frontage and colonnades, the bulk and moustache of New Zealand Prime Minister William Massey appears from a balcony, flanked by James Allen and Joseph Ward.

Massey luxuriates in the adulation. Victory, he insists absurdly, 'is an honour that is due to the Anzacs, to the boys from Australia, New Zealand, and the islands of the Pacific … Our boys on Gallipoli bore the heat and burden of the day, and the remains of many of them will lie on those bleak hills until the last trumpet sounds, but they will never be forgotten.'[1]

Backed by the Corinthian columns of the Bank of New Zealand building, the Justice Minister Thomas Wilford mounts a chair to be seen above the crowd. 'Turkey will be swept for ever out of Europe,' Wilford exclaims, 'across to the shores of Anatolia and to far [Ankara]. The breath of Turkey blights, withers, and destroys, and the foot of Turkey desecrates the soil upon which it is placed. The bloody murders the Turks have committed in Armenia should not be allowed to go unpunished, and the rulers should be brought before the bar of civilisation to answer for their crimes.'[2]

Word spreads across Australia with a shrill shriek of telephones. Offices, shops, warehouses and factories go up in applause. Work stops. Restaurants close. Schoolchildren sent home. A five-minute cacophonous peal of bells at noon, from Bendigo and Ballarat to Newcastle. Liners in Sydney's harbour let loose foghorns and whistles. A salvo, a blast of celebratory artillery in Hobart.

Amidst the throng outside *The Age*, jostling to glimpse the cable announcing surrender, a single plaintive, stumbling, feeble voice attempts the first few bars of *Rule Britannia*. Within a second, a riotous rendition along the avenue. *The nations not so blest as thee must in their turn to tyrants fall …*

One woman, overheard in a Melbourne street: 'My boy is fighting in Palestine. Perhaps they will let him come home now.'[3]

Less than two weeks later, Germany, riven by insurrection and revolution behind the lines, sues for peace.

So ends the war that is supposed to end all wars.

In Istanbul, a bearded sallow-looking figure slips through empty streets. He wears a ragged German uniform. An escapee's disguise. Krikoris Balakian, brother to Haroutiun Balakian, survivor of the zone of genocide, witness to extermination, a 'living martyr' risen and made to walk again, on his way to see his ailing mother.

They share an ecstatic, furtive embrace.

'Mother', Balakian whispers.

'Oh, my sweet child!'[4]

The bishop immediately sets about writing a memoir of his experience, what will eventually become the monumental work *Armenian Golgotha*. But on 13 November, he emerges to witness the Allied navies steaming their way up the Dardanelles to take control of the vanquished Ottoman Empire.

He dons a greatcoat and hat and hires a small gondola to cross the Bosporus. His Muslim boatman does not know that he carries an Armenian bishop once marked for execution. He tries to commiserate:

> *Effendi*, what bad times we're living in! What black days we have fallen upon! Talaat and Enver have destroyed the fatherland, picked up and fled, and left us to our fate. Who would have believed that a foreign fleet would enter Constantinople so illustriously and that we Muslims would be simple spectators?

Balakian, aiming for some kind of comfort, tells him: 'These black days will pass too; don't worry.'[5]

The bishop climbs through ecstatic Pera to the hill at Taksim. A panorama of cold steel and turbulent water as the combined French, British, Italian and Greek flotilla slip ominously towards shore. The *Agamemnon* drops anchor by Dolmabahçe Palace. A squadron of biplanes buzz the cool sky. The city watches on, 'mouths and eyes wide open.'[6]

Balakian ventures back to Pera, where surviving Greeks and Armenians rejoice drunkenly in the streets. The flags of Allied nations flutter from shops and offices. Girls throw flowers from balconies.

'The Muslims had withdrawn behind the grated windows of their houses, watching in silence.'[7]

The French General Louis Franchet d'Espèrey trots pompously into the ancient capital on a white horse. Behind comes an occupation force: Allied soldiers, intelligence agents, diplomats and commissioners.

French soldiers occupy the southern region of Cilicia. Italians march into Antalya. Crucially, Greek fighters seize control of the famous port city of İzmir.

Article 7 of the Mudros Armistice empowers them to take over any area if security is threatened. Article 24 entitles them to intervene military if any disorder erupts in the 'Armenian provinces'.

They do not know just how un-Armenian those provinces have become.

Behind the occupation force, in turn, come humanitarians: volunteers for the Red Cross, Near East Relief (NER) and the Lord Mayor's Fund (LMF); Quakers and Mennonites; veterans and medics; reformers and nurses; teachers and mechanics. In early 1919, a flotilla of freighters depart New York laden with food, clothing, prefab buildings, motor trucks, and fifteen decommissioned French army field hospitals complete with beds, surgical instruments and drugs.[8] Some daring individuals simply book a train and arrive on their own, hoping to help. Together, these first responders lay the foundation for a vast and intricate operation of relief.

Among that number is a brave and hard-headed young nurse from New South Wales named Isobel Hutton serving with the Australian Imperial Force in Palestine. She demobilizes as soon as possible and joins the American Red Cross, taking charge of a hospital set up in an abandoned Ottoman barracks in Aleppo.

Under her charge, around 6,000 'wearied, frightened, hungry, dirty' and 'half-animalised' Armenians, many suffering medieval illnesses like tuberculosis and typhoid. Most have not been properly fed, clothed or washed in over a year.⁹ With the aid of local volunteers, Hutton works to provide a semblance of order and sanity to that hospital. A visiting Red Cross inspector remarks that it seems impossible 'that one nurse could bring peace out of chaos singly and so speedily'.¹⁰

'Go anywhere you like to-day among these people and you will find thousands of them bearing some mark of Turkish atrocity,' Hutton will write later of these Armenians:

> Women with their bodies seared by fire, the result of being forced through a circle of straw, after their clothes had been sprinkled with kerosene. Some with maimed limbs, because of fighting for a daughter's or sister's honour. Little children limping for the rest of their lives because the tired little legs could not carry them faster on some occasion of deportation. Young girls with the whole face disfigured with many tattoo marks and a hundred such things too terrible to dwell on … One needs to have lived through it, seen the pillaged homes, where everything of value has been stolen or destroyed; ministered to them in their anguish of mind; nursed and fed and cared for them till such time as they were any way like fit to shift for themselves, before even a dim idea of the frightfulness can be arrived at.¹¹

Hutton's grim work is supported by compatriots, now free from the pressures of war work, free to give their spare change to the Armenian relief cause. In mid-1919 the Victorian Friends of Armenia inaugurates a fresh collection drive with a massive advertisement stretching the length of a page in *The Age*, imploring Australians to give in aid of 'the vast refugee hosts … driven forth into the deserts and wilderness to suffer unspeakable horrors and to die of violence, hunger and exposure,' victims of a 'deliberate and diabolical plot'.¹²

Between them, the people of Melbourne, Sydney and Adelaide pool together £11,000 for the LMF by August 1919.¹³ By November, New Zealanders have heeded the call. From Aotearoa, contributions to the LMF reach £2671.¹⁴

But what Isobel Hutton sees and experiences is but a sliver of a vast and almost insurmountable catastrophe, every victim suffering physically and mentally, the lingering permanence of inflicted horrors.

NER's workers try to bring a degree of normality to their lives. Of course, 'normal' is not a word possible in the Armenian vocabulary in the immediate aftermath of an apocalypse. 'Normal' means at last one meal a week, or maybe a roll of rags to use as a blanket. Rootless, displaced, homeless. The very base of their being rent.

Somewhere between 85,000 and 150,000 Armenians remain in the Syrian deserts.[15] The authorities do not know how many orphans or assimilated women are alive in the interior – the Armenian Patriarchate suspects as many as 50,000 women are still in captivity.[16] Tens of thousands of Armenians and Assyrians find shelter in the semi-functioning Armenian Republic. At Gyumri, a former Russian barracks houses 25,000 orphans.[17] Unable to comprehend what has befallen her people, Zabel Yessayan distracts herself from her inability to write by working amongst these children.

They range in age from toddlers to late adolescents, and become one of NER's principal missions. Many of them have been targeted as part of the CUP's policy of assimilation, of subsuming them into the dominant culture, destroying their distinct identity, their religion, giving them new names, their tongues no longer able to utter the language of their birth. Many more have been plucked from the arms of families during deportation, or, perhaps most tragically of all, were sold by them, in the hope they might survive the death march.

For girls, and some boys, sexual violence – outrage – is so common that Karen Jeppe, a Danish relief worker of supreme compassion, states in the mid-1920s that of the thousands of Armenian women she has tended to, *all but one had been abused*.[18] Some girls bear unmistakable signs of depraved captivity: deep blue tattoos of shame across their faces and hands, impossible to remove.

NER, supported by British military police, works to retrieve these kidnapped children. Rescue homes are established in Istanbul and Aleppo. Under pressure from feminist groups, the League of Nations launches a Commission on the Deportation of Women and Children, which declares all forced conversions illegal, obliging the government to return trafficked youth.

Emily Robinson, secretary of the Armenian Red Cross and Refugee Fund of Great Britain, even compares the return of young Armenians to the repatriation of PoWs when she addresses the League. 'Many scores of thousands of Armenian women and children are still detained in Moslem houses where they have been captive since 1915,' she notes:

> The Armistice provided for the release of 'all prisoners of war.' Only the men were released and the terms of the Armistice as regards women have not been carried out. Some of us who have this matter much at heart earnestly trust that the League [will intervene] … The present state of things is hazardous in the extreme to the cause of peace in the East besides being a scandal and a disgrace to the civilization of the 20th century.[19]

Despite NER's staunch work, it is slow. Many stolen Armenians are adults by the time they are rescued, or manage to rescue themselves.[20] Karen Jeppe records thousands of pages of testimony, including that of a woman named Zabel who gets herself to the Aleppo safehouse in 1926. Zabel's experience is indicative of many thousands of other Armenians held against their will across a collapsing empire:

> In the beginning of the deportation, Zabel's father was separated from her family and was sent in an unknown direction. Zabel was exiled with her mother, 5 sisters and a younger brother … Near Veranshehir, they collected all the beautiful girls, and distributed them among the Turks and the Kurds. The rest of the caravan had to go further on in the deserts to die. Zabel had been the share of a Kurd, who married her. She lived there 11 years, unwillingly, til an Armenian chauffeur informed her that many of her relatives still were living in Aleppo. Having made her escape in safety, she reached Ras al-Ain, from where by our agent she was sent to us.[21]

'Rescue', however, is not always a liberating experience, but a fraught one.

Armenian children taken at a very young age sometimes refuse to leave their new homes when relief workers come to find them. A small number of children, it is true, have been adopted out of a sense of genuine caring, and are converted to Islam because of culture and custom rather than malice.

Stanley Kerr, an American humanitarian, visits an Arab sheikh in Aleppo province with several Armenian children in his household. Kerr finds them safe and well cared for. 'Now are you going to take these children from me, after I have protected them during the past four years?' the sheikh asks him. 'I have no choice,' Kerr replies.[22] He is bound by duty to return them to their community. But what is their community, after half a decade? The Arab village or the Armenian?

Kerr's story is not unique, but it is illustrative of the ideology of early humanitarianism, and NER's task in particular. For all its progressive thinking, NER's workers barely attempt to help those Turkish, Arab or Kurdish innocents in the war's wake. Little effort is made to ease their conditions of immiseration. Many NER workers have primitive views about Islam and the people who live beyond Europe's frontier, and attempts to rescue Armenian children from Muslim homes or 'harems' – while earnest and honest in intention – reeks of superiority.

And as NER's mission evolves from triage to rehabilitation, the semi-colonial nature of their work grows clearer. They are attempting to make Armenians the 'vanguard of a new, modern, and moral community' under Protestant American tutelage.[23]

While nursing the skeletal form of a proud people back to some semblance of health, NER seeks to restore Armenians to a defined homeland that never really existed, to reconstitute a nation from thin air.

As the weary work of succour continues, the British government sets about punishing the Ottomans for siding with Germany, for carrying out the extermination of the Armenians, upholding their vow of 29 May 1915 to hold 'personally responsible' all perpetrators of 'crimes against humanity'.

In British minds, partition of the Ottoman Empire goes hand-in-hand with condemning the killers. Prime Minister David Lloyd George insists that a 'heavy punishment will be meted on them for their madness, their blindness, their crimes,' a punishment harsh enough to 'satisfy even their greatest enemies.'[24] Rear Admiral Richard Webb, assistant high commissioner in Istanbul (and former commander of the battlecruiser HMS *New Zealand*), goes further still:

> Punishing those responsible for the Armenian atrocities means punishing all Turks. That is why I propose that the punishment, on the national level, should be the dismemberment of the last Turkish Empire, and, on the individual level, putting on trial the senior officers on my list so as to make an example out of them.[25]

Carving up foreign territory is easy enough – the British have been doing it for centuries. But what court is going to hear about the annihilation of Armenians and Assyrians, or the forced removal of Greeks? Even if such a court does exist, what law could its defendants be tried under? No legal instrument for the prosecution of genocidaires exists.

The Hague Conventions of 1899 and 1907 speak of 'principles of humanity' and 'public conscience' and lay out the rules for how one state should treat another, but no provision is made for how a state should treat its *own* citizens. During the War, military commanders can be held responsible for any crimes, yet this does not extend to political leaders of a nation. The idea of 'crimes against humanity' is only that – an idea, an ethical principle.

An Allied commission set up in January 1919 explores these legal quandaries. It considers forming an international court or a special British-led tribunal, which only produces a further dilemma: the accused will still be tried retroactively – after the law is created – which is obviously indefensible.

The commission's report, passed up to the Council of Ten in Paris, eventually rests its case on the 1907 Hague Conventions, neutering any attempt to create a truly international criminal court, or any legislation outlawing crimes against humanity.[26]

Independent of the Paris deliberations, the British foreign minister, minister for war, and first lord of the Admiralty meet to scratch out their own policy. The rulebook they produce allows British diplomats in Istanbul to send long lists of suspects to the barely functioning Ottoman government demanding they be arrested or transferred to Malta for safekeeping.

Ottoman ministers respond with fury. As a riposte, they insist that any potential criminals ought to be tried on their own soil, under their own laws. They ask the British to hand over evidence which can be used at trial – a request duplicitously denied. The ministers even go so far as to suggest placing impartial foreign judges on the courts, or convening a joint British-Ottoman military tribunal. Both reasonable ideas are rejected.[27]

Ottoman civil society, like the rest of the world, is well aware of what has happened to their fellow Armenians, Assyrians and Greeks during the war. In excoriating polemics, newspapers demand to know why Talât, Enver and the others have been allowed to flee instead of face trial. Some call for their execution, for their 'heads to be ripped from their bodies, laid on the chopping block … then hung from the obelisk in front of Topkapı Palace!'[28]

Furious debates rage in Parliament, that neutered institution. MPs fume at each other, laying blame for so many deaths. Turkish MPs shout down their Armenian or Greek counterparts or deny them time on the floor, perhaps because their speeches cut to the heart of a truth some do not want to hear.

Mattheos Nalbandian, who had seen his entire family deported, gives a brave recitation of the evidence, of the trauma. 'Gentlemen, these things are not tales from *One Thousand and One Nights*; these are the facts, just as they occurred, and our distinguished assembly should express regret over them and weep':

> Both world opinion and the victims will demand an accounting and compensation, and the Turks will have to provide it … Redemption is possible, but we must find every person who committed these crimes and we must punish them, and we must return and restore those rights that were trampled and abused. And after this we will go before the civilized world as a delegation and declare that we are going to do this, even it means punishing one hundred thousand … this is the soundest and most righteous path.[29]

The only option left for the new Ottoman government which takes charge in November 1918 is to try suspected genocidaires in their own courts – in the vague hope that it might please the British and earn them greater leniency at the Paris Peace Conference – to stave off dismemberment.[30]

An early attempt at some form of justice: the Fifth Commission, a parliamentary committee tasked with publicly questioning CUP officials and officers. Former Prime Minister Said Halim, among others, takes the oath, but stalls, pleads, sidesteps and diverts blame to any other government office and agency but his own, insisting that no systematic attempt was made on the lives of Armenians.

The deportation law was to protect the army's rear, he reasons. A necessity, but 'the implementation was a disaster'. And anyway, Said Halim insists: 'I heard about these disasters after they had already happened. In the end it was the Ministry of War that informed us of the reasons behind all this … That's where you need to ask, because I am unable to say anything that would convince you otherwise.'[31]

Already denials are being formulated.

The Fifth Commission's failure to excavate any helpful answers leads to the creation of a new body, this time with strong powers: to subpoena documents, search houses and offices, question witnesses, order arrests and place suspects under surveillance. Tasked with leading this investigation is an official with intimate knowledge of the genocidal apparatus: Hasan Mazhar, former governor of Ankara, sacked for refusing Talât's orders to deport Armenians.

The Mazhar Commission soon discovers, in a series of raids on CUP headquarters and the homes of its leaders, that the perpetrators purged and destroyed the records of the Special Organization and the Central Committee, and any surviving statistics on deportations and killings closely kept by Talât's Interior Ministry.[32]

Nevertheless, after two months of probing, investigators produce thick files on 130 suspects. They are handed over to tribunals initially overseen by civilian judges. By the opening of proceedings, the tribunals become extraordinary courts-martial, staffed with military judges and prosecutors.[33]

These trials will bring Armenians face to face with their executioners once more.

The first case to come before Court Martial Number One indicts the leaders of Yozgat, a district of Ankara. Out of 33,000 Armenians, 31,000 had been deported. Eighteen-year-old Eugenie Varvarian had been among them. Asked to give evidence, she testifies that the district governor, Kemal Bey, had given orders to slaughter deportees. Eugenie repeats his words back to him, across the courtroom: 'Kill them, kill them; if you don't, I'll kill you.'

That girl, Kemal retorts, is a 'liar who didn't know what she was talking about'.

Eugenie responds: 'Kemal is lying when he says that he didn't massacre Armenians. Did all the Armenians commit suicide? Where are most of them now?'[34]

In April, the main trial opens in Istanbul. Twenty-three suspects indicted. Only half appear in court, including ex-Prime Minister Said Halim, CUP ideologue Ziya Gökalp and İsmail Canbolat, Talat's successor at the Interior Ministry.

Talât, Enver, Drs Şakir and Nâzım are sentenced to death *in absentia*.

Other hearings for lower-ranking suspects stretch on for months. Judges use the time to authenticate some 293 files of incriminating secret documents which survive the CUP's textual purge: copies of coded telegrams ordering deportations and massacres.[35]

However rigorous the detective work, the courts-martial are wildly susceptible to political interference. Twelve different cabinets will hold power between November 1919 and November 1922, and the zeal of the prosecutors often depends on whichever political wing is in control. At times, the tribunals are lenient or forestalled by corruption. At others, they resemble show trials for cleansing the Ottoman state of the CUP and its sympathizers.[36]

Setrag Karageuzian, an Armenian investigative magistrate at the Trabzon trial, bemoans the lack of will to prosecute genocidaires. After nearly four months of probing in an attempt to build a case, he comes to the conclusion:

> (1) The Ottoman government did not intend to punish those responsible for the massacres or the other culprits or to see that justice was done. Its sole aim was to deceive Europe and America and public opinion in the civilized countries; (2) the program of Union and Progress is a crystallization of the mentality of the Turkish people; (3) the great majority of the state officials, gendarmes, officers in the gendarmerie, police chiefs and policemen who organized and carried out the deportation and massacres are still in the posts they held then. Consequently, they will never want the investigations to succeed. The state officials have created as many difficulties as possible in order to bring our mission to naught. The police and gendarmerie, instead of arresting the accused, producing witnesses, and carrying out the orders given them, forewarn the guilty, that is, their former accomplices, of all pending actions; (4) with the means currently available, nothing can be done to apply the principles of justice.

In sum, Karageuzian labels the courts-martial a 'well-constructed farce'.[37]

No perpetrator should ever put itself on trial. That way injustice lies. But still, decrepit, failed and hubristic though they may be, these tribunals mark the first time in history that a case of premeditated mass murder, carried out by a state against its own citizens, has been tried in a court of law.[38]

Believing themselves imminent victors, the Allies had signed a litany of covert accords and secret deals during the war, squabbling for the carcass of Ottoman territory: the Constantinople Agreement (1915); the Hussein-McMahon Correspondence, the Sykes-Picot Accord and the Balfour Declaration (1916–17); the Saint-Jean-de-Maurienne Agreement (1917); the Fourteen Points, and the Four Principles (1918).

All of them promise contradictory or self-negating settlements.

For months after the Armistice, they jostle over maps, cleaving the empire into sectors of influence, occupation and control. The Ottoman government's own pleas are met with ridicule: David Lloyd George calls their submissions to the Paris Peace Conference 'good jokes'. American President Woodrow Wilson scoffs that he has 'never seen anything stupider'.[39] Imperialism by derision.

An eventual plan decided between Britain, France and Italy at San Remo in April 1920 bisects, amputates and throttles the empire. Britain gets mandate control over Iraq and Palestine. Syria and Lebanon go to France. Greece is formally granted the area around İzmir.

Remaining regions fall under zones of economic influence: France the Cilician coast, Italy the Mediterranean cities of Antalya and Konya. Crucially, Anatolia's eastern provinces are set aside for the creation of Armenian and Kurdish mandates, with the potential to become totally independent. Only the smallest sliver of Asia Minor remains.[40]

This draft partition plan is written up as the Treaty of Sèvres, a settlement far more ruthless and draconian than the Versailles Treaty notoriously imposed on Germany.

Istanbul's government will grudgingly, meekly swallow it whole on 10 August 1920.

However, a burgeoning movement rising from Anatolia's chaotic depths poses an upstart challenge to imperial powers, to the Ottomans' powerlessness, an insurgency forged in the ashes of the CUP.

Part of a stay-behind plan drawn up by Talât and his accomplices during the fraught days of the Gallipoli campaign and enacted the night before they fled, the scheme officially dissolves the CUP but keeps intact its secret networks. Front groups form, the most important of them called *Karakol*, or The Guard. Its goals are simple and twofold. Protect CUP members from prosecution in the event of defeat and organize a resistance movement against attempts to carve up the country.

Special Organization leaders stockpile guns and ammunition in secret caches to be picked up by insurrectionary operatives.[41] These shadowy cabals also interfere with the ongoing courts-martial in Istanbul by smuggling suspects to safety. Two remaining killers – Halil Kut Paşa and Dr Mehmed Reşid, the Butcher of Diyarbakır – both escape in this way (though Reşid, in a rare display of a guilty conscience, commits suicide soon after).[42]

All of its members are lifelong CUP members with a duty to a collapsed regime. They are, as ever, obsessed with that most critical question of all: *How can we save the state?* Yet when the Greek armies occupying İzmir advance inland in mid-1919, claiming their promised spoils, the cadre takes on the charisma and mystique of popular rebels.

But they lack a figurehead. A leader.

10

The golden chain of mercy

A rusty, clattering tramp steamer cuts the Black Sea's stormy waters, bound for the Anatolian port of Samsun.

Aboard, passengers double over with nausea. One of them nurses lingering pain: infections of the ear and kidney that had knocked him out of the last year of war. He is a man café and mess hall gossips revere as a capable if tempestuous commander, cool in resolve but prone to arguing with superiors, a man made a hero by his defence of Gallipoli on Red Sunday, of Chunuk Bair, the Caucasus, Syria and Palestine. Mustafa Kemal.[1]

Like the officers he travels with, Kemal is a Turkish Nationalist, though one less fired by expansionist dreams than Enver was. More of a hard-headed pragmatist, devoted to the concept of sovereignty. Although a CUP man since before the 1908 Revolution, he is largely untainted by the crimes of his comrades. But not for much longer.

Army insiders – likely CUP agents – have secured him a military inspectorate in the far east, where the Allied grip is the weakest. Working alongside close friend Kâzım Karabekir, he begins to covertly organize disparate cells of loyalists, officers and *Karakol* operatives into a fully fledged rebellion, fulfilling the purpose of Talât's stay-behind plan.

When the British find out what Kemal is up to, they order him sacked. Forever one step ahead, he instead resigns from the army, adopting the guise of a dissident once more. In his resignation letter, he explains that the new movement has been launched 'to save the sacred fatherland and the nation from the threat of disintegration, and in order not to fall victim to Greek and Armenian designs'.[2]

Between July and September 1919, the fledgling Nationalists hold two congresses, thrashing out ideas on how to deal with foreign occupation. They announce their intention to 'preserve the integrity of the Ottoman Empire and our national independence and to protect the sultanate and the caliphate'. Under

Figure 17 'Mustafa Kemal, hero of Gallipoli'. Credit: Printed in Rafael de Nogales, *Four Years Beneath the Crescent*, New York: Charles Scribner's Sons, 1926.

Kemal's sway, the Nationalists vehemently oppose the creation of a new Armenia in the Six Provinces. Even the return of refugees and survivors – a game of demography – must be opposed.

Preservation, in other words, is essential. No land should be ceded, nor political or religious institutions abolished. Further, Kemal keenly understands that the prosecution of genocidaires is intimately connected with Allied attempt at partition. For Kemal, as for the British, trying perpetrators of the Armenian Genocide in court is analogous to a new Armenia in the east or an expanding Greece in the south. He sees both as an existential threat. Any appeals to justice for Armenian victims and survivors are a challenge to authority and integrity.

These simple and defiant points make up *Misak-ı Millî*, the National Pact.[3]

In December, Kemal shifts his base of operations from Erzerum to Ankara, making his home in a grand mansion that once belonged to an Armenian merchant. A new headquarters for what Kemal believes is a war of liberation, of independence.

Desperately seeking relief, desperate to escape the blighted desert, Armenian and Assyrian survivors head north for nearby Cilicia, for the protection of British occupation troops.

They crowd a ring of coastal and inland cities – Adana, Mersin, İskenderun, Urfa, Maraş – in their tens of thousands, entreating the British for financial aid, for their homes back, for a steamer ticket west, for at least one meal a day. Nationalist propaganda and the provocations of armed irregulars have already made the surrounding countryside a no-go zone.

By the end of 1919, in line with the deals set out in the Sèvres, a French administration replaces the British. The French troops are mostly Africans: colonials made to do the clean-up work of empire. Accompanying them, several thousand Armenian volunteers of the Légion arménienne, prone to acts of revenge against local Turks.

Here, in Cilicia, the Nationalists will make their first strike.

Kemal orders his lieutenants to move against the northernmost town of Maraş, where some 22,000 Armenians are seeking refuge, where the French garrison is ill-prepared to defend them. On the outskirts, desultory murders. At least two a day, mostly Armenians searching out food.

The French bungle a retaliatory crackdown, arresting members of the local Turkish elite on the night of 21 January. In response, Nationalist guerrillas open fire on French patrols and haul artillery guns to the Taurus foothills overlooking the town, invoking a siege.

Two days later, a pogrom follows: Armenians shot or bayoneted where they stand. Eight hundred flee for a church, only for the church to be burned down, with them inside. One witness notes the deep pits dug at the edge of town, 'men tied in bunches of three, and led to the edge of it, and then shot and dumped into it, dead or alive.'[4]

The toll, after almost three weeks of blockade and butchery: 800 French dead; 10,000 Armenians cut down.[5] Above all, the Nationalist banner raised. This is their modus operandi. Their campaign to oust the Armenians – and by proxy, the French – spreads to surrounding cities.

The British react to news from Maraş with exquisite blunder. On the night of 15 March, armoured cars roar through Istanbul's streets, bound for the war ministries, for the parliament buildings, a tightening of the occupation and a warning to the limp Ottoman government to curtail Kemal's insurgency.

A defiant Kemal, now with a taste of blood, calls for Members of Parliament to make their way to Ankara. 'Today,' he cables, 'the Turkish nation is called to defend its capacity for civilisation, its right to life and independence – its entire future.'[6]

On 23 April 1920, almost five years exactly since Red Sunday, Mustafa Kemal inaugurates the Grand National Assembly from his de facto capital, in essence creating a situation of dual power: two rival governments in one state. In Istanbul, the collaborationist monarchy. In Ankara, Nationalist insurgents.

This renewal of atrocities will be the backdrop for a fresh wave of humanitarianism in the British Dominions, a more fervent undertaking in New Zealand and Australia on behalf of those doomed by Mustafa Kemal.

With the Great War's end, women ascend to the leadership of the Armenian committees in Australasia: the badge-sellers and ledger-minders and letter-writers, forming the vanguard, energized by an embryonic human rights agenda, embracing 'the Armenian relief cause as an extension of their maternal care'.[7]

Among this bold, assertive number is Melbourne opera singer Cecilia John, a radical pacifist who ardently believes that 'all wars, just or unjust, disastrous or victorious, are waged against the child'. John, along with Vida Goldstein and Adela Pankhurst (of the famous suffragette family), forms the Women's Peace Army. When the (gloriously named) social reformer Eglantyne Jebb establishes the London-based Save the Children Fund (SCF) in 1919, John and her colleagues move swiftly to establish Australian SCF branches in every state with the support of the Women's International League for Peace and Freedom and the National Council of Women (NCW).

Sydney feminist Eleanor MacKinnon, member of the NCW and the National Women's Club, joins the executive of the New South Wales Armenian Relief Fund, and will later help to nationalize the Australasian Armenian Relief Fund, editing its official journals. Lady Cara David, a prominent feminist and liberal, is essential to efforts in New South Wales too, helping form committees in areas outside the major towns and cities.[8]

Aside from these dedicated feminists, Australians organizers also have a significant propaganda advantage: moving images.

In January 1920, the NSW committee takes delivery of seven reels of nitrate film: *The Auction of Souls*, a story adapted from the experiences of Aurora Mardiganian, who had been in Diyarbakır during the apex of Dr Mehmed Reşid's bloodletting.

The Auction of Souls had been filmed in, of all places, the Californian desert and on the beaches of Santa Monica in late 1918, locals dressed up as Ottoman soldiers or Armenian peasant women. Remarkably, or cruelly, Aurora plays herself in the movie, though often shooting stalled when she broke down mid-scene, terrified of the actors in red fezzes – an open case of shell shock, or, as it will come to be called, post-traumatic stress.

The resulting picture is highly sensationalised and ultraviolent. Mass killings. Piles of dead bodies. It struggles to pass the censors in Britain. Of course, these depictions are nothing against the reality. Aurora explained this to the directors as they were preparing a scene featuring Armenian women crucified on well-constructed crosses, long hair prudishly obscuring nude bodies:

> The Turks didn't make their crosses like that. The Turks made little pointed crosses. They took the clothes off the girls. They made them bend down. And after raping them, they made them sit on the pointed wood, through the vagina. That's the way they killed – The Turks. Americans have made it a more civilized way. They can't show such terrible things.[9]

However sanitized, or however shocking, *The Auction of Souls* proves immensely popular in Australia. After a first showing in Sydney, the papers praise its 'Zolaesque realism' and warn: 'Those who wish to be entertained should stay many miles away from it, but those who would learn how a small nation was nearly exterminated, even though their hearts are wrung when they are gaining the knowledge, should see it. It kills for all time the phrase which was popular during the early days of the war, that "Johnny Turk is a gentleman" '.[10]

The film's release is preceded by a vast spread in the *Sunday Times* telling Aurora's story, leading to a week-long run of continuous showings at the town hall.[11] It then premieres in Melbourne before getting a nationwide billing, a share of every ticket going to Armenian relief funds.

In New Zealand, the first highly mobilized appeals come as part of an empire-wide relief drive for Save the Children in early 1920, the British government promising to match every donation pound for pound. It is principally for starving children throughout Eastern Europe, but Armenians feature prominently in the campaign literature as the most desperate for aid.

Again, women in the YWCA and the WCTU form the backbone of the operation, the debut SCF committee forming in Auckland in March.[12] A public week-long appeal in June sees subscription lists posted in churches, factories, warehouses, government buildings and offices.[13] A total: just under £13,000 raised, the bulk by churchgoers.[14]

The SCF committee in Dunedin calls for a 'week of pity' in July. Appeals published on the front page of the *Otago Daily Times* inform readers:

> Thousands of children perished in the Near East last year, because of starvation. All who could be accommodated were taken to refugee camps and orphanages … Many of the children were clad in only one cotton garment; they suffered with chilblains until their little fleet burst. Pneumonia, influenza, pleurisy … all the ailments of winter united in undermining their physical strength. Their power of resistance weakened by privation, exposure, and malnutrition was not great, and thousands succumbed. All through the winter it meant not the digging of one little grave, but one big grave every day. Give and Save a Life!'[15]

The Otago appeal hopes to raise £10,000. The total: £15,000, including donations from Southland. The southern appeal is so successful that its chief organizer travels to Christchurch to school their committee on tactics. In September volunteers canvas door-to-door throughout Canterbury.[16] 'Twenty shillings will clothe a child and feed it for a week,' *The Press* reminds its readers. The total in Christchurch by December: £10,000.[17]

With the governor general as its patron, the Wellington branch organizes street collections, and receives donations from the Labour Party. The total: £4,000 by year's end.[18]

Altogether, New Zealanders amass £50,000 for Save the Children, funnelled through the Minister of Internal Affairs to London.[19] Much of the donation is diverted to Austria and Eastern Europe to combat famines, but a valuable £2,000 makes its way to the LMF.[20]

Even with such bountiful support, the Republic of Armenia is struggling.

Landlocked, its administration confined to the gritty town of Yerevan, a population made up mostly of survivors and refugees – far from the lustre of its nearby neighbours Tbilisi and Baku. Armenia's only hope for safety and security rests in the promises made in Sèvres.

But these are mere pencil marks on a subdivided map. For all the Allied talk of restitution for the Armenian people after what they have faced, little is forthcoming. Just as it has been since the nineteenth century, foreign powers express their sympathy for the Armenian plight but do nothing to enforce treaty terms or provide armed protection. Mustafa Kemal understands this well. 'A frontier which is not defended with bayonets, force, and honour,' he says, 'cannot be secured by another principle.'[21]

He orders the smashing of the Republic, putting to death any hope of an Armenian home in Anatolia. 'It is indispensable,' Kemal tells Kâzım Karabekir, commander in the east, 'that Armenia be annihilated politically and physically.'[22]

Karabekir's corps, invigorated with Soviet guns and gold, advance eastwards, into the Caucasus – a repeat of his invasion in 1918. Armenian defenders fight bravely, but they fight with faulty rifles, with a clutch of generals prone to squabbling and insubordination.

Kars falls. Another massacre. Armenian soldiers stripped, deported west. Widespread looting. More butchery practised in the streets – for three whole days. Six thousand dead. Blood-sopped snow, a *Winterreise*. Karabekir is carrying out his orders well.

Hemmed in, facing that promised annihilation and a choice between two evils, Armenian leaders turn to the Soviets as their last hope. A presumptuous, arrogant cable from Moscow: 'The Central Committee of the Russian Communist Party has decided to establish a Soviet regime in Armenia. The Revolutionary Committee has already arrived.'[23]

At midnight on 3 December, the Armenian Republic, not even 1,000 days old, is subsumed back into a Russian fold. To complete the tragedy, Soviet negotiators demand that Armenians give up their claims and entitlements in the Treaty of Sèvres.

The Six Provinces, the Armenian homeland, lost forever. Mount Ararat, that most sacred symbol, is on the other side of the border.

Persecution continues. Mustafa Kemal expands his ravaging campaign in Cilicia, with its imperilled Armenians, many of them now too fearful to venture beyond the limits of the province's cities. Out there, Nationalist guerrillas roam. Farms and vineyards and orchards go untended. Famines wither and wilt.

One by one, Cilicia's cities fall under siege. At Antep, encirclement lasts an entire year. At Hacin, Armenian defenders and survivors are reduced to eating horses, donkeys, cats, then the leaves and bark of trees. The gristle of desperation.

Nationalist salvos thump periodically at the desolate swampy fringes of Adana, where the refugee camps are.

This is not the prize the French imagine: not a zone of influence so much as a zone of lost lives and sunk costs. Their goal had always been Syria, not Cilicia. In October 1921, the French barter with Armenian lives, agreeing to abandon the region to the Nationalists in exchange for a few railway and mining concessions. A secret annex in the Ankara Agreement obliges the French to leave behind significant war material – rifles, ammunition, artillery – to be deployed by Kemal's forces.

With the French exit, an Armenian exodus. A stream of souls downwards to the coast. At Mersin, the only trade is in passports and ferry tickets, passage to İzmir or Istanbul or South America or Athens. Exiles sell their belongings for a pittance at the ports, or burn them. Some Armenians even walk *back* to Aleppo, where they had been deported to, where they had escaped from.

Faced with the likelihood of thousands of defenceless orphans falling into Nationalist clutches, the relief agencies – NER, LMF, Red Cross – hastily organize a network of convoys and routes to spirit the children to Syria, Palestine and Lebanon: a mass *kindertransport*, caravans by train and by foot.

Behind them follow Turkish refugees and new Nationalist administrations. As if crystallizing the continuity between the CUP's genocidal practices and the Nationalists' mop-up operations, Kemal's National Assembly reinstates the Law on Abandoned Property, helping themselves to the spoils of spoliation.

At Adana's train station, one can find two columns of people heading in opposite directions. Overnight, it transforms from an Armenian city to a Turkish city. Just twenty-four months earlier, Cilicia's Armenian population had been over 100,000. By 1922, it is around 22,000.[24]

Loyal Lincoln Wirt has seen this before: the smell of filthy camps; gaunt stares of parentless children; feeble recoiling of women humiliated. As a Red Cross Commissioner on the Western Front, as a NER organizer among the first to embark for Syria in February 1919 – Wirt is familiar to it all.

Michigan-born, a flush of white hair parted across his crown, Wirt is emblematic of American protestant missionary zeal. Early in his career, he had pastored in Newcastle, Sydney and Brisbane. There, he trained his gift for passionate oratory – learning to shout for crowds while retaining empathy in his voice. For NER, these are invaluable tools. Returning to the United States, he embarks on a long tour and by 1920 can claim to have had a hand in establishing

Figure 18 'Reverend Loyal Lincoln Wirt'. Credit: Evan Wirt and Family.

NER committees in *every state of the union*. And in 1922, he keeps heading west – over the Pacific, to internationalize the movement.[25]

He embarks from San Francisco in January, landing in Japan, China, Korea, the Philippines and Hawaii before mooring in Australia, his old flock, in May.[26]

By now, Wirt's stump speech is well prepared: part history lesson, part rallying cry. He emphasizes the extent of Armenian suffering and pleads for relief of any kind for survivors. In a sincere and impassioned rhetorical style, his argument proves convincing to anyone who hears it.

Loyal Wirt kicks off his Australian tour in Hobart, June 1922, where he unveils a soundbite. My mission, he tells a collection of leading Tasmanian clergymen, is to 'stretch a golden chain of mercy across the Pacific, with a link in every country'.[27]

The Hobart meeting establishes a precedent that will be followed in every place Wirt steps foot: the assembled audience passes a unanimous resolution expressing sympathy for Armenians, and a relief committee forms on the spot, staffed by leading notables of the city.

He tells a large audience at the Melbourne town hall a day later that 'half the [Armenian] nation had been exterminated', describing children 'thrown into the gutter where they were picked up and carried away in carts like rubbish'.[28] The resulting appeal catches the attention of Thomas Walter White: the Australian pilot, Anzac captive and witness to genocide. He quickly signs his support, becoming a staunch advocate for the cause.

After addressing audiences in Sydney alongside the Australian nurse Isobel Hutton and supported by leading Australian feminists like Cara David and Eleanor McKinnon, Wirt sweeps across the Tasman to New Zealand.

An *Auckland Star* reporter gives a portrait when he arrives on 17 July 1922: 'Short, smart, dapper, with penetrating be-glassed eyes, and all the efficient push of the American businessman, combined with the cultured manner of the American professional.'

Yet Wirt's efficient push in Auckland runs into trouble immediately – a drive for Russian relief is taking place at the exact same moment. In tune to popular sympathies, he reasons thusly: 'I would not take one penny away from the Russian relief work, but I would like to point out that the Russians, the Poles, and of course, the Belgians, all had a Government of some sort behind them. The Armenians have nothing at all. They have no friend at court.'

Repeating his clarion call about the 'golden chain of mercy', he tells the reporter of NER's successes in setting up hospitals and orphanages, providing a constant flow of supplies to ravaged areas. 'There is yet so much to do. We do not want money so much as food and clothing. The Australian people have promised a relief ship and a unit of workers. Is it too much to ask for a 1000-ton ship loaded with produce and workers from New Zealand?'[29]

To a gathering of clergymen and ministers of the city the following day, the American shows an NER propaganda film called *Alice in Hungerland* and lectures on the history of the Armenians. This history, repeated throughout the tour, is somewhat skewed, inflating the tolls of dead and dispossessed or exaggerating the numbers of Armenians who were able to fight back against their oppressors.

Half-truths or not, the holy men pass a resolution 'expressing deepest sympathy with the suffering people of the Near East, especially with Armenian Christians', and endorse the idea of preparing a ship to be sent in aid.[30]

At the invitation of Auckland Mayor James Gunson, Wirt gives a 'stirring appeal' to a public meeting at City Council chambers the next day, appealing not for gold, but for 'food, wheat, wool, milk, blankets, and old clothing and leather'. Again, attendees express their support. A relief committee forms, and Gunson pledges to gain the blessing of William Massey's Reform government.[31]

Success continues. Prolonged applause greets the charismatic American at a civic reception in Wellington. (Letters from Massey and Reform MP for Wellington Sir John Luke express their regret at failing to attend). For the powerful men gathered, Wirt introduces a new note of bluster. The *Evening Post* quotes him as saying: 'If he had his way, he would appeal, not for foodstuffs, but for gunboats; not for money but for fighting men; but now that could not be. Any war raged on behalf of Armenia must be with the use of moral weapons, not military ones.' For his peroration, a note from the just-formed Auckland committee is read out: 'We will do our share,' they challenge. 'We will match whatever Wellington does, and then some.'

Robert Wright MP, who during the war wielded the treatment of Armenians as a war cry, follows Wirt on stage. 'Farmers are complaining over their inability to find a market for their beef,' he notes, '[and yet] the Armenians are dying in thousands of starvation! Would it not be possible to purchase beef from the farmers at reduced prices and send it to the relief stations in Armenia?'[32]

Suitably buoyed, the audience passes a unanimous motion 'expressing its deep sympathy with the endeavour that is being made to render relief to the suffering people of Armenia'. A committee begins, with Wellington's mayor as its chairman.[33]

Wirt then ventures south to Dunedin, where he gives three lectures, then back up to Christchurch where he speaks to civic reception attended by the deputy mayor, also the Red Cross executive in the city, and a meeting of religious leaders, each of them pledging to hold an 'Armenian Sunday' in their churches.[34]

By the time he returns to Wellington to catch a ship back to Sydney, Wirt has convinced New Zealanders to set up relief committees for Armenians in every major city with prominent political and clerical figures in charge.

'My heart has been touched a hundred times by the generous and sympathetic response which the people of New Zealand have made to my appeal for the saving of our Armenian brothers,' Wirt states as he departs. 'Not long, I trust, shall it be until the Australian mercy ship, accompanied by the New Zealand mercy ship, will sail by tragic Gallipoli into the Dardanelles.'[35]

But plans for this mercy ship hit a significant snag. Before sailing off, Wirt meets with Prime Minister William Massey, who is seemingly the only person not bowled over by Wirt's fulsome vows for aid – even the evocations of 'tragic Gallipoli'. Asked in Parliament what the government plans to do for Armenians, Massey merely promises that any donated goods can be transported freight-free on the railways. But he declines to sponsor a mercy ship outright. 'Charity [begins] at home', Massey grumbles, 'and in view of the conditions prevailing in the Dominion', he will not promise much.[36]

Again the generosity and solidarity of ordinary people. Again the recalcitrance and apathy of political leaders.

Mustafa Kemal has fulfilled his first condition, to not fall victim to 'Armenian designs'. Their dreams of a homeland in Anatolia have been snuffed out. Now, he turns to his second, and more formidable condition: the Greeks.

A Hellenic army has marched far inland from their base at İzmir, occupying an enormous portion of western Anatolia, confident of British backing. In March 1921, they seize Afionkarahissar – site of the Anzac PoW camp – before being halted by Nationalist forces. The Greeks forge ahead again in July, this time breaking through and threatening the Nationalist seat of power in Ankara. As they evacuate their wives and children, members of the National Assembly demand that Mustafa Kemal take over direct control of the army. He agrees, in early August 1921, and dons a grubby tan field uniform once more.

Under Kemal's command, the Nationalists withstand a massive assault along a sixty-kilometre front at the Sakarya River for three weeks.

The result is a stalemate, but it crushes the morale of Greek soldiers. They have pushed too far past any land to which they can reasonably lay historical claim. Some wonder why they are fighting *at all*. Soldiers begin deserting in their dozens, while their diplomats beg the British government – or, more specifically, the philhellene Prime Minister Lloyd George – for more arms, money and moral support. Outnumbered in cabinet, Lloyd George refuses, urging them to dig in.

For Kemal, the Ottoman Greek population is indistinguishable from the foreign-born Hellenic army. Both represent an occupying force, a breach of sovereignty and a barrier to ethnic homogeneity.

As in Cilicia, an integral part of his military campaign are cleansing operations, closely following Talât's model wielded against the Armenians: decapitation of town and village elites, decimation of military-aged men, deportations, mass rape and seizure of property. Against Pontic Greeks – those who live on the Black Sea coast, well behind the front lines – the Nationalists wield their greatest, most pitiless fury.

The town of Bafra, near Samsun, is most representative. The local Greek elite are invited to a dinner party, where they are all murdered. A roundup, then massacre, of young men. A unit of irregulars, functioning not unlike the Special Organization, pillage houses, then escort columns – several hundred at a time – to nearby villages, to nearby gorges over a period of weeks. One man pays his executioners 300 lira for the privilege of being shot, rather than hacked.[37]

At Cappadocia, Greek community leaders appeal to the British for protection: 'Our populations', they write, 'find themselves totally at the mercy of ... Kemal. It is impossible to describe the terror, tortures, ordeals and exactions...Mass hangings are the order of the day ... Soon ... nothing will be left but ashes and the silence of death.'[38]

Unlike a half-decade earlier, Ottoman Greek civilians have some protection. They can flee towards the front lines and the occupation zone. But in that zone, Turks suffer vast depredations at the hands of a gruff and uncaring administration. It is often Ottoman Greek refugees who carry out vicious reprisals – deepening immiserations, fuelling Nationalist propaganda.

Kemal rejects all appeals from the Allies to cease his military and genocidal campaigns, even rebuffing an offer of a hollowed-out Sèvres settlement. He stakes everything on a decisive, annihilating victory.

By August 1922, the Greek and Nationalist armies are evenly matched. Towards the end of the month, Kemal makes a lightning strike, an offensive so shattering and total that Hellenic forces are put into immediate retreat, turning tail for the coast. They carry out a policy defined by all who witness it as 'scorched earth': blowing up bridges, torching Turkish towns, villages and crops, killing their residents and looting what they can find.

Within two weeks, the defeated army, trailed by tens of thousands of ethnic Greek civilians fearing the rapid advance of the incoming Nationalists, shuffle towards the grand port of İzmir.[39]

In Australia, Loyal Wirt's plan for a mercy ship is not stalled by the government. Its date for departure set: September 1922.

As preparations are made, Wirt completes his Australasian tour. By the end of August, he is in Adelaide, setting in motion a large church-led campaign

Figure 19 ' "Anzac Bread!" The *Hobson's Bay* departs Princes Pier, Melbourne'. Credit: Evan Wirt and Family.

throughout South Australia and the Northern Territory which leads to the donation of a motorized ambulance costing some £200.⁴⁰

A nearly brand new, 14,000-tonne Commonwealth passenger liner named *Hobson's Bay* is handed over for transport and loaded, on 2 September, with £250 worth of dried milk powder, £150 in woollen materials and £100 in raw leather. The *Hobson's Bay* departs for Melbourne, where great lumbering cranes load 100 tonnes of flour (around 4,000 sacks) on board. While resting in port, an immense banner hangs over the side: AUSTRALIAN FLOUR FOR STARVING ARMENIAN CHILDREN.

Wirt tails the ship by rail to Perth, from where it finally departs on 15 September. Joining him aboard are a handful of Australian missionaries and activists, including Hilda King, a prominent Christian organizer, and Sydney couple Ernest and Mary Bryce, the latter well known among feminist circles in the city.⁴¹

They are sailing towards a conflagration.

Charles Dobson has been in İzmir for only five months. With his Greek wife Eleni, in his role as an Anglican vicar, he works closely with the British authorities. They respect his service, for he has seen combat before.

Born in Christchurch, New Zealand, a minister to hard-scrabble coal towns on the West Coast, and at Gallipoli and on the Western Front, a participant in full charges 'over the top' thirteen times, winning himself a Military Cross.[42] But never has this handsome thirty-six-year-old Anzac veteran 'witnessed anything so horrible' as what happens when Mustafa Kemal's war of liberation crashes against İzmir on 9 September 1922.[43]

Dobson hears rumours and suspicions from all quarters – British diplomats, American officers, Greek clerics – that Kemal will sack the city, in peacetime

Figure 20 'Charles Dobson'. Credit: Tyree Studio Collection/Nelson Provincial Museum.

a refined and elegant place. But he does not believe it – until the first waves of destitute refugees, Greeks and Armenians alike, overrun the hospitals and congest the streets. Dobson protects a few of them in his own churchyard.

The first appearance of Nationalist troops – a cavalry unit – does not spark alarm. It is when the infantry arrive that the looting begins. Down at the packed waterfront, Dobson finds civilians with gunshot wounds, and tends a man trampled by horses who dies later that night – a night filled 'desultory rifle-fire and screaming'.

The next morning, 10 September, with the aid of a Turkish policeman, Dobson commandeers a cart to collect the dead laying strewn amongst roadside debris. Their bodies are buried in an Orthodox graveyard.

Mustafa Kemal enters the city, victorious. He tells two American naval commanders that 'the situation now demands that the Greeks and the Armenians leave Anatolia'.[44]

A day later, hastening from consulate to church to railway station, Dobson stumbles across a large group of men, around 200, 'sitting down on their haunches … with a Turkish guard standing over them'. He later hears from an 'absolutely unimpeachable source' that these chained men were later butchered with bayonets. At dusk, he finds an unattended cart in a square

> covered with a rough sort of matting which was thrown over, but was not sufficient to hide the nature of the contents of the cart, there were women and babies, and the body of a young girl … they were all dead. I pulled it aside to look at them; they had all been shot. This girl – I do not know what age she would be; she was a thin sort of girl, and she had not reached womanhood, although you would not call her a child – was shot through both breasts, and there were other evidences that she had been outraged.

On the morning of 12 September, Dobson meets with the British vice-consul, sitting in the yard of the embassy. A sudden crash: a man's body flung into the wall of the building from an adjoining roof. Dobson leaps up, finding an Armenian, alive. On the roof nearby, a squad of Turkish soldiers aiming their rifles. He yells at them, in English, to prevent them pulling their triggers.

On 13 September, as refugees and foreigners alike scramble for lifeboats, amid a general deterioration, Dobson ventures to the Armenian quarter of İzmir. A scene of chaos: one man 'lying on the road who had been shot through the thighs … He had a great clot of blood which had formed which I could not attend to'. His screams go unheeded. 'Another man had been struck in the jaw and a very large part of his face had been knocked up. Up the side streets there were shots fired.'

As evening falls, the New Zealander finds himself, along with his wife, infant child and their Greek nurse, standing on the wharf, jammed together with hundreds of other refugees waiting for the mass of Allied ships in the harbour to rescue them. On the quay, the Smyrna Theatre advertises its latest show in electric lights, great block letters two feet high, an absurd mocking of the scene: LE TANGO DE LA MORT.[45]

Only when Dobson and his family are aboard the *Bavarian* does he notice the fire.

An immense pillar of dense smoke spirals from the Armenian quarter, where he had been hours earlier. As the steamer pulls away, the blaze blasts through the city, towards the sea. Beautifully white architecture turned gold and crisp in the heat, silhouetted against molten sky.

'An enormous conflagration,' Dobson notes, 'just one sheet of flame ... getting more terrible all the time ... You would see the outline of a building and then that building would catch fire too, and nearer and nearer it was bursting through actually on the water front.'[46]

In the storm, cafés, consulates, cinemas, schools, churches, all eviscerated. Two-thirds of İzmir burn in a rage for a full forty-eight hours. The poorer Turkish quarters are untouched.

The prickling smell of charred flesh hangs over the Mediterranean. Below the waves, drowned bodies drift. Bits of bodies: escapees churned to pieces by ship propellers.

Greeks, naturally, blame Turkish Nationalists for the holocaust, accusing them of torching a predominantly Christian city as revenge. Nationalists indignantly point out the stupidity of razing a prize they've just conquered. Charles Dobson writes a report on his experience which makes it into the hands of British Foreign Minister Lord Curzon. The Anzac veteran will go to his death convinced that Turkish soldiers are responsible:

> I was astonished ... to find how unwilling some circles were to believe the culpability of the Turkish troops in the burning of [İzmir]. It seems to me that the firing of the city by the fanatic element of the Turkish Army was the natural culmination of the breakdown of restraints imposed by military necessities, and of the unbridled indulgence of xenophobia.[47]

After docking briefly at Suez and Beirut, the *Hobson's Bay* reaches Istanbul, anchored near Galata Tower. On deck, Loyal Wirt receives urgent orders from NER to dispatch some of the mercy ship's cargo to the Greek islands, to Greece

Figure 21 '"Just one sheet of flame...getting more terrible all the time": HMS *Iron Duke* in the foreground as Izmir burns'. Credit: *London Illustrated News*/Mary Evans Picture Library.

itself, where tens of thousands of people are starving – İzmir's warehouses and stores having been incinerated. Within hours, a significant load of flour is transferred to an auxiliary steamer, bound for needy people.[48]

Wirt notes the brittle irony in this expedition. The supplies pass 'through tragic Gallipoli, where many brave Anzacs from Australia and New Zealand had laid down their young lives, face to the foe. And now the unhappy victims of this same foe were to be fed with bread from their homeland, as if to complete the work for which they died, Anzac bread!'[49]

Mustafa Kemal has his victory, his annihilating liberation. With İzmir's embers still hot, he issues a decree: 'Permission to leave Turkey is hereby granted to all Greeks and Armenians ... This permission is valid until September 30, 1922. It is hereby declared that those, who after [that] date ... are in a position of impairing the public peace ... will be deported.'[50]

Permission, indeed. Throughout Anatolia, people run like rivers to the coasts, to the railway terminals and ports – sites of thievery and desperation. By the end of September, more than 190,000 Ottoman Greeks and Armenians have fled İzmir and its surrounds, ferried in bucketing boats to mainland Greece. The very last to leave are the remaining Greek and Armenian villagers of Gallipoli.[51]

In the remains of Ottoman Europe, some 250,000 Greeks flee westward. Observing the exodus, a cub war correspondent, the young Ernest Hemingway:

> Twenty miles of carts drawn by cows, bullocks and muddy-flanked water buffalo, with exhausted, staggering men, women and children, blankets over their heads, walking blindly along in the rain beside their worldly goods ... Nobody even grunts. It is all they can do to keep moving. Their brilliant peasant costumes are soaked and draggled ... A husband spreads a blanket over a woman in labour in one of the carts to keep off the driving rain. She is the only person making a sound. Her little daughter looks at her in horror and begins to cry. And the procession keeps moving.[52]

Within a year, Greece is hosting more than a million displaced persons. Tent camps in the ruins of the Parthenon. Squalor in the royal boxes of Athens's Opera House.

But the War of Independence, as it will come to be called, is still not yet fully won.

The British remain in control of the strategic areas of Istanbul and the Dardanelles, clinging to the idea that somehow Sèvres might still be enforced. Winston Churchill and David Lloyd George invoke the 'sacrifice' at Gallipoli seven years earlier as justification for a last stand. 'If the Turks take the Gallipoli Peninsula and Constantinople,' Churchill bullishly warns, 'we shall have lost the whole fruits of our victory.'[53] He cables the prime ministers of New Zealand, Australia, South Africa and Canada in mid-September 1922, begging for troops to hold the Straits.

Strangely, only the New Zealand government willingly offers to back him, volunteering a battalion of Kiwi men. The others politely decline, or do not even bother to reply.[54]

Lloyd George and Churchill will not get their last stand, anyway: their Liberal–Tory coalition collapses, vanquished in November's elections. Sèvres is a lost cause.

At Lausanne, Switzerland, in the early months of 1923, the Nationalists win their greatest victory yet. By refusing to deviate from their National Pact, they are able to finally found a sovereign state with barely any concessions to foreign powers at all. The idea of a greater Armenia is not mentioned, illustrating just how miserably the Allies have failed to keep their promises.

The Lausanne Treaty is signed on 24 July 1923. Turkey's Anatolian borders are set. The last British soldiers leave Istanbul in October, and later that month, Mustafa Kemal becomes president of the Republic of Turkey. He will later take the honorific *Atatürk*, meaning 'Father of Turks'.[55]

By then, only 10 per cent of Armenians living in the Ottoman Empire in 1914 remain – 'the most successful murderous cleansing achieved in the 20th century'.[56]

A long time ago, in 1916, from his perch in turbulent Petrograd, the New Zealander Harold Williams, a famed hyperpolyglot, sat down to write a regular dispatch to the London *Daily Chronicle*. His subject was the Armenians, and their homeland.

The Turks 'have done their utmost to blot out the Armenian name,' Williams wrote. He wondered if 'Armenia' is anything more than a 'historical conception'. No people, he noted, 'have suffered such a cruel fate'. Not the Belgians, Serbians or Poles.

Then again, Williams pondered: 'Perhaps some thousands are still in hiding, waiting for deliverance … Perhaps in the end a fragment of the nation will be gathered together to begin once again, not for the first time in its history, the slow plodding march through the ages.'[57]

11

An old paper mill

Listen. The rhythmic rumble and crash of an ocean pale, churning. Above, warm thermals buffet birds as they fish. By the shore, by the bronze beach, a team of NER workers find an old paper mill: low stone buildings dilapidated and weary-looking. Fresh water runs in a trickle close by. Behind, there is green on the hills, verdant with orange trees and olives ripening in the heat.

This is Antelias, a tiny seaside town in Lebanon, part of Greater Syria under French occupation. Here, NER decides to build one of the many dozens of safe homes for Armenian children – a space of succour and a relative kind of comfort.

The orphanage that will be built here represents most movingly the deep, inexorable connections between New Zealand, Australia and the Armenians. For this place comes to be called the Australasian Orphanage, overseen by two Cantabrians: John Knudsen and his wife Lydia.

John Henry Knudsen: born in Christchurch in 1890, to a Norwegian father, Gabriel, and an English mother, Elizabeth. Lydia Helen Davidson: born six years later in Auchenblae on the rough far east of Scotland, and barely eleven years old when she lands in Wellington in 1907.

John attends the prestigious Christ's College school, works as a clerk and accountant for a brewing company, is called up to serve in the Canterbury Regiment in 1917, two months before his twenty-seventh birthday. He doesn't make much of a soldier, spending his war on the Western Front and in various British hospitals for a variety of illnesses. He demobilizes in Egypt in 1919, where his mother has been a British Red Cross volunteer since 1916.[1]

Perhaps inspired by her charitable example, John signed up for the American Red Cross before jumping ship to NER. His skills as a bean-counter prove useful, and he is posted to the dark heart of the post-war crisis: Aleppo, with its bleak deserts and bleaker residency of impoverished Armenians. John becomes treasurer of the Aleppo NER office, then rising to assistant director, then assistant director for the entire Syria-Palestine area under Howard McAfee.[2]

John's work is not only heartbreaking, but also dangerous. Mustafa Kemal's Nationalists have as little time for relief workers as they do for Armenians and Greeks. In early 1920, John embarks on a mission in Cilicia alongside Levon Daghalian, a representative of the Armenian Union, a Turkish translator and another Armenian servant. Racing to catch up with a departing French convoy on the road from Kilis to Gaziantep, their car hits a rut, stunting the engine. Crowding around the battered vehicle assessing the damage, they take fire from a gang of Turkish guerrillas.

Taking cover behind their machine, the interpreter wraps a white handkerchief around the barrel of his own rifle and waves it vigorously. He approaches the shooters. They cease fire and emerge from their own hiding places.

The party, the interpreter explains, is American. This does not placate the guerrillas at all. They bundle up the stranded motorists and march them in the direction of town. John Knudsen, feeling indignant about the interruption, has to be prodded along with whacks from a rifle butt. For around forty-five minutes they walk, fearing at every stop that they would be killed. John never lets on that he understands Turkish. He fears for Daghalian and the servant, far more vulnerable than he for being Armenian.

The gang presents them to their commander, who after some negotiation, promises to protect Knudsen and Daghalian. But them alone. Their car is burned, and the pair are sent back to Kilis two days later. Their Armenian servant is never heard from again.[3]

John is hardly the most imposing man, standing at five-foot-seven, but has a certain stolid certainty about him, with lucid blue eyes and neatly barbered fair hair. In some photographs, he even appears severe: starched collar and dark suit, thin lips drawn tightly. Nevertheless, Lydia Davidson, barely into her twenties with sandy brown hair and a button nose, saw something in him, and he in Lydia.

The two young Cantabrians marry in Cairo, on the other side of the world, in June 1920. Two ceremonies, days apart, first at the British consulate, and then a church service.[4] After John's scrape in Cilicia, they decide on a quieter life. One with fewer bullets.

The couple move to Beirut, travelling through the network of NER orphanages in the region, helping out where they can. Eventually, they are chosen to oversee the renovation of the old paper mill at Antelias.

A large gang of children is already on site by the time John and Lydia Knudsen arrive, housed in low-slung drab tents propped up by wooden planks. They need to build the place from the ground up, to make it fit for human life. And so, the boys are put to work under John's supervising eye, working through the summer and autumn of 1922 to build infrastructure and a set of connected dormitories wrought from strong Lebanese timber. Every nail is hammered in by the soon-to-be residents.

By November, the work is done.

No doubt John and Lydia would stand together with their backs to the Mediterranean, admiring their work: the abrupt U-shape of the orphanage, framed around a large dirt playing field divided from the beach by a rickety wire fence. To the right stands a two-storey stone-clad main office, behind it a low and long building where the children will learn their new trades. Outside the arch of the orphanage gate, the girls wash laundry in the nearby river. The new dorm rooms run parallel to the beach along the back border, and on the left an open clearing for communal meals. Clean. Orderly. Prideful.

When he meets John and Lydia after his successful tour of New Zealand and Australia in December 1922, Loyal Wirt suggests that this new complex be given the name 'Australasian Orphanage'. It sticks.[5]

The initial roll call is 1,700 children, 200 of them girls. The first load of supplies arrives on the *Hobson's Bay* dispatched from Australia in September, escorted by Hilda King, the Melbourne volunteer who will stay for three years at Antelias, tending the kids.

Their motto is 'Hold Fast to Honour'.[6]

Figure 22 'The completed orphanage, as viewed from the beach'. Credit: Missak Kelechian Collection.

For Armistice Day in 1922, the orphanage staff, the boys and girls, local consuls and clergymen file out to the Allied cemetery on the main road to Damascus. Arranged against the coming cold, they stand in an array of shades: the French in white and gold and navy; Maronite, Catholic and Armenian priests in flowing black robes; dignitaries in the dress uniform of their countries; and multi-ethnic locals in an array of colours and emblems.

Lydia makes and lays the wreath for Indian graves.[7] A French band plays the *Dead March*, and they sing O *God Our Help in Ages Past*:

Our hope for years to come
Be thou our guide while life shall last
And our eternal home.

Days at Antelias are divided between morning and afternoon, the earliest hours devoted to languages (English, French and Armenian), arithmetic, geography, history, all taught with pupils sat on the dusty floor of a wooden hut. Their uniforms are long shorts and white blouses, though regulation long wool socks are often discarded in the heat. Girls learn sewing and other home-making skills.[8] Sometimes classes are trooped down to the seaside, taking their lessons in the sand, clutching their dog-eared and rare textbooks while a teacher stands lecturing, farcically, in full suit and tie.

After chaotic lunches in the open – children lined up with their plates in long rows knee-to-knee – come the trade classes: a foundation in life and a way to earn a living: carpentry, shoemaking, tailoring, blacksmithing, and the most vital vocation of all, baking. Boys and girls learn trades equally, partly the grim necessity of having a survivor population of mostly females, but evidence too of NER's self-proclaimed progressive bent, and the feminist outlook of its administrators.[9] There are around forty teachers, vocational experts and 'mothers' (essentially matrons), some of them overseas humanitarians, like the Knudsens, or Lebanese locals, or other diaspora Armenians.

During summer months, the boys hold sporting contests: a short sprint track marked in the dirt with chalk, friends powering along under the matrons' gaze or attempting to leap a rickety high jump without even a lumpy mattress to break their fall.

Institutions like this are central to NER's mission of building a 'new Near East', with rehabilitated and educated Armenians as the foundation of this new 'civilization'. 'It may be doubted if any American organization has ever had an opportunity equal to ours in shaping the future of the Near East,' a report to

Figure 23 'Lydia Knudsen (L) and Hilda King with a young orphan'. Credit: Missak Kelechian Collection.

NER's head office in New York reads. 'The 100,000 children now under our care, wisely guided will become the leaders in a New Era in the Old World. They will be the trained agriculturists, the mechanics, merchants, manufacturers, bankers, educators, lawyers, doctors, governors and rational leaders of the New Near East'.[10]

The Orphanage complex also contains a shelter house that serves as temporary accommodation for refugees and survivors that criss-cross Anatolia and Syria in search of home, work and family.

In early 1923, some 600 Assyrians show up at the orphanage, sent by ship from Istanbul to be escorted to British-held Iraq, where several thousand of their compatriots – for whom Robert Nicol gave his life – reside after the mass exodus from Urmia in 1918. The boat that carries them to Antelias in turn takes some 800 Greek children over the sea to Athens and its overflowing camps.[11]

Hilda King, in a letter to the *Sydney Morning Herald*, relates the brief and despairing reunions in a territory with such a vast and ever mobile refugee community: two NER workers, who had been bringing Armenian children from Harput to Aleppo, encounter a gang of workers toiling on a railroad. They had been forced out of Anatolia and are still held in slavery, mending the tracks for no pay and little food.

As the convoy of children passes by the workers, one man looks up and catches sight of his own little son. The father can only hold the boy for a brief moment. Hilda King can only assure him that his son is in good hands. She promises, fitfully, reassuringly, to reunite them one day. The boy has protection. The father has nothing.[12]

Asdghig Avakian has spent almost all of her youth and young womanhood in orphanages. She knows their rules and codes, their smells and routines, the deep longing for missing family they inevitably provoke.

Her earliest memories date to an orphanage in Harput. Her mother, unable to provide education or upbringing after her husband died, placed her there when Avakian was two years old. It was clean and safe, courtesy of the heavy missionary contingent. Asdghig, whose name means 'little star', recalls the coterie of girls she lived and played with, the trips to nearby lakeside beaches, and the moment when her mother returned many years later, waiting by the gates. They embraced tenderly.

'With tears running down her cheeks she held me at arm's length and smiled lovingly, tenderly and sadly, obviously admiring how much I had grown. Then she pulled me towards her again, kissing my forehead, my eyes, my cheeks, neck, face, lips, and hands, drinking in insatiably my warm and excited breath.'[13]

For all the love and affection, Avakian felt like a stranger out in the world, after so much time away. Her old home was stranger still, overtaken by the tall, strict, brutish man her mother had married. He was abusive, so she clung to her mother as her only protection. Their brief moments together working in the fields were their happiest – 'an oasis of kindness in this desert of hatred and cruelty'.[14]

There was no respite. She recalls the day the CUP gave its order for extermination, waking up one morning to 'dreadful noises' – the moans and cries of women in the street as the men of the village were being collected and sent away under armed escort. Her stepfather was taken too – one bully for another. The town crier went among the houses warning the rest to prepare for deportation.

Wasting no time, Avakian's mother bundled together some food and coaxed a donkey down a dark road, her daughter propped up atop it. She was being returned to the orphanage of her youth. And when they reached it, her mother was exhausted, dehydrated, collapsing at the gates where they had once reunited.

'She took me into her arms, pressed me to her heart, looked into my eyes, smothered me with kisses, inhaled my breath deeply through her nostrils, her tears falling into my hair and eyes.'

She asked for a drink of some kind. Avakian rushed to the kitchens, filling a ladle with water. She returned to find, standing there in the courtyard with a wooden spoon held limply in her hand, her mother had vanished.

The orphanage's sisters gathered, sobbing quietly.[15]

Quality of life dropped drastically during the years of war, blockade, deportation and immiseration. Diseases took hold. Food was little. Any education was done in Turkish, not Armenian.

From the high barred windows of the compound, the girls could look out into the Protestant church across the way, which the Ottoman authorities had requisitioned, using it as a waystation for deportees heading south. Some girls, Asdghig among them, developed an illicit scheme to launder the deportees' clothes. She acts as runner, collecting soiled bundles from outside the church walls, and throwing them back over when they were clean.

Avakian survives the genocide in that orphanage, which is taken over by NER when they arrive. But with the Nationalist advance, her time in that secondary home was up.

She is one of the many thousands escorted by NER to safety between 1920 and 1922. On these *kindertransports*, most have to walk the distance. Asdghig Avakian gets the luxury of a train.

And it is on this train, passing over the mountains after leaving Aleppo, that Asdghig sees an ocean for the first time – the Mediterranean – and the 'seething metropolis' of Beirut.

'The green plants thrilled us,' Avakian will remember, 'as did the warm and sunny atmosphere … We felt that now our journey had really come to an end. We had arrived.'[16]

Descending the mountains, her group of Armenian orphans arrive at Antelias, where they camp for a few days in large tents amid pine trees and orange orchards – fruit they have never seen before in such abundance.

A few days later, Avakian and her friends are taken down to the Australasian Orphanage, through the narrow entrance gate, onto the bright field, the ocean gently lolling against the coast. They are bathed outside, in the sun, behind a screen of bushes. Their first meal there consists of bread 'and some black, bitter, salty things which were called olives'. The children spend their first days playing in the open air.

'Our hearts were filled with joy, and for the first time for a long time we felt happy.'[17]

Unlike Avakian, Haroutiun Dilanian knows nothing of orphanage life until he reaches Antelias.

Until the soldiers came to his hometown of Maraş and took away his father, promising to put him to work on the *Baghdadbahn*, where the Anzacs prisoners were. Until nine-year-old Haroutiun's entire family – one brother, three sisters, beloved mother – was deported. Until they marched desert-ward, to the Aleppo camps. Until he was separated from that family and taken in by an Arab shepherd.

For a loaf of bread a day, Haroutiun worked the sheep. Until he lost one, and fearing the wrath of his new master, fled on a stolen donkey to a German military camp. He survived by 'eating what the donkey ate', until the corners of his mouth were stained green from wild grass.

Until he stumbled to Damascus in 1917, sleeping in the streets with other orphans, stealing food, and finding Armenian women spinning and weaving fourteen-hour days in a factory. One of those women, a survivor too, noticed little Haroutiun lingering at the edges of the shop. She bathed him. And he slept. Until he pried his eyes open to find another tear-stricken woman before him. His mother.

Realizing that it was no dream, they 'cried from happiness for hours' together.

Until after the war. Until Haroutiun Dilanian and his mother returned to Maraş, only to be forced out again by the Nationalists. Until his mother really was killed.

Until he arrives at Antelias, aged sixteen in 1922, and is given the number 384 – a number that he will carry with him when he emigrates to Australia in 1971.[18]

Not long after her deliverance, Asdghig Avakian falls ill with malaria. Her treatment at the hands of one of the matrons demonstrates that however much Antelias may have been a haven from the barbarities of the outside world, orphanages are still ruled by the cane.

Exhausted, vomiting, suffering from fever, Asdghig drags herself from bed, and crawls out to the corridor, where a 'Superior' discovers her, whipping her with a stick and shouting that she should have reported her illness earlier. Only the intervention of a kinder sister stops the beating, and she is taken to the clinic for treatment.

'We were sufficiently accustomed to hardship and suffering to accept each new blow as it came,' Avakian writes of this bitter incident. 'Our lives had been conditioned to accept occasional cruel and unfair treatment as an ordinary part of living.'[19]

Souren Antoyan, a survivor also from Harput and another *kindertransporter*, observes that while he was given a chance to become human again after the experiences of the genocide, it is still an exceedingly tough existence. He arrives at the Australasian Orphanage in Antelias in 1925, aged ten years. 'Life was very difficult,' as he describes it:

> The orphanage told us that they couldn't give us enough to satisfy our hunger. They could only feed us enough so we could survive. We never had enough. We often went to bed hungry. When we had the opportunity to leave the orphanage we would go out to the fields and collect herbs and orange rind, crush them and eat them to satisfy our hunger.[20]

Asdghig Avakian is somewhat unique among the thousands-strong roster of the Australasian Orphanage. She does not stay there for most of her childhood, as many others do, and is given a route out a few months after arriving.

One day, she is called along with some of the older girls to line up outside the school superintendent's office, where two missionaries inspect them. The sister who had helped Avakian during the malaria bout speaks highly of her, and she is promptly selected for training as a nurse at the American University Hospital in nearby Beirut.

She packs twelve brightly dressed dolls and a Bible – her only possessions. She is fifteen years old.

Asdghig works diligently, and eventually rises to become night supervisor at the Hospital, attaining an independent station in life so that she could write a memoir – *Stranger among Friends* – a luxury never considered for so many of the Australasian Orphanage's boys and girls, who slip into the kinds of modest lives history tends to obscure.

In early January 1923 the *Hobson's Bay*, which had taken the first batch of relief supplies to Antelias, departs Australia once more.

Aboard is Reverend James Cresswell, a congregationalist, 'the model of an earnest, modest, South Australian dissenting minister, a sober figure of the kind taken for granted in suburbs and country towns across the state.'[21] While ministering, he had become deeply involved in Armenian relief work, fighting for a people who, as he put it, 'had been broken on the rack'.[22] He wrote pleadingly to Australian government ministers asking if they might consider adopting Armenian children en masse – an idea rejected because it clashes with 'White Australia'.

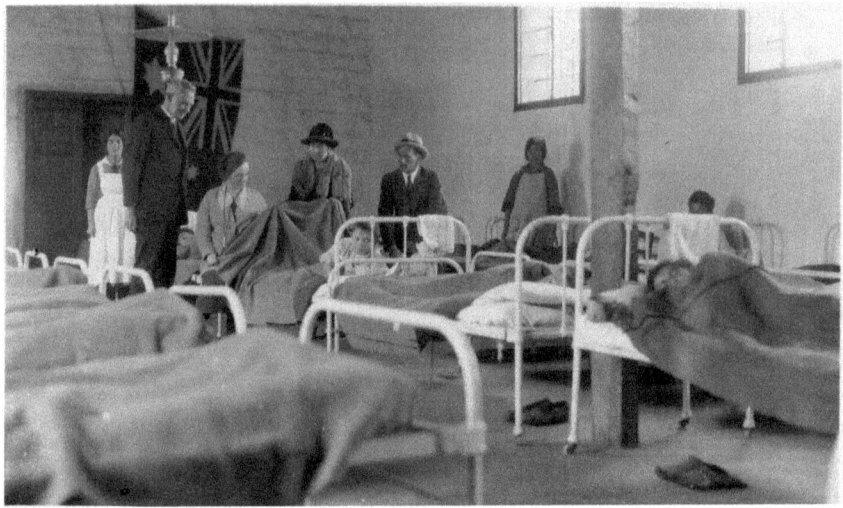

Figure 24 'In the dorms, James Cresswell (standing) inspects donated blankets with (L–R) Lydia Knudsen, Hilda King, and John Knudsen'. Credit: Missak Kelechian Collection.

In December 1922, Cresswell is appointed National Secretary for the Armenian Relief Fund of Australasia – a loose union of those committees still associated with NER. Its executive asks him to undertake a survey tour of NER's efforts across Anatolia, Syria and Greece.

He lands from the Mediterranean in mid-January 1923, travelling through Palestine before reaching Antelias on 13 February.

At the orphanage gate, as water laps the shore nearby, Cresswell is warmly greeted by John and Lydia Knudsen – Lydia being six months pregnant. (In April that year, Lydia gives birth to John Alexander Knudsen. The couple joke that they can't work out John Jr's nationality, born as he is to New Zealand parents of Scottish and Norwegian stock by an American nurse at an Australasian institution in Syrian territory under French control.)

An Armenian teacher gives an address to the minister, thanking the 'representatives who live in that big island which we call Australia'. The teachers and the children have little to give in return for the charity of Australians and New Zealanders, but they 'send their sincere love and gratitude', and give Cresswell an embroidered tablecloth made by the orphans, in the hope it will be taken back and displayed during relief committee meetings.[23]

John and Lydia escort the Reverend around the orphanage, inspecting the long dormitories, watching over the boys as they eat lunch, seeing them at work on their trades; bending leather into shoes; folding flour into loaves; viewing the carpentry shop where chairs and little wooden tricycles are crafted, the latter sent off for the youngest of all in other orphanages.

At the end of the tour, Cresswell and the boys pose for a photograph to be distributed back home, crowding around (and on) the iron-balustraded staircase to the main office building draped in a large Australian flag. John Knudsen appears in the corner of that photograph, the brim of his hat tipped back coolly against the sun.

Late one night during Cresswell's stay, eleven frightened Armenian boys arrive at the orphanage, having travelled several hundred kilometres in a few days.

'Most of the fellows were so much waifs of the world that they could not remember their parents and few of them even knew their own names,' Cresswell writes in his diary. Lydia Knudsen, doing her best to comfort the boys, escorts them into the main dormitory and lays them down.

During her rounds later that night, Lydia finds some of them huddled together under one blanket 'like little puppies'. Not wanting to disturb their sleep but needing to reassure them of this strange new world in which they had found themselves, she takes the smallest one in her arms. Lydia asks him where he's come from.

He replies confidingly, in a whisper as he nestles her sleepily, that he has 'come from God'.[24]

Reverend Cresswell tours the other NER orphanages in Lebanon before journeying up to Aleppo, made into an epicentre of suffering again, after the victory of Kemal's Nationalists: refugees clad in rags gathered from the 'rubbish heaps of years'. In caves dug out from hillsides, he describes a frantic multitude in his diary:

> No words seem adequate to describe the misery that must be the portion of the inhabitants. A few yards inside the light was very dim, then failed altogether and it was necessary to use a lantern ... Here were women pale and emaciated, here children with swollen abdomen indicating results of starvation diet. Again one saw a little babe pinched and pallid. Another just four weeks of age lying on a tiny bundle on the floor – one among thousands of the suffering children in this group.[25]

The vast orphanage system is barely able to contend with the sheer numbers of sick and needy.

Cresswell ventures over the Mediterranean to Greece, where, unlike Armenians, Ottoman Greeks expelled from Anatolia at least have a nation state to tend them, though Cresswell finds the refugees' situation is no less dire.

In April the Reverend embarks for Soviet Armenia itself, travelling along Turkey's northern Black Sea coast, and then back through the Dardanelles, where at the invitation of an officer from the Imperial War Graves Commission, he pays his respects to Anzac bones.

At Arıburnu, he realizes the place 'had kept but a few traces of those terrible days in which, under a storm of shot and shell, our lads landed upon its beach'.[26]

Almost three years after the end of the war, New Zealand's own relief funds, finally, click into gear.

On a Monday evening in September, a crowd squeezes into the Soldier's Club Hall on the corner of Cuba and George Streets in Palmerston North. Jimmy Nash, the town's beloved mayor and Reform MP for the region, introduces the evening's speaker: Reverend S Robertson Orr.

The minister had heard Loyal Wirt speak and takes up his mantle, delivering it to the provinces. Orr is something of a passionate amateur. He knows barely anything about Armenians, colouring them as people who 'preferred to die than forsake their religion', and falsely claiming that Armenians numbered around 25 million a century earlier before the majority were killed by 'the Turk'.

Nevertheless, Orr is passionate and eloquent. He understands the urgency of the cause. He is sympathetic to his audience – a modest farming community – when they think 'of home and their own needs when an appeal for help is made'. But they, Orr says, 'had not seen their children butchered, their daughters betrayed'. He concludes with a ringing endorsement of NER, and a committee forms on the spot.[27]

The appeal for Armenian relief proves curiously popular in this rural part of the country. One drive takes place during the same week as the Çanak Crisis, when Prime Minister Massey offers up New Zealand troops to defend the Dardanelles. Collection buckets in churches. Lectures in Fielding. Donations flood in.

The Manawatu branch raises £138 in cash and assorted goods worth around £600.[28]

Stirred by Loyal Wirt's oratory, the Otago Armenian Relief Committee campaigns hard 'on behalf of the sorely-persecuted and starving Christian people of Armenia', regularly running prominent ads in the *Otago Daily Times*, hosting lectures and organizing donation cans for churches.[29] As in Australia, many women become passionately involved, holding collections in the bucketing rain.[30]

By January 1923, the Fund has received £441 in cash and a sizeable quantity of goods.[31]

Wellington's committee organizes appeals with the mayor's treasurer doubling as their own. St Andrew's on The Terrace is used as a store for donated goods.[32] Joseph Nathan, a well-known trader, donates thirty-five cases of dried milk with a value of £135.[33] By September 1923, just over £320 in cash has been squeezed from the capital.[34]

Train cars and shipments pour into the capital from around the country, carried free by freight lines and shipping companies, as per William Massey's meagre promise.[35] Under relief committee rules, cash donations are used to buy non-perishable goods like preserved food, clothing, leather and blankets.

And in early May 1923, twenty tonnes of assorted children's clothes, boots, flannels, rugs, flour, oatmeal, sugar, rice, tinned goods and dried milk are packed up in zinc-lined cases and shipped – free of charge on the Huddart Parker line – aboard the former troopship *Ulimaroa* to Sydney. From there, that precious cargo is reloaded onto an Australian ship, to be dispatched for the Australasian Orphanage.[36]

The orphanage receives the goods with great gratitude, the Knudsens reporting back to the New Zealand Red Cross that the cases opened up 'in splendid condition'.[37] Loyal Wirt sends a letter too, writing that 'the lot of the Armenian children had been made much brighter' by the goodwill, the generosity and the solidarity of the New Zealand people.[38]

Campaigners get another surge in donations when Reverend Cresswell lectures in Auckland and Wellington on his way back to Australia, singing the praises of the Knudsens, imploring that are no workers for whom he felt a greater appreciation.[39] And another when, from February through April 1923, Dr Armstrong Smith, chief European organizer for Save the Children, is warmly received by dignitaries and large crowds in Wellington, Auckland, Christchurch, Palmerston North and Napier.

'Familiarity with huge figures has blunted our susceptibilities,' Smith tells a reporter in Christchurch, trying to ward off sympathy fatigue. 'Think rather in terms of a fellow human being with the same capacity for suffering – and for gratitude – as yourself. Think in terms of the little children – many of them orphans, who have no one to care for them in that mad rush of panic-stricken humanity'.[40]

To ram home his point, Smith shows a film at each lecture. Silent celluloid beams the suffering of another world into theatres and town halls:

Some of the pictures thrown on to the screen were painful illustrations of the almost impossible task undertaken in [Smith's] noble work. Little chaps, scarcely alive, naked, with ribs almost protruding through their tender skins. Legs – or rather horribly distorted, ill-nourished, and twisted shapes – eyes aflame, but looking beyond the earthly sphere wondering when their turn will come. That was the picture burned into the minds of Dr Armstrong Smith's audience last night; that represented truly, or as nearly as mere pictures can, the real meaning of starvation and its loathsome partners, disease and decrepitude.[41]

After these great bursts of giving, spurred by two of the largest aid organizations in the world, support from Australians and New Zealanders for Armenians continues until the end of the 1920s, long after the world's attention has turned from them.[42]

In 1926, a jovial and dedicated volunteer worker named Edith Glanville will set sail for the Middle East – with no official documentation but a letter of introduction from the NSW premier.[43] Her eldest son had been killed going ashore at Gallipoli as part of the second wave on Red Sunday, and Glanville never recovered from the shock, his death weighing heavily on her decision to throw herself into Armenian relief work. 'My son was killed at Gallipoli,' Glanville explains, 'and when I heard how the Armenians had suffered at the hands of the Turks I felt that I who had suffered should do my best to help.'[44]

Even with this bountiful sympathy, resources are always thin. Taken together, the amassed charity from Australia and New Zealand only just manages to keep the Australasian Orphanage afloat.

In September 1923, nearly ten years on from the beginning of the genocide, John Knudsen takes on an international role, travelling with the organizer Ernest Bryce to Geneva on behalf of the Australasian Relief Fund, plotting ways to keep donations flowing and survivors protected, even after so much has already been given.[45]

Two years later, with the orphanage winding down, John and Lydia Knudsen decide to move on. John follows the same route south as Asdghig Avakian, becoming the secretary of the American University Hospital in Beirut – a position he holds until 1930. From there, he never returns to New Zealand, instead working as a hospital administrator in Tasmania and New South Wales.[46]

Hilda King leaves the orphanage in 1925 too, abandoning her post due to illness and stress. Back in Australia and bed-bound, she yearns to return to the boys she helped raise. A journalist visits her, and asks whether the children might, through care and education, forget their bleak pasts.

'No,' King replies, 'and I don't think they will ever really forget. But they are young, and while they are happy and busy the memory of their past is kept in the background.'[47]

By 1929, all of the boys have graduated, sent out into the wider world with their missionary education and their trade training. It is often a difficult struggle for them, Lebanon remaining a poor country until the 1960s. The site of the orphanage is sold by NER to the Armenian Catholicosate, its buildings razed, and a gorgeous cathedral built in their place.

Now, listen. The sound of the Mediterranean lapping the shore can still be heard, that shore where two nations at the bottom of the world chose to establish a place of care and succour and education. A haven from destruction. Several thousand Armenian lives passed through this place, their well-being overseen by an accountant and a nurse from Christchurch, New Zealand.

The deep bonds formed there, in those years, remain alive in spirit and in memory.

12

Paper Eichmanns

1923. Year Zero. 'The new Turkey has absolutely no relation with the old Turkey,' Mustafa Kemal declares. 'The Ottoman state has gone down in history. Now, a new Turkey is born.'[1]

The final moribund remnants of the Ottoman Empire are wiped away. Mehmed VI, the last sultan, shuffles hands in pockets out the back door of Dolmabahçe Palace, his throne and dynasty abolished. The Caliphate follows in March 1924.

Finally, at this moment of apparently immaculate conception, the president gives his answer to that old question: *How can we save the state?*

An authoritarian one-party dictatorship, blended with extreme ethno-nationalism: Kemalism. Turkey for the Turks. And then, only for certain *kinds* of Turks: under Kemal's new secular vision, those not throwing off their Muslim faith are expunged from the structures of power, and all religious institutions are strictly controlled. Homogeneity, sameness, consistency – these qualities are enforced, then prized above all others. A total repudiation of the pluralism, however flawed, of the Ottoman state.[2]

All culture, all intellectual life flows from above. Even in this repressive age, Turkey has one of the most all-consuming censorship laws in the world, prohibiting 'any publication at odds with the general policies of the state'. Liberal, Left, even hard-Right newspapers and journals are shuttered, their presses dismantled. Civil society does not exist. Show trials – 'Independence Tribunals' – humiliate dissidents, those who rebel from that sameness. Public institutions purged of 'coup plotters'. A new penal code imported, basically unaltered, from Fascist Italy. Elections are entirely ceremonial, a way to mobilize an exhausted, traumatized population behind Kemal's Republican People's Party.[3]

Atop it all, Mustafa Kemal: heroic saviour, beloved father, honoured leader, cherished teacher. A monumental and totalizing personality cult surrounds him.[4] The sheer number of statues, plaques, paintings and tributes in Kemal's likeness – inconceivable years earlier under Islamic rules about human depiction – is enough to make Josef Stalin pine in envy.

For Turks who have endured so much in the plummeting aeons after the 1908 Revolution – a seemingly endless succession of wars, of ever-escalating cycles of repression, of famine and requisition, of seeing their neighbours powdered to ash – this is no consolation.

Below Kemal, a loyal regime utterly stacked with war criminals, mass murderers and genocidaires. Because this is not Year Zero, after all. Even as it publicly disavows the CUP, Kemalism grows directly from it. Save for the escaped Central Committee, its leading men are identical.

Şükrü Kaya, former chief of the İAMM, flees British custody in Malta, later to become interior and foreign minister under Kemal. He escapes alongside Ali Ishan Sâbis, the general who decimated Urmia in 1918, who goes on to become the National Assembly member for Afionkarahissar. Before his death in 1924, Ziyâ Gökalp joins Dr Nâzım as a deputy, and has a hand in drafting the constitution. Both Kâzım Karabekir, the commander ordered to annihilate Armenia 'politically and physically' in 1920, and Abdülhalik Renda, responsible for massacres in Muş and Bitlis, serve as Speakers of the National Assembly. Celal Bayar, instrumental in the deportation of Greeks in 1913–14, will later rise to be Turkey's third president.[5]

Dozens of other former police chiefs and CUP men are granted positions as district and province governors. Roughly 80 per cent of Ottoman bureaucrats and civil servants keep their jobs in the new republic. Some 90 per cent of army officers continue to serve through the end of the empire, into the Republican era.[6] Little wonder, then, that in 1925, the dictatorship begins to shatter the Kurds, the last large minority in the country, adapting the tactics, deploying the weapons, and even wielding the same destroyers of Armenians, Assyrians and Greeks against them.[7]

To fashion the infant Republic, born in war and nurtured by siege, these men and this regime dislocate Turkey in time. The past really will be another country.

Prime Minister İsmet İnönü writes that it is 'not only necessary to eradicate centuries-old traditions, beliefs, and customs, but to *efface the memory as well*'.[8] Şükrü Kaya tells the Assembly to applause that 'every nation makes its own history'.[9] From 1928, they oversee a ground-up re-education of Turkey's population in a new Latin alphabet to replace the old Ottoman script, cutting the people off from their written past completely.[10] Such reforms plunge into pseudo-scientific absurdity with Kemal's 'Sun Language Theory', positing that Turkish is the original meta-tongue of humankind.[11]

In place of this real past, a grand foundational mythology. At the centre of it, a heavy pall of silence which smothers the memory of exterminated Armenians, Assyrians and Greeks. No one will dare ask where all the Christians went, nor question where the wealth of a new Turkish bourgeoisie, the economic base of the Republic, comes from. To speak of these crimes is a tightly enforced taboo.

For the ruling Kemalists, Armenians and Armenia itself are a reminder of the fragility of the Ottoman state, a fragility which cannot be allowed to afflict Turkey.

They consider themselves victors, successfully fending off the Treaty of Sèvres, killing any plans for an independent Armenia once and for all. Any talk of Armenian treatment at the hands of the CUP is considered a prelude to claims for more territory or monetary reparations, therefore threatening the sovereignty and security of Turkey itself.

Mustafa Kemal places this anxious 'Sèvres Syndrome' at the heart of a counterfeit history he had created from thin air while leader of the insurgent Nationalist movement. His first instinct was to blame the victims. 'Whatever has befallen the non-Muslim elements living in our country,' he says three months after moving to Ankara, 'is the result of policies of separatism they pursued in a savage manner, when they allowed themselves to be made tools of foreign intrigues and abused their privileges.'[12]

On 24 April 1920 – the fifth anniversary of the beginning of the genocide – Kemal rose in an open session of the newly created National Assembly to dispute that his predecessors had exterminated an entire people. 'Where in our country had massacres of Armenians taken place?' he asks rhetorically. 'Or where are they taking place?' He decries

> those who, out of political expediency, have acted to incite the entire world against us in order to destroy the positive public opinion that is emerging and to prevent the entire world from recasting their negative opinion of us, have in the end *falsified and proclaimed this bogus Armenian massacre, which consists of nothing but lies* ... and have thereby poisoned the entire world against our devastated country and against our oppressed nation with this terrifying accusation.[13]

In private, Kemal is slightly less fulsome. To a closed session of the same assembly, he alludes to an 'incident that somehow had taken place during the Great War.'[14] A week later, he refers to 'bloody incidents ... between Armenians and our nation'.[15] The closest he ever gets to the truth comes much later, in a lecture to some Ankara notables, in which he calls the genocide 'unfortunate events'.[16]

Kemal elaborates on this theme when he makes a sprawling address in the capital to a congress of the Republican People's Party in 1927. It lasts from 15 to 20 October: thirty-six hours and thirty-one minutes of bombast and stamina. It comes to be called *Nutuk*, or 'The Speech', published in book form and distributed throughout the country.

Quite deliberately, Kemal intends *Nutuk* to be a heroic official version of the history of Turkey and its founding – the sacred scripture of the Republic. In it, Kemal describes the genocide as 'cruelties and murders' while blaming the CUP (in essence, his own regime) without mentioning it by name. He stresses instead that 'Christian elements ... were at work all over the country, either openly or in secret, trying to realise their own particular ambitions and thereby hasten the breakdown of the state'. He compares Armenians to the Greek army fought during the Independence War, asserting that 'Muslims had been compelled to suffer from the cruellest acts of violence' and that 'some Armenians who had been saved from deportation had, in disobedience of orders, attacked their own protectors'.

Then, Kemal inflates sporadic but vengeful bloodletting committed *by* Armenians *against* Turks during the post-war period into a paranoid conspiracy. He justifies the subjugation of the Armenian Republic by claiming that 'after the Armistice of Mudros the Armenians did not cease for a moment to massacre the Turks en masse in the interior of Armenia as well as in the border districts ... Armenian atrocities became intolerable'.[17]

Truth inverted. Kemal's constructed narrative is upside down, a tale of innocent Turks suffering at the hands of marauding Armenians trying to carve their own territory from the hallowed nation, echoing Talât Paşa's own justification for annihilation. It is a recasting of history to the benefit and exoneration of perpetrators.

This version will survive in Turkish historiography, and therefore Turkish public opinion, for a long time yet to come.

Denial of the Armenian Genocide begins in this vacuum, this vast void of memory.

In the turbulent decades following the war, and despite the great sympathetic outpouring of the relief movement, fewer and fewer people pay care to Armenians, or Armenia itself locked behind the Iron Curtain, another colony of Red expansion. In the late 1920s and 1930s, British and American foreign policy performs a galling volte-face, preferring to back the Turkish Republic as a check against the Soviet Union, a tactical ploy for the Middle East's oil. Armenian survivors carry their trauma into diaspora, settling into new lives in faraway places, like Australia and New Zealand. In lieu of any determined bid to commemorate the genocide outside their fragmented, insular communities, the cataclysm falls from light. Even though that old catchphrase 'Remember the starving Armenians' persists, a general kind of amnesia afflicts public memory.

One man, however, keeps the flame alive: Raphael Lemkin, a Jewish lawyer from Poland.

Lemkin was born with the coming of the twentieth century. An early and voracious reader, he seemed to have a sense of justice and ethics hardwired into the fibre of his being – perhaps the price of growing up in a country where pogroms against Jews are an annual festivity.

As an adolescent, Lemkin reads about what happened to Armenians during the First World War, just over the Black Sea. He is aware of the Allies' charge of 'crimes against humanity' made in May 1915. 'More than 1.2 million Armenians killed,' he notes, 'for no other reason than they were Christians.'[18] The thought stuns him. And he is stunned still further when, while studying law in Lviv, he follows a sensational trial taking place in Berlin.

On 15 March 1921, a young Armenian veteran of the Caucasus Front approached the suited bulk of Talât Paşa on a Berlin avenue. Soghomon Tehlirian says nothing as he fires, the bullet shattering Talât's spinal cord, burrowing through his brain, exiting just above his left eye. He falls. Thick black blood pools on the pavement.[19]

The kill order came from the ARF, part of a wider conspiracy of assassination they termed Operation Nemesis. In the years after, they will successfully execute former Prime Minister Said Halim, Special Organization chief Dr Bahaeddin Şakir and ex-Navy Minister Ahmed Cemal. The Soviets got Ismail Enver in 1922, leading a gang of Muslim rebels in Tajikistan.

The ARF also orchestrate Tehlirian's eventual trial in Germany: a plea of insanity mingled with a concocted story of traumatic neuroses brought on by his 'experiences' in the zone of genocide, deliberately designed to bring the Armenian tragedy to the wider world. A jury takes just two hours to exonerate him.

Raphael Lemkin does not know that Tehlirian acted as part of a conspiracy of revenge, nor does he recognize the falsehoods of his defence. He insists that Tehlirian should not have acted as 'self-appointed legal officer for the conscience of mankind,' yet the young lawyer is astonished and troubled that it takes an assassination to bring the Armenian experience into a civil courtroom for the first time.[20] Lemkin questions his professors: How is that an entire people can be killed and no one tried for it? The reply is the same one given by the British in 1919: national sovereignty reigns supreme, and no statute exists to outlaw such a thing.

While Lemkin serves as a public prosecutor in Poland in the early 1930s, Adolf Hitler and his National Socialists brawl their way to power in Germany. From the very earliest days of German fascism, its leaders have grafted the Turkish struggle onto their own: studying, obsessing over, taking inspiration from, trying to emulate how one figure, a dominating strongman, eradicated meddling minorities and created a pure *völkisch* state from the ruins of empire.[21]

To the Nazis, Kemal heralds 'the coming of a new age'.[22] For Hitler himself, Kemal is a 'shining star in the darkness'.[23] He keeps a bust of the Turkish Führer, his most 'cherished possession'.[24] And when Mustafa Kemal finally succumbs to a life of heavy drinking, aged 57 on 10 November 1938, Nazi newspapers are filled with moist, flowery tributes. An ironic note, for 10 November is the final day of a frenzy: *Kristallnacht*.

Raphael Lemkin reads *Mein Kampf*, Hitler's morbid jail rant, a manifesto for the extirpation of all Jews and the colonization of Europe, and rightly sees it as a 'blue-print for destruction'.[25] He writes pamphlets articulating his doubts about weak international law, sketching the outlines of a code that can outlaw mass killing by governments, what he calls 'barbarism', and mass destruction of culture, or 'vandalism'.[26]

In 1939, as Hitler and Stalin's combined armies extinguish independent Poland between them, Lemkin flees, becoming a victim of the very crimes he is trying to define. Unlike so many millions, he escapes to Sweden where he collects decrees and ordnances issued from Berlin, studying how Nazi power operates towards minorities in its conquered territories. He reaches the United States and combines his analysis of this legal minutiae and his ideas on international law into a hefty volume called *Axis Rule in Occupied Europe*, leaden with a full 400 pages of appendices.

Chapter 9 introduces a brand new word and concept to the world: Genocide. The prefix *geno* means 'race' or 'tribe'; the suffix from *caedere*, means 'to kill'.

Its introduction is tragically timely. The *Shoah* is underway.

Through his analysis of Nazism, and always keeping the Armenian case at the back of his mind, Lemkin evokes genocide as a *process* of elimination rather than a singular event, beginning with the disenfranchisement of a targeted group, the removal of their legal rights, the destruction of their bodies, and the eradication of their culture and memory. His most radical thought of all is to suggest that genocide, like crimes against humanity, can occur *outside* times of war.

Turkey, ruled by Kemal's close lieutenant İsmet İnönü, does not join the Second World War, preferring to stay anti-Communist. But it does bow to Nazism's influence. İnönü unleashes a spree of official anti-Semitism. Returning the compliment, Hitler digs up Talât's body and sends it in a carriage swathed in swastikas back to Istanbul where it is reinterred, with full honours, on Liberty Hill.[27] A revenant, returned.

There is, after all, no real neutrality in a fight against fascism.

After Europe's liberation, as the crematoria burn out, Lemkin strives to have his new idea and new word included in the indictment at Nuremberg. He proves to be a single voice alone in the wilderness, a stooped figure in a shabby brown suit, haranguing lawyers and officials. Allied prosecutors accept the notion of crimes against humanity, but refuse to use 'genocide'. The word is employed in the closing statements of the tribunal as a descriptive term, not a legal one. Lemkin is defeated.

But he has his great victory a few months after final sentences are handed down – the payoff for his dogged persistence The United Nations General Assembly adopts Resolution 96, which overrules the Nuremberg omission and accepts genocide as really existing in international law. Spurred on, Lemkin drafts the Convention on the Prevention and Punishment of the Crime of Genocide, adopted by the UN on 9 December 1948. Article Two:

> In the present Convention, genocide means any of the following acts committed with intent to destroy, in whole or in part, a national, ethnical, racial or religious group, as such:

(a) Killing members of the group;
(b) Causing serious bodily or mental harm to members of the group
(c) Deliberately inflicting on the group conditions of life calculated to bring about its physical destruction in whole or in part
(d) Imposing measures intended to prevent births within the group
(e) Forcibly transferring children of the group to another group.[28]

Genocide is a unique concept, emphasizing collective identity in a tranche of burgeoning human rights law which stresses the agency of individuals. Lemkin's contribution is singular, and he will be among the first to use the phrase 'Armenian Genocide' in 1949 as part of his campaign to have the Convention ratified.[29]

For all this, though, Raphael Lemkin will die penniless and alone in 1959. But his championing of justice survives imperishably.

For fifty years, silence has been the Armenian default. In diaspora, the family home holds secrets. Mothers, aunts, grandmothers may speak tiredly, reluctantly of what happened in the 'old country', but there is precious little collective grief, no air let in on shared traumas. In the Armenian SSR itself, the regime vacillates between grudging acceptance of past experience and cold repression.

But on 24 April 1965, a strange thing happens.

More than a 100,000 demonstrators throng Yerevan, doused in great tides of water by the city fire department as they hurl bricks through the windows of the Opera House, where the party elite are holding their own private commemoration. They demand acknowledgement from the Communist Party. They demand their old land, their old homes back.

It is dangerous, this demonstration. In such a totalitarian state, all dissent is snuffed out by the KGB or crushed under the tracks of *Panzerkommunismus*.[30] It is a system which had imprisoned then executed Zabel Yessayan, the bravest of them all, for no other reason than she was a writer. Some Armenian students even manage to picket the Turkish embassy in Moscow. The uprising – the largest ever held in the USSR – first leads to the removal of the local Party secretary, then the regime granting permission for a memorial to be built at Tsitsernakaberd.[31]

The year 1965 is a genuine Year Zero.

Popular feeling spreads throughout the Armenian diaspora. On the floor of the United Nations, the foreign minister of Cyprus speaks of the 'twentieth century's first genocide'.[32] The Lebanese parliament passes a motion demanding reparations for Armenia. In the United States, rallies are held from coast to coast, from Boston and New York to Los Angeles and Winston-Salem. Commemorative speeches are heard in the Senate, and the governors of Maine and Massachusetts define Armenians' wartime experience with that new term: genocide.[33]

It seems spontaneous, this explosion of feeling. But it has been gnawing away, ever so slowly, in the souls of survivors and their descendants. The 1965 movement reanimates the Armenian diaspora to campaign and fight for recognition and justice, if not restitution.

Those in favour of genocide recognition, however, uncover a yawning gap. There is precious little scholarly work on 1915 and its aftermath. Ambassador Henry Morgenthau's memoirs, Armin T Wegner's photographs and the British historian Arnold Toynbee's *Blue Book* all presented immediate evidence, but the baton has not been taken up. Indeed, the case is the same for the *Shoah*: only after 1961 and the trial of leading Jew-killer Adolf Eichmann in Jerusalem does the Holocaust emerge as an essential field of academic study and remembrance.

It is not until the 1970s that Armenian historians begin working rigorously on the subject. This small group, which includes Richard Hovannisian, Vahakn Dadrian and Levon Marashlian, is gradually joined by other non-Armenian writers, including the American Robert Jay Lifton and Frenchman Yves Ternon.[34] Even then, early scholarship is hamstrung by the need for its earliest researchers to *prove* the charge of genocide. To do so, they accentuate the elements that most closely resemble the Holocaust – mass slaughter by killing squads, concentration camps, industrialized deportation – while ignoring the critical ways 1915–23 does not compare to the Final Solution, like forced religious conversion and the mass assimilation of Armenian children.

But just as this dignified and critically important work gets underway, demands for recognition take a dark turn. Revenge.

In the mid-1970s, radicalized Armenians take up terroristic violence to advance their grievances. Inspired by other nationalist revolutionaries – especially the Palestinians of the PLO and PFLP – the (clunkily named) Armenian Secret Army for the Liberation of Armenia and the ARF-linked Justice Commandos wage an international shooting and bombing campaign. Between 1973 and 1984, they will assassinate thirty-one Turkish diplomats and members of their families, including children.[35]

Two attacks are carried out in Sydney and Melbourne, the former killing consul general Şarık Arıyak and his bodyguard, the second causing severe bomb damage to the consulate.[36]

Later, many of these young men will regret their actions as unconscionable and inhuman. Worse, such tactics are counterproductive and self-defeating: any legitimate questions of justice, understanding, reconciliation or reparation are stained with the depravity of terrorism.

Worse still, the bombing and hostage-taking induce that Pavlovian reflex instilled in the gut of Turkish politics: threatened sovereignty, threatened existence. It gives the Turkish ruling elite a perfect excuse.[37]

In 1980, the Republic's military junta abandons its policy of stressed silence and responds to calls for recognition by formulating, imposing and propagandizing a (semi-)coherent form of Armenian Genocide denial.[38] At the suggestion of an officer in charge of the National Security Council's Intelligence Department, a quasi-academic research group is set up with close ties to the Ministry of Foreign Affairs. This group's task is to scour available archives for material, cataloguing favourable documents then passing them on to pre-selected and approved authors – many of them former diplomats and bureaucrats.

By 'opening' the archives, the regime can claim they are taking positive steps towards an honest dialogue. But from the very start, as Foreign Minister Mesut Yılmaz explicitly states, their goal is 'primarily to render ineffective the claims of Armenian genocide'.[39]

In rapid succession, these officials publish books which, in a scattershot manner, seek to counter any suggestion that the CUP deliberately and systematically exterminated Armenians (or Assyrians and Greeks). The deportations were merely precautionary measures in military zones. There were no death squads. There was no mass sexual violence. There was no assimilation. There was no mass plunder of property. The CUP did not withhold aid. Armenian claims of victims well over 1 million are incorrect: perhaps 300,000 died, largely due to conditions of the war.

The most tendentious authors go further, reaching into justification: the Armenians were treasonous, either allied with Russia or preparing a revolution. There was no genocide, but if there was, *they deserved it*.[40]

The number of official and semi-official 'histories' in this manner rises sharply, from one book published on the subject between 1976 and 1980, to twenty-one books between 1981 and 1985. These warped and inverted editions legitimate arguments within the Turkish state, but they also form the backbone for textbooks issued to Turkish students at secondary schools and universities.

To support this internal propaganda effort, government censors bowdlerize foreign books written by non-Turkish authors, excising offensive passages. Notably, Alan Moorehead's seminal book *Gallipoli* deals with the genocide over three pages and twelve paragraphs, discussing the responsibility of the CUP, the reasons for their actions and the trajectory of the genocide itself. In the Turkish edition, this section is scissored down to two paragraphs lacking any detail or context.[41]

Thus, denial is reproduced first as silence, then as a shout, now with a narrative, a well-rehearsed argument, a bibliography, and an index, ready for export.

Built in to the new, vigorous policy of denial is a dissatisfaction with simply disputing scholarship, in keeping the manufactured argument between tweed-clad academics. The junta goes much further, embarking on an international campaign of influence-buying, misdirection, bullying, blackmail and open threats. Any parliament, university, movie studio, activist, religious group, human rights organization, publishing house, newspaper or political faction that so much as mentions the dreaded 'G-word' draws their fire.

The United States, with its large Armenian diaspora, becomes a principal battleground. From the mid-1980s the Turkish state pours millions of dollars into public relations and lobbying firms, hoping to sway civil society groups. The Assembly of Turkish American Associations, an astroturf front invented solely to counter the Armenian diaspora lobby, pressures universities and schools, begging for First Amendment protection, filing vexatious lawsuits in an attempt to push their line.[42] Every anniversary of the Armenian Genocide, on cue, full-page denialist propaganda ads appear in major newspapers and on central city billboards, funded by oblique front groups.[43] Perhaps most perversely, they suborn Jewish political groups to their argument, accentuating the primacy and uniqueness of the Holocaust to suppress Armenian experience.[44]

In a perfect illustrative web of denialism and realpolitik, the Turkish government establishes the Washington-based Institute of Turkish Studies (ITS) in 1982 (supplemented with cash from military contractors like General Dynamics and Westinghouse) ostensibly to fund scholarships, host conferences and 'play a key role in furthering knowledge and understanding of a key NATO ally of the United States'.

Its first executive director is Heath Lowry, student of Stanford Shaw, who in turn studied under Bernard Lewis, one of the first Western historians to adopt the Turkish denialist line. As head of the ITS, Lowry pens columns in the press denying the genocide and lobbies Congress to defeat recognition motions. And in 1994, without ever producing a full-length scholarly work or teaching at an American university, Lowry is granted the Atatürk Chair in Turkish Studies at Princeton University – a tenure openly funded by the Turkish government.[45]

Lowry keeps in close contact with his benefactors, and carries out their wishes. Turkish Ambassador Nüzhet Kandemir asks him to find a copy of Robert Jay Lifton's 1986 book *The Nazi Doctors*, disturbed that it contains mention of the Armenian Genocide. Lowry dutifully finds the book, reads it and compiles a long letter of reply, noting all the pages the genocide is mentioned and listing the sources Lifton uses.

'Our basic problem,' Lowry writes, as if addressing a close friend,

> is with authors such as [Vahakn] Dadrian, [Helen] Fein and [Leo] Kuper, each of whom are now serving as sources for authors such as Lifton. These facts make

it rather difficult to register our unhappiness with Lifton per se ... I strongly recommend that it be pointed out to Ankara that Lifton's book is simply the end result of the Turkish failure to respond in a prompt fashion to the Dadrian articles, and the Fein and Kuper books. On the chance that you still wish to respond in writing to Lifton, I have drafted the following letter.

This draft letter expresses 'shock' at references to the '*so-called* Armenian Genocide *allegedly* perpetrated by the Ottoman Turks ... ' and goes on to accuse Lifton of using 'questionable' sources and being 'careless'. The Turkish ambassador then has Lowry's letter retyped almost verbatim on official embassy stationery, signs it and sends it off.

When Robert Lifton receives the letter, their collusion is plain. He is stunned to find enclosed, by some bureaucratic slip-up, the Ambassador's letter, Lowry's suggested draft *and the original memo*.[46]

Lifton responsibly publishes all three letters in an article about academic ethics, and circulates a petition against Turkish denialism which appears in the *Washington Post* and *New York Times* signed by such revered names as the poets Seamus Heaney and Derek Walcott, the titanic Holocaust historians Yehuda Bauer and Raul Hilberg, writer of *The Crucible* Arthur Miller, *Sophie's Choice* author William Styron, denial expert Deborah Lipstadt and the essayist Susan Sontag.[47]

Even with Heath Lowry and the Turkish government's shameless corruption exposed and denounced, he will never resign from Princeton. Such is the power of money, and denial.

The ITS's model of obfuscation, repudiation and manipulation survives, too. A deliberate muddying of scholarly waters. An entire Potemkin village inhabited by denialists attempting, not unlike climate change 'sceptics', to ferment 'debate' and 'doubt' about 'official narratives', to insist that there is genuine competition between a rancorous, racist, persecutory 'Armenian view', and a modest, reasonable, curious 'Turkish view'.[48] In a perfect simulacrum of mock grievance and sanctimonious anger, one head of the Assembly of Turkish American Associations exclaims:

> Turks are the new Jews. Genocide crowds are the new KKK ... Facts, figures no longer matter to these lynch mobs ... They insult, intimidate and terrorize ... They already have their chosen verdict in their minds which comforts their anti-Turkish bias: Turks are guilty and there is no need to discuss this verdict; it is execution time ... get the rope![49]

A wave of revolutions sweeps through Eastern Europe in 1989, putting an end to the Soviet Union. Armenians liberate themselves in 1991.

Turkey immediately recognizes the Second Republic, but then cuts off diplomatic relations when Armenia falls once again into a catastrophic war with Azerbaijan over Nagorno-Karabagh – a strip of disputed territory shorn from the First Armenian Republic and gifted to the Azeris by Stalin in the 1920s.

The end of the so-called Cold War threatens to end the alliance between Turkey and the United States, a relationship which gave Turkey its international prestige after joining NATO in 1952. Helpfully, US foreign policy pivots from Turkey's north to Turkey's south during the First Gulf War. American jets pound Iraq from Turkish airbases.

It is this military–industrial–national security apparatus that prevents recognition in America, presidents consistently succumbing to intense Turkish lobbying efforts whenever motions come close to passing through the Senate, as in 1984, 1989, 1990 and 1995. Jimmy Carter and Bill Clinton refer obliquely to 'massacres' or 'tragedy'. Only Ronald Reagan, the coldest warrior of all, ever mentions 'genocide'. In 2000, the Turkish government even goes so far as to send its own National Assembly members to Washington ahead of a resolution vote in Congress, repeatedly warning that airbases in Turkey will be closed to US planes and lucrative defence contracts cancelled. That motion meets a demise when the State Department officially warns that Turkey 'could not guarantee the safety of American citizens ... in light of unforeseen violence'.[50]

In this tone of voice, the tactics of denials applied on Capitol Hill are applied on other governments, too, each with their own uniquely grotesque threats.

Two weeks after the scotched US Congressional vote in 2010, Sweden's parliament agrees by a majority of one to recognize the Genocide. Turkey withdraws its ambassador, while Prime Minister Recep Tayyip Erdoğan, remarkably and without irony, threatens to *deport* tens of thousands of Armenian workers. 'I may have to tell these [Armenians] to go back to their country because they are not my citizens,' he blusters. 'I don't have to keep them in my country.'[51]

During a mass in Rome during the hundredth anniversary, Pope Francis chastised Ankara's denial policies. 'Concealing or denying evil,' Francis sermonized, 'is like allowing a wound to keep bleeding without bandaging it.'[52] In response, Turkey recalls its ambassador to the Vatican, and hauls in the Holy See's representative in Ankara to condemn the Pope's remarks. Foreign Minister Mevlüt Çavuşoğlu writes that 'religious authorities are not the places to incite resentment and hatred with baseless allegations'.[53]

Erdoğan's administration nevertheless is susceptible to matters of public perception. Even as he sharpens denial at home, he fashions new tactics for use abroad.

In 2014, the president makes a statement misinterpreted as a significant break with past denial policy. He speaks of 'shared pain' and the 'duty of humanity to acknowledge that Armenians remember the suffering experienced in that period'. But he gives that suffering no more weight or importance than 'every other citizen of the Ottoman Empire'.[54] Obfuscation is still denial.

He further uses the pretext of Turkey's frozen diplomatic relations with Armenia to propose a bilateral 'Truth Commission' composed of 'historians and other experts from our two countries to study the developments and events of 1915'. Such a group 'would shed light on a disputed period of history' and 'constitute a step towards contributing to the normalization of relations between our countries'.[55]

This olive branch is sharpened at both ends, for it seeks to frame the Armenian Genocide as a squabble between competing nationalisms, rather than a matter of truth, law and moral justice that demands global mediation.

Nevertheless, the most critical act of recognition comes in June 2016 from Germany, the Ottoman Empire's ally during the First World War, whose soldiers and diplomats at the very least consented to the mass killing.

With extreme viciousness, the Turkish government jeopardizes a recently inked deal with Germany to house refugees fleeing the Middle East and North Africa, treating vulnerable and stateless people as pawns in their denial attempts. Prime minister Binali Yıldırım claims outright that there is no 'shameful incident in our past that would make us bow our heads'.[56] A spokesperson for Erdoğan asserts that 'having committed the largest genocide in modern history, Germany resorts to lies about Ottoman Armenians to relieve itself of guilt'.[57]

Such ugly rancour is drowned out by the intelligence and honesty of Cem Özdemir, the German Green Party co-chair of Turkish heritage and sponsor of the Bundestag motion. He addresses the chamber in a tone befitting the intense seriousness with which Germany has considered its blackest periods. 'There can be no question about the appropriateness of time when talking about unimaginable savagery like genocide,' he states. 'Just because we were complicit in this horrible crime in the past does not mean that today we are going to side with the deniers.'[58]

Between the identities of the Republic and the Diaspora, there is a third kind of Armenian: those who endure in Istanbul, perhaps as many as 100,000 of them, some of the only Armenians who survive in the land of their ancestors. From this isolated community, an oracle arises.

Hrant Dink: born in 1954 in Malatya but a child of the old capital's orphanages, its heady cosmopolitanism and fractured politics and rich culture. For Dink, an Armenian heritage and a Turkish nationality are not exclusive but reconcilable – exemplified by *Agos*, a weekly newspaper he edits, printed in both languages, reviving, after a long severance, a noble traditional of bi-lingual publishing common in Istanbul before 1915.

In the pages of *Agos* and in innumerable television appearances, Hrant Dink urges reconciliation between Turks and Armenians. He bravely, openly confronts the momentous silence that walls off any discussion on the genocide from public debate. His columns and essays, written with considerable skill and poetry, attempt to convince his countrymen not to obscure or ignore their history, but to consider it seriously and honestly.

He frames his argument as one for Turkey's future: the ultimate goal, he insists, is a radical widening of democracy. From that, everything else will follow.[59]

Dink observes acutely that paranoia and fear towards Armenians are the 'fundamental mortar in the construction of Turkish national identity.' (In Turkish, *Ermeni* is often deployed as a common slur.) 'Remove that mortar, that hatred of the other, and the identity may collapse.'[60] Therefore, he insists, the movement of recognition, for democracy, for the revivification of Turkish civil society, must move gently so as to not trigger the Pavlovian reflex of suspicion and threat. First must come a process of 'comprehension', because 'denial, or recognition, without comprehension will benefit no one':[61]

> When you attempt to implement [recognition] in societies where knowledge is not free, the real paradox appears of its own accord. In societies where the right to know cannot be sufficiently exercised, if people talk about and argue only for knowledge they have access to, how will you then assess that as a crime? Having defined it as a crime, will you have managed to include the perpetrator on your side in the struggle against genocide? If the man only knows that much, and acts according to the mentality he has formed on the basis of that knowledge, what kind of change will your law bring about in his mentality? ... In the end, it is not that Turkish society knows the truth but still denies it, it is *defending what it knows to be the truth*.[62]

For writing and for speaking, for appealing to truth and decency, Dink is hounded by ultranationalists and by the government, much like his close friend and genocide scholar Taner Akçam, who for years has to check for bombs under his car every morning. Dink is prosecuted under Article 301 of the Turkish penal code for 'denigrating Turkishness' – the same arbitrary and punitive law wielded against the Nobel-winning novelist Orhan Pamuk.

Dink is acquitted the first time they try him. At the second trial, he is sentenced to a suspended six-month jail term, which he appeals to the European Court of Human Rights.

On 19 January 2007, while awaiting a third trial, he publishes a column documenting his struggles, his tone riven with palpable resignation and exhaustion. He notes that his computer is filled with threats against his life. He takes them to the prosecutor's office, but never hears anything back. There is yearning though, too: 'What my family and I have been through has not been easy,' he writes. 'I have considered leaving this country at times ... But leaving a "boiling hell" to run to a "heaven" is not for me. I wanted to turn this hell into heaven.'[63]

Later that day, on the doorstep of *Agos*, just past 3.00 pm, Hrant Dink is shot twice in the head – the gunman a teenage fascist.

He falls forward. His blood flows slowly along the pavement, seeping into the cracks between the flagstones. A blotched white sheet is placed over his body, held down at the corners by bricks so that the world can't see what they did to him.

The assassination of Hrant Dink, a courageous writer who committed no crime, is genocide denial's ultimate expression. Denial kills.

A conclusion: Lying side by side

The great psychoanalyst Sigmund Freud observed, as a century of empire turned to a new age of nations, that 'in the origins of the traditions and folklore of a people, care must be taken to eliminate from the memory such a motive as would be painful to the national feeling'.[1]

Nations are built on forgetting. All citizens, knowingly or unknowingly, carry this enforced silence. To engineer a useable past, we stifle that which is embarrassing or distasteful. Anything that prompts a shiver of discomfort or disquiet slips into the chasms between history. Then, heroism is embellished, tales of supremacy and victory let loose on the common consciousness.

Between them, New Zealand and Australia and the Republic of Turkey do not share much, but they do share this: the defilation, traducing and decimation of their minority indigenous populations.

Terra nullius: the virgin unknown lands. Their peoples tamed by convict larrikins and pioneers, or bushmen and farmers, by armies and militias. Refashioned in the image of the metropole, reinforced over and over again by codification and blood quantum and land clearance and frontier war. Did Australia not have its own policy of aggressive assimilation? Were children not seized from their mothers, spirited to compounds, their distinct cultures, beaten, abused, raped out of them – as with the Armenians? Were Māori lands and property not plundered, their defenders cut to pieces, their language expunged – like the Assyrians?[2]

These barbarisms are the preconditions of the nation. Without such a process, they would not exist. This is the pain in the 'national feeling', a pain that must be eliminated from memory. To absolve the crime at its heart, a mythology is therefore required. A miraculous tale, easily digestible, easily repeated.

For Turkey, there is the father-soldier Mustafa Kemal and his hiving of the Republic from the shattered timber of empire. The man who redeemed a people by completing an extermination, who brought peace and security. In New Zealand and Australia, it is the Anzac story that has become myth.

Any mortal doubt about that combat was long ago excised, all uneasy hearts chloroformed. The reality of a miserable, humiliating defeat was forgotten. The name Gallipoli and the memory of troops who served there were raised to the highest vaults of nationhood, but with their blood and pulped flesh and scarred minds purged, leaving only a shell into which the supposedly herculean, jocular qualities of the Anzac soldier were poured. The diggers' virtues were adopted as national virtues.

It was instant, this mythology. Erected just weeks after the Red Sunday landings by the British war correspondent Ellis Ashmead-Bartlett. A breathless dispatch from the front line of fantasy.

Of the invasion, he described 'New Zealanders and Australians, whose blood was up, instead of entrenching [rushing] northward and eastward searching for fresh enemies to bayonet'. Of wounded men ferried back to hospital ships, Ashmead-Bartlett noted their joy at knowing that 'they had been tried for the first time and not been found wanting'. There was, he insisted: 'no finer feat during this war than this sudden landing in the dark and the storming of the heights ... Raw colonial troops in these desperate hours proved worthy to fight side by side with the heroes of Mons, Aisne, Ypres, and Neuve Chapelle'.[3]

After the ignominious withdrawal from the peninsula, Ashmead-Bartlett toured New Zealand and Australia lecturing, reinforcing this courageous view.[4] And by the first commemoration of Anzac Day, its metaphorical value was already in place. *The Sun* gave a perfect assessment on 24 April 1916:

> To-morrow is the first anniversary of our baptism of fire whereby we became a nation, and one which, we believe, is destined to take a great part in the future of a regenerated world. We are still a very small nation with a brief, though not uneventful history, *but the real beginning of the national consciousness of Australia and New Zealand was made on that eventful April 25* of last year, when the youth of these two outposts of democracy made its unexampled assault upon the cliffs of Gallipoli. It is to the heroism and gallantry of our men that we pay tribute to-morrow, for they, the citizen soldiers of two young countries, by their bravery and sacrifice have conferred honour upon us.[5]

However much the political, theological or commemorative adornments of Anzac Day have morphed or mutated, these beliefs have never changed. Thus Bill Gammage, author of *The Broken Years*, can describe Anzac in quasi-religious language a half-century later as 'Australia's Westminster Abbey, the fount of her traditions, the shrine of her nationhood, the tomb of her kings'.[6]

New Zealand and Australia were, of course, not laboured into being on the dusty scrubland of the Aegean coast. Although limited commands were given to each expeditionary force, New Zealanders and Australians did not fight under their own flag, but rather the Union Jack, as constituents of the British Empire. And it bears remembering that Istanbul – the waylaid prize of the Anzacs – was promised to Tsarist Russia, perhaps the cruellest of the nineteenth century's autocracies. It was Russian troops, not Anzacs, who would have marched into that ancient city.[7]

Regardless, over decades of parades and marching bands, of solemn assemblies and recitations of The Last Post, Anzac Day became the de facto day of nationalist celebration. As more wars followed – the Second World War, Korea, Malaya, Vietnam – Anzac Day devoured them, subsuming their unique political contexts and effects into the dominant mythology. Even Armistice Day, marking the end of the First World War and honouring the much larger number of men and women who served and fought and died in the pit of France, fell out of favour.[8]

Trumpeted ideals of unity and congeniality were deployed as barriers against doubt, dissenting opinion and criticism. The Anzac tradition, representing as it does the very founding of the nation, ought to be above 'politics'. As Maureen Sharpe has described, 'The day, the area, the troops and the word "Anzac" itself, attained a sanctity that required them to be protected from any disrespect. Any criticism or misuse was seen as an insult to the dead.'[9]

This is how the impermeable fortress, the ego-defence, of Anzac mythology came to be.

For sixty-five years, the national mythologies of Turkey on the one hand, and Australia and New Zealand on the other, were separate. There was no contact, no intertwining.

Even up to the fiftieth anniversary of Anzac Day, ceremonies of mourning were lopsided. Voyagers – mostly veterans, envoys, military men and their families – landed at Gallipoli and paid their respects, merely tolerated by their Turkish hosts.[10] The day, 25 April had little resonance for them; their moment of commemoration comes earlier, on 18 March, marking the punishment of Churchill's treasured fleet.[11] And the Republic never tended Anzac graves: that duty fell to the Imperial (later Commonwealth) War Graves Commission.

There was no Special Relationship, little inter-governmental cooperation. Australia only established diplomatic ties in the late 1960s. New Zealand's connections with Ankara were, as one Ministry of Foreign Affairs briefing paper describes them, 'generally insubstantial'.[12] It wasn't until June of 1985 that New Zealand embassy officials in Tehran floated the idea of having cross-accredited ambassadors.[13]

The first whisper of deepening ties emerged in 1981, almost entirely by happenstance. Turkey's relations with traditional Western allies were in disrepair. Searching for new diplomatic partners, the staunchly Kemalist military junta under General Kenan Evren suggested to Canberra that the tiny shoreline at Arıburnu where the Australians landed on Red Sunday could be renamed *Anzak Koyu*, or Anzac Cove.

By 1984, approaching the platinum anniversary of Anzac, Australian Prime Minister Bob Hawke had taken personal interest in the proposal and officially announced the plan. The Turkish junta then pushed further: a condition for the renaming was required, a quid pro quo, some kind of reciprocal gesture. General Necdet Üruğ, Chief of the Turkish General Staff and a powerful figure in the regime, proposed that a bust of Mustafa Kemal be placed somewhere in Canberra in exchange.[14]

Hawke was seduced by fierce lobbying from the Turkish embassy in Canberra, and pushed for quick planning within his administration. The Australian War Memorial (AWM), however, explicitly ruled out placing any monument to Kemal on their grounds. An eventual deal struck with Ankara allowed for a monument – an intimidating bas-relief of Kemal's face and an accompanying plaque – to be placed on Anzac Parade, directly opposite the AWM.[15]

Upon hearing of these discussions, New Zealand requested to join in the deal. A twin monument and memorial park were planned for Tarakena Bay, Wellington – a site supposedly chosen for its resemblance to the stony shores of Arıburnu.[16]

The New Zealand decision was met with indignation from two groups. First, Greek and Cypriot communities incensed by Turkey's occupation of Cyprus. Second, the Wellington Māori Council, which pointed out that the land selected was the historical site of a *pā* – a sacred site in Māori culture.[17] The irony went unnoticed: a monument built to an ethnic cleanser built on lands that had been ethnically cleansed. Rather than heed, or even respond to these protests, planning was 'carried out under fairly strict secrecy'.[18]

The Australian monument to Kemal was unveiled on schedule for Anzac Day 1985. Present on the day, Turkish Foreign Minister Vahit Halefoğlu, under the protection of the Australian SAS.[19] The minister then flew the Tasman, and attended the dedication of the memorial park at Tarakena Bay. Five years later, the New Zealand monument to Kemal was finally open to display. Part of the edifice was a container of soil from the freshly renamed Anzac Cove donated by the Turkish government.[20]

Those years, which not coincidentally saw the Turkish state construct and refine its genocide denial policy, were witness to a widespread revival of Anzac traditions after vicious and protracted and noble protests against the Vietnam War had threatened them. Peter Weir's film *Gallipoli* was released in 1981, and Maurice Shadbolt's play *Once on Chunuk Bair* followed in 1982. Ceremonies at Anzac Cove began to be broadcast live on television and radio. The idea of young Australasians backpacking to Gallipoli gained prominence – that obligatory thanatourism, that morbid rite of passage.

Only then, seven decades after Red Sunday itself, were the first building blocks of the Special Relationship rammed into place. And from that day forward, Mustafa Kemal was valorized and revered in cult-like terms. He became a central figure in Anzac mythology alongside General Birdwood, William Malone and Simpson's Donkey.

Hence Bob Hawke was able to say at Gallipoli in 1990, that 'it was through his brilliant defence of the Gallipoli Peninsula … that the great Mustapha Kemal Atatürk demonstrated the singular qualities of leadership which enabled him subsequently to create the Turkish Republic'.[21] Or as New Zealand Foreign Minister Winston Peters explained in 2007: 'After the war, it was Mustafa Kemal Atatürk, a divisional commander at Gallipoli and later founder of the Turkish Republic, who paved the way for reconciliation. His generous words, which are engraved on the battlefield here and on the memorial to Atatürk back home in Wellington, continue to have resonance for New Zealanders and will never be forgotten'.[22]

In 2012, Julia Gillard summarized the flowering of this Special Relationship, promising to name the centenary year of 2015 as 'the year of Turkey in Australia'.[23]

And in 2017, memorialization continued. A new monument, unveiled in Pukeahu National War Memorial Park: a sheet of iron bearing the Turkish star and crescent designed and built by the New Zealand Defence Force's official artist, who worked closely on commission with the Turkish government, and was obliged to sign a non-disclosure agreement.[24] The New Zealand government had no involvement in its planning or creation, and *received it as a gift*.

At the unveiling, flanked by Turkey's ambassador, Minister for Culture and Heritage Maggie Barry intoned – with all the sincerity that she could summon –

that this new memorial was 'a testament to our international relationships, and the shared values, the freedoms and the quality of life our countries have fought for and continue to support today'.[25]

The individual mythologies of Turkey, and New Zealand and Australia were finally merged, enshrined in a Special Relationship, in ceremony and remembrance.

On all these memorials, including the gigantic granite slab found at the southern end of the cemetery at Arıburnu, there is a verse. Mustafa Kemal's Words to the Anzac Mothers:

> Those heroes that shed their blood and lost their lives ... You are now lying in the soil of a friendly country. Therefore rest in peace. There is no difference between the Johnnies and the Mehmets to us where they lie side by side here in this country of ours ... You, the mothers who sent their sons from faraway countries, wipe away your tears; your sons are now lying in our bosom and are in peace. After having lost their lives on this land they have become our sons as well.

These moving words have been repeated annually for as long as it seems modern memory can reach back. Prime ministers and dignitaries recite them as their perorations, an appeal to lofty, conciliatory, poetic ideals – a palliative balm for the wounds which are the First World War's legacy.

If Anzac Day really is a sacred and revered national day, then these words are the most imperishable of the liturgy, equivalent to John McCrae's *In Flanders Fields* or Laurence Binyon's *For the Fallen* for their undying promise of remembrance.

It used to be said – is still said – that a 700-strong delegation organized by a British navy association visited Gallipoli in April 1934. It was said that they were addressed by Şükrü Kaya, the Turkish Interior Minister and acting Foreign Minister of the day. This genocidaire, chief expeller of Armenians, principal looter of their property, read a speech given to him by Mustafa Kemal. Kaya's speech featured those now immortal Words to the Anzac Mothers. After that, they weaved their way into Anzac hearts.

But no one present that day heard them. The British and Australian press covering this significant event did not mention Kaya giving a speech, nor recalled hearing a sentiment so moving that it instantly became part of commemorations.[26] When Kemal died four years later, no obituary in any country deigned to mention the seismic words, nor do any major biographies either.[27]

Figure 25 'Mustafa Kemal (L) with Şükrü Kaya in 1927'. Credit: unknown.

Kemal did, in fact, send a rather more mundane message to the British ambassador. It read: 'I am much touched by your cordial telegram. I send warmest wishes to all of you during your devout pilgrimage.'[28] (In printing this message, the *New Zealand Herald* referred to Kemal, as was custom, as the 'Dictator of Turkey'.[29])

Nearly twenty years later, in 1953, Şükrü Kaya gave an interview for a special edition of a pro-regime Turkish newspaper. It is in this interview that something like the words attributed to Kemal appear for the first time. Here, Kaya claims he gave an address on behalf of the president in 1934 which read:

> Those heroes that shed their blood in this country! You are in the soil of a friendly country. Rest in peace. You are lying side by side, bosom to bosom with Mehmets. Your mothers, who sent their sons from faraway countries! Wipe away your tears. Your sons are in our bosom. They are in peace. After having lost their lives on this soil they have become our sons as well.[30]

They share a general similarity of form and an emotional resonance with the passage now so familiar, but they are not the same, and the sentence 'There is no difference between the Johnnies and the Mehmets to us where they lie side by side here in this country of ours' does not feature at all. And again, nobody at Gallipoli that April day in 1934 ever recalled hearing Kaya give a speech.

There is only Kaya's claim that they are Kemal's words.[31]

Nevertheless, a chance encounter between a retired Turkish schoolteacher and an Anzac veteran at Gallipoli led to them entering the now-shared lexicon of remembrance – onto those feted monuments.

The schoolteacher carried a guidebook to Eceabat published in 1969 which included a verbatim copy of Kaya's 1953 version. He read them to the Anzac veteran, who, suitably delighted, asked for them to written down in translation, and took them home to Brisbane where they were read again at an Anzac veterans meeting. From there, they passed into the hands of Gallipoli serviceman Alan J Campbell, who was in the process of finalizing an Anzac memorial in Brisbane.

Campbell wrote to the Turkish schoolteacher with the guidebook, who in turn passed Campbell's letter on to the head of the Turkish Historical Society with a promise that the verses would be fact-checked and their provenance proven. The Historical Society, soon to become the state's key propaganda arm in its denial policy, only found Kaya's 1953 interview. This was considered proof enough, and Alan Campbell was provided again with an English translation.

The quote (as claimed by Şükrü Kaya in 1953) was inscribed on a small plaque on the Brisbane monument in 1978 – but with significant alterations. The plaque calls Mustafa Kemal 'Kamel Ataturk' and asserts he gave the speech at Quinn's Post cemetery in 1931.

Most importantly of all, Campbell himself *invented* the sentence 'There is no difference between the Johnnies and the Mehmets to us where they lie side by side here in this country of ours.'

This crucial, summarizing line appeared nowhere else but on Campbell's memorial.[32]

These Words to the Anzac Mothers, therefore, are fraudulent. Mustafa Kemal never wrote them, spoke them, nor thought them, in 1934 or any other time. They are idols to untruth.

Both the New Zealand and Australian governments, during their planning to build the Kemal memorials, barely bothered to check their provenance. There were doubts in Bob Hawke's office and at the National Capital Development Commission. Similarly, Bob Cater, Assistant Secretary, Special Duties in Wellington was concerned about 'the wording agreed with the Turks and Australians', and requested Dr Jock Phillips, Chief Historian at the Historical Publications Branch and a respected intellectual, review draft language and make it 'more accurate'.[33]

But these verifications were never carried out, mostly for reasons of expediency. And regardless, fact-checking of a quote provided by the Turkish regime of their most deified national figure would be diplomatically insensitive.

Thus, a discomforting reality: the most iconic refrain of Anzac Day, a plea for healing and unified grief, words of amelioration, words that now define the Special Relationship, come from a mass murderer. But then, they did already.

Once the Special Relationship was made solid, glued with the Words to the Anzac Mothers, New Zealand and Australia were bound to Turkey's national story, obliged to guard Turkey's myths just as closely as their own, for they are one and the same. Revealing the true basis of one nation would also reveal the other.

The ease with which the Special Relationship was created was only possible because of the yawning hole dug by Australasian historians, these archaeologists of the Gallipoli campaign, these builders of paper towers. They committed themselves to fashioning an anthology in which the Armenians, the Assyrians, and the Greeks and their fate are barely mentioned.

To do so, they had to avoid, obscure and ignore primary material that was always available: the diaries of Anzac PoWs littered with the bodies and ghosts of Armenians; Stanley Savige's memoir of his efforts to save Armenian and Assyrian refugees from Van and Urmia in 1918, and his account of Robert Nicol's sacrifice; the lingering memory of the Armenian relief movement as a popular force in the interwar years.

It took forty years, until Alan Moorehead's *Gallipoli*, published in 1956 and bowdlerized in Turkey itself, for any historian of Anzac to draw the obvious link between the Dardanelles campaign of early 1915 and the early stages of the Armenian Genocide.[34]

But even as this classic text formed the very basis for modern Anzac historiography, Moorehead's successors ignored his observations for another fifty years – until the Australian public intellectual Robert Manne pointed to the gap in the pages of *The Monthly* in 2007:

> [Despite] the fact that the Armenian Genocide was one of the great crimes of history; despite the fact that it took place on Ottoman soil during the precise months of the Dardanelles campaign; despite the fact that that campaign is regarded as the moment when the Australian nation was born; so far as I can tell, in the vast Gallipoli canon, not one Australian historian has devoted more than a passing page or paragraph to the relationship, *or even the mere coincidence,* of

the two events. Concerning the Armenian Genocide, in the space of two large volumes on Gallipoli, Charles Bean is silent; Les Carlyon gives the issue three or four lines; John Robertson allows half a page.[35]

Then again, of course someone like Charles Bean, mythmaker supreme, would be *silent*. He had already made his position clear in the debate – rife in the New Zealand and Australian press at the time – on whether to regard the Ottomans, and subsequently the Turks, as guilty or innocent, gentlemanly or unspeakable, Jekyll or Hide, or to even consider that a contradiction was possible. Recall his contemporaneous doggerel: 'For though your name be black as ink … You've played the gentleman.'

And then nothing, again. It took almost another ten years, until after the centenary of Red Sunday, for Vicken Babkenian and Peter Stanley in their vital, pioneering work *Australia, Armenia & the Great War* to revive the linkage, suggesting the existence of 'the Gallipoli trigger'.[36]

And still, after all the bluster of the centenary, there is no mention of the genocide in either the AWM's exhibits or in the celebrated *Gallipoli: The Scale of Our War* at Te Papa in Wellington seen by millions. Allowing the destruction of the Armenians, the Assyrians, the Ottoman Greeks into this hermetic storehouse of fairy tales would reveal the entire edifice to be absurd on its face. A pulling back of the curtain. A lifting of the carapace.

Every effort must be made to protect that shared national mythology – even outright genocide denial.

On 1 May 2013, the upper house of the New South Wales state parliament passed a motion. It honoured 'the memory of the innocent men, women and children who fell victim to the first modern genocides' – those carried out against Armenians, Assyrians and Greeks.

Although the motion was tainted by being brought by Christian chauvinist Fred Nile as a veiled assertion of anti-Muslim sentiment, it still condemned 'all other acts of genocide as the ultimate act of intolerance', and stressed 'remembering and learning from such dark chapters in human history' so that 'crimes against humanity are not allowed to be repeated'.

It did not indict or criticize, or even name the Turkish government, or Turkish people in general, yet it rightly attacked 'attempts to use the passage of time to deny or distort historical truth'.[37]

Predictably, depressingly, the NSW motion drew a fuming, vociferous response from Turkish ministers and diplomats.

Just a week after the parliamentary session, Turkish Foreign Minister Ahmet Davutoğlu warned in a statement that 'although the solid friendly relations existing between the peoples of Turkey and Australia will not deteriorate because of this unilateral decision … its negative repercussions are nonetheless inevitable'.

Anyone who questioned the 'very special relations that exist between our peoples' or tried to 'damage the spirit of Çanakkale/Gallipoli will … not have their place in the Çanakkale ceremonies where we commemorate together *our sons lying side by side in our soil*'.[38]

When asked by Australian broadcaster ABC whether Davutoğlu's threat implied that members of the NSW parliament would be banned from Gallipoli commemorations, Turkish consul general in Sydney Gülseren Çelik merely replied, 'Yes'.

Çelik went further in a letter to NSW MPs, dismissing the witness testimony of Anzac PoWs as being fabricated. Even the local council of the Gallipoli area was employed to attack the motion: 'We announce to the public that we will not forgive those who are behind these decisions and that we don't want to see them in Çanakkale anymore.'[39]

In this manner, and in this tone of voice, complete with an appeal to the spirit of the Words to the Anzac Mothers, the shared sacredness of Anzac Day was employed as a weapon of blackmail to impose genocide denial on foreign powers. It was a threat that showed immense disrespect not only to Armenians, Assyrians and Greeks, but also to the supposed Anzac spirit of reconciliation.

And yet. The threat worked.

On the eve of the centenary, the New Zealand government made its first ever statement on the Armenian Genocide, the first clarification of its position since William Massey's letter of 1916:

> New Zealand considers that the resolution of historic issues between Armenia and Turkey including appropriate terminology is best left to the parties directly concerned to work through.[40]

This terse response seems inane and inoffensive on the surface – a reasonable position to take on something apparently not essential to traditional New Zealand foreign policy. In fact, it is a formulation borrowed from the United Kingdom and – until late 2019 when the House and Senate finally passed motions of recognition – the United States: a 'straw man' formula which allows countries to wriggle out of public pressure by appealing to a desire to see relations normalized between Turkey and Armenia. As if, again, the question of genocide recognition was merely a question of competing nationalisms.

However, internal correspondence between Ministry of Foreign Affairs and Trade (MFAT) officials and the foreign minister's office reveals a deliberate calculation to avoid offending or angering the Turkish government and therefore jeopardizing Gallipoli commemorations.[41]

MFAT's permanent briefing file on the question of Armenian Genocide, consulted by officials in order to write that statement, makes direct reference to Turkey's furious response to the NSW recognition motion.[42] The briefing file notes Ahmet Davutoğlu's threat specifically, that anyone who tried to 'damage the spirit of Çanakkale/Gallipoli will … not have their place in the Çanakkale ceremonies'.

The briefing file's conclusion then states that there will be no recognition 'given New Zealand's strong interest in ensuring the centenary commemorations Gallipoli go smoothly next year'.[43]

To be clear: Turkish threats to ban dignitaries from the hallowed ground at Gallipoli directly informed the foreign minister's statement of Armenian Genocide denial.

Then again. Even if New Zealand or Australian officials had given some thought to going to Yerevan, going to the forbidding monument at Tstisernakaberd for the centenary, the Turkish administration deliberately attempted to curtail it, stretching their commemorative programme back a day, to 24 April – a date with no meaning to the Gallipoli campaign, or to its memory.[44] (On that day, the determined Armenians and Turks who walked, shoulder-to-shoulder clutching red carnations, from the suburb of Sultanahmet to Haydarpaşa, retracing the footsteps of those arrested on Red Sunday, found themselves swamped by crowds of Antipodeans looking for their buses to Gallipoli.[45])

This MFAT briefing file was consulted again when, during a visit to the country by the eminent scholar Taner Akçam in 2018, Prime Minister Jacinda Ardern quoted from it.

'When it comes to those issues around terminology and so on,' she said during a press briefing, 'those are issues we have left for [a] reconciliation process between those parties who are involved … We leave it to those directly involved to work through those issues through that reconciliation process.'[46]

But then, Ardern had the temerity to claim that the government had '*always acknowledged* the significant and tragic and large-scale loss of life of the Armenian people at the time of the dissolution of the Ottoman Empire. We have, and we continue to do so … New Zealand has *always acknowledged* that large scale loss of life.'[47]

If Ardern was gesturing towards William Massey's 1916 statement, she did not say so. If she was unaware of Massey's position, then 'always acknowledged' is a self-serving fabrication.

Either way, a similar echo is found in official equivocations in Canberra, hinting at collaboration between foreign ministries.

'Turkey has protested strongly at instances of genocide recognition internationally and in Australia,' Foreign Minister Julie Bishop wrote in August 2015. 'The history of our shared experience with Turkey at Gallipoli is an important tie that binds us.'[48] And further:

> The Australian Government is deeply sympathetic to the Armenian people for the horrific and tragic loss of life and suffering which occurred at the end of the former Ottoman Empire … There is no question that these events (which included massacres and forced marches) took place … They had a devastating effect on Armenian identity, heritage and culture, an effect which has been borne by subsequent generations. These terrible events and their victims should not be forgotten.[49]

Tragedy, at least in the Euripidean sense, implies thwarted innocence, something fated to happen. But the Armenian Genocide was not a tragedy. It was a crime and ought to be considered as such by liberal governments who wish to be seen to be upholding an international framework of human rights that was, in part, borne from that very crime to begin with.

Rather than consider openly and honestly what happened to the minorities of the Ottoman Empire during the First World War, the New Zealand and Australian governments choose instead to suppress it and deny it, in favour of protecting one of the most sacred and revered days in the national calendar. It is a unique denial, too, for no other nations are so enmeshed in Turkey's politics of remembrance, not so committed to this field of memory.

In doing so, they not only deny the Armenians, Assyrians and Greeks harshly earned recognition, but the experiences of their own citizens: Anzac PoWs – otherwise venerated – who saw the genocide with their own eyes. Men like Thomas White, Edward Mousley, Charles Dobson, Leslie Luscombe. Or those of the Dunsterforce like Stanley Savige and Robert Nicol who saved lives. Or those thousands who were so moved as to donate to the Armenian relief movement, or even volunteered to lend their succour in a time of crisis, especially women like Lydia Knudsen, Isobel Hutton and Hilda King.[50]

Had the Special Relationship not emerged during the 1980s, then perhaps the New Zealand and Australian governments could acquit themselves of having to care about an issue like the Armenian Genocide. Yet it is precisely this Special Relationship that makes their denial all the more bitter, solipsistic and coldly calculating: better to protect one's own mythology than challenge a falsehood.

Because, after all, there is an enriching truth buried under the weight of mythology.

Veterans cried together. Men who once tried to skewer and blast each other stood on Gallipoli's hilltops and shore, arm-in-arm, and wept. For lost comrades, lost innocence, for their own burdening traumas. These moments cannot be faked, nor can they be maligned.

Their desire to sink arbitrary differences and consider the inheritance of that conflict shoulder to shoulder served as an example to those at home. To see the flags of those three countries flown together over the heights of Chunuk Bair when they were once arranged in opposition makes us pause in contemplation and hope that maybe, just maybe, a bond of peace can be forged in dark hours.

This ought to be the model for the Anzac Special Relationship: simple, unadorned mourning and remembrance, without the resort to a grand myth, without having that awful question asked: Do we remember the dead of the Dardanelles, or the dead of Der Zor?

Denial, Deborah Lipstadt once imperishably wrote, is the 'final stage of genocide' because it 'strives to reshape history in order to demonize the victims and rehabilitate the perpetrators'. That statement was polished and refined by Elie Wiesel, the Holocaust survivor who signed an open letter protesting Turkey's denialism in 2000: 'The executioner always kills twice, the second time through silence.'[51]

Within the last few decades, great numbers of ordinary, brave Turkish citizens faced with a monolithic government determined to snuff out all liberties have rebelled against this double murder.

Hrant Dink's funeral in 2007 was a galvanizing event: mass rallies in several cities, tens of thousands carrying placards and posters inscribed with solidarity slogans in Turkish *and* Armenian. We Are All Armenians. We Are All Hrant Dink.

His death was a catalyst. Those people who signed a 2008 petition titled 'I Apologize' asserted: 'My conscience does not accept the insensitivity showed to and the denial of the Great Catastrophe that the Ottoman Armenians were subjected to in 1915. I reject this injustice and for my share, I empathise with the feelings and pain of my Armenian brothers and sisters. I apologise to them.'[52]

Turkish historians, following the revolutionary example of Taner Akçam, began examining the glaring holes in their own discipline, strove to throw off the weight of mythology. Oral histories kept quietly alive throughout eastern Anatolia prove to a new generation that before the founding of Republican Turkey, other people lived there, even as their cultural artefacts, their ruins, their churches, were left to rot over a hundred winters.[53]

In 2004, Turkish lawyer Fethiye Çetin published *My Grandmother*, a memoir that broke open a gargantuan taboo. Çetin discovered that although she had been brought up to believe she was a Turk, and a Turk alone, her grandmother had been an Armenian orphan, stolen from her family.

There is no estimating the number of Turks who unknowingly carry the weight of this ancestry. It could be in the millions. Only the Turkish government knows with any certainty, keeping special codes for its citizens in the Civil Registry: 1 for Greeks, 2 for Armenians, 3 for Jews, 4 for Assyrians, 5 for other non-Muslims. The state, hidden from public view, can trace each person's heritage back to at least 1923 and the Treaty of Lausanne.[54]

In February 2018, the Turkish government opened up those race-coded databases for the first time. With a few clicks, citizens believing themselves to be of unblemished Turkish stock like Fethiye Çetin found ancestors of Armenian, Greek or Balkan descent.

For some, it was a chance to chase a European Union visa. For others less opportunistic, the shock was palpable. Suddenly, they were introduced to the caution and fear that had long been the burden of Turkey's minorities – the sense that their lineage might make them a target of the state's limitless and discriminate oppression. Journalists speculated that opening the databases was a calculated political move: all the better to further fracture and splinter society between the 'pure' and the 'impure'.[55]

In the same year, Avedis Hadjian released *Hidden Nation*, a bountiful, lyrical account of what he terms *azaltılmış halklar*, or minoritized peoples, the verb form altered, not unlike the Spanish *desaparecido*, to indicate those who had been forcibly 'disappeared' – the progeny of entire generations of Armenian, Assyrian and Greek girls and boys stolen and assimilated.[56]

For many of these minoritized peoples, there is no route back to their ancestors. They are Turks now, or Muslims. They do not feel (or are too afraid to feel) the pull of a maligned identity. For others, halting attempts to reclaim what was lost. Some joined the Armenian Church, others Assyrian Apostolic or Chaldean Catholic congregations – the closest they can get to their forebears.

For a poignant few, a composite identity can be forged from family ethnicity, language, religion, culture and provincial custom. But it is still an identity borne of sublimation: somewhere in their past, an ancestor was robbed of their faith and language and life.

Many Kurdish groups, descendants of accomplices to the genocide, atone and grieve with their Armenian neighbours. In Diyarbakır, scene of the worst bloodletting, Kurds, Armenians and some Turks united to rebuild a ruined church – a restoration of what was once lost. Surp Giragos became the locus for a nascent Armenian community in the region, drawing to its elegantly curved arches all kinds of minoritized peoples, its symbolic power potent, emblematic of the inching progress made against terrifying silence.

It was Primo Levi, a gentle Italian chemist and survivor of Auschwitz, who laid a curse against those who forget, who do not tend to the past.

In his verse epigraph to *If This Is a Man*, Levi scornfully addresses 'You who live safe in your warm houses, You who find, returning in the evening, hot food and friendly faces'. Remember those who had no home, comfortable or otherwise. Who had no sustenance. Who could only stare into a crowd and find malevolent eyes.

Of the extinguishing of a people, Levi instructs us: 'Meditate that this came about.' Carve their experience into your hearts, their unheard words, 'Or may your house fall apart ... May your children turn their faces from you.[57] '

Progress, after all, is only possible through action. Dishonesty and denial do not incur debts to the future. There will be no inevitable reckoning. What remains, what is left, is only duty and responsibility to memory – unceasing and permanent. To the unnamed unreturned voiceless, to those dead awoken and made to speak once more.

Notes

Chapter 1

1. Alyson Wharton, *The Architects of Ottoman Constantinople: The Balyan Family and the History of Ottoman Architecture* (London: I.B. Tauris, 2015), 1
2. Peter Balakian, *The Burning Tigris: The Armenian Genocide and America's Response* (New York: HarperCollins, 2003), 23–8; Donald Bloxham, *The Great Game of Genocide: Imperialism, Nationalism, and the Destruction of the Ottoman Armenians* (Oxford: Oxford University Press, 2005), 43.
3. Srbouhi Dussap is among the most pioneering of female Armenian writers, heavily involved in charity and educational work. See Victoria Rowe, *A History of Armenian Women's Writing: 1880–1922* (London: Cambridge Scholars Press, 2003), 21–30.
4. Christopher J. Walker, *Armenia: The Survival of a Nation* (Second Edition) (London: Routledge, 1990), 99–100.
5. 'In a span of twenty years, from 1862 to 1882, immigration of the Muslim population of the Balkans and Russia increased the Ottoman Muslim population of Anatolia by at least 40 per cent,' from Bedross Matossian, *Shattered Dreams of Revolution: From Liberty to Violence in the Late Ottoman Empire* (Stanford, CA: Stanford University Press, 2014), 12.
6. Louise Nalbandian, *The Armenian Revolutionary Movement: The Development of Armenian Political Parties through the Nineteenth Century* (Los Angeles: University of California Press, 1963), 53–4.
7. Raffi (trans. Jane S. Wingate), *The Fool* (Los Angeles, CA: IndoEuropean Publishing, 2009), 12.
8. Matthew 5:39, King James Version.
9. Raffi, *The Fool*, 110.
10. Raffi, *The Fool*, 254–65.
11. Raffi, *The Fool*, 263.
12. Bloxham, *The Great Game of Genocide*, 41–2.
13. Vicken Babkenian and Peter Stanley, *Armenian, Australia & the Great War*, Sydney: New South Publishing, 2016.
14. Bloxham, *The Great Game of Genocide*, 44.

15 George A. Bournoutian, *A Concise History of the Armenian People* (Second Edition) (Santa Ana, CA: Mazda, 2003), 260–3.
16 Bloxham, *The Great Game of Genocide*, 45.
17 This phrase is borrowed from Miéville, *October*, 11.
18 Nalbandian, *The Armenian Revolutionary Movement*, 90–103.
19 Nalbandian, *The Armenian Revolutionary Movement*, 104–31.
20 Nalbandian, *The Armenian Revolutionary Movement*, 151–78.
21 Quoted in Balakian, *The Burning Tigris*, 56.
22 Ronald Grigor Suny, *'They Can Live in the Desert But Nowhere Else': A History of the Armenian Genocide* (Princeton, NJ: Princeton University Press, 2015), 110; For instances of massacre from small provocation, see Benny Morris and Dror Ze'evi, *The Thirty Year Genocide*, 56, 74, 87, 92, 97, 103, 113.
23 Italics added. Verheij, 'Diyarbekir and the Armenian Crisis of 1895', 124–6, quoted in Suny, *They Can Live in the Desert*, 117–18.
24 Johannes Lepsius, *Armenia and Europe: An Indictment* (London: Hodder & Stoughton, 1897), 18.
25 For a definitive account of American relief involvement, see the first ten chapters of Balakian, *The Burning Tigris*.
26 A sample of the Australian material: 'Armenian Horrors: Fearful Holocaust', *Argus* (AU), 20 May 1896, 5; 'Horrible Massacres: Children Buried Alive', *West Australian* (AU), 23 October 1896, 5; 'Eight Thousand Butchered: Three Thousand Roasted Alive', *Sydney Morning Herald* (AU), 20 May 1896, 7.
27 'The "Unspeakable Turk" again!', *Grey River Argus* (NZ), 20 November 1894, 2.
28 'The Chartered Monster', *Evening Post* (NZ), 28 December 1896.
29 See Kate Ariotti, 'From Unspeakable to Honourable: The Great War and Australian Narratives of the Turks'; Jeremy Salt, 'Johnny Turk before Gallipoli', in *Before and After Gallipoli: A Collection of Australian and Turkish Writings*, ed. Rahmi Akcelik (Melbourne: Australian-Turkish Friendship Society Publications, 1986), 22–3; also, the entirety of Edward Said's *Orientalism*.
30 'Disgusted with the Turks', *South Canterbury Times* (NZ), 25 November 1896, 3.
31 Minutes of 1896 Annual Convention, quoted in Babkenian, 'Australian Women and the Armenian Relief Movement', 115.
32 'For Armenia', *Otago Witness* (NZ), 6 August 1896, 41.
33 Armen Garo, *Bank Ottoman*, 205–6, quoted in Suny, *They Can Live in the Desert*, 123.
34 Zabel Yesayian, 'Ink'nakensagrut'iun', 60–1, quoted in Rowe, *A History of Armenian Women's Writing*, 32.
35 *Zohrab: An Introduction*, selected and translated by Ara Baliozian (Kitchener, ON: Impressions, 1985), 70.

Chapter 2

1. Stanford J. Shaw and Ezel Kural Shaw, *History of the Ottoman Empire and Modern Turkey, Volume II: Reform, Revolution, and Republic: The Rise of Modern Turkey 1808–1975* (Cambridge: Cambridge University Press, 1977), 258.
2. See the section 'Positivism as a Method: The Implementation of a New Political System', M. Sait Özervarlı, 'Positivism in the Late Ottoman Empire: The '"Young Turks" as Mediators and Multipliers', in *The Worlds of Positivism: A Global Intellectual History, 1770–1930*, ed. Johannes Feichtinger, Franz L. Fillafer, and Jan Surman (London: Palgrave Macmillan, 2018), 85–7.
3. Erik J. Zürcher, *The Young Turk Legacy and Nation Building: From the Ottoman Empire to Atatürk's Turkey* (London: I.B. Tauris, 2010), 98, 104.
4. Andrew Mango, *Atatürk: The Biography of the Founder of Modern Turkey* (New York: The Overlook Press, 2000), 69.
5. Gaïdz Minassian, 'The Armenian Revolutionary Federation and Operation "Nejuik"', in *To Kill a Sultan: A Transnational History of the Attempt on Abdulhamid II (1905)*, ed. Houssine Alloul, Edhem Eldem, and Henk de Smaele (London: Palgrave Macmillan, 2018), 51.
6. Dasnabedian (ed.), *Nyuter Ho. Hi. Ta. Badmutyan Hamar*, vol. 4, p. 198, in *To Kill a Sultan*, 52.
7. Mango, *Atatürk*, 70.
8. Quoted in Hans-Lukas Kieser, *Talaat Pasha: A Father of Modern Turkey, Architect of Genocide* (Princeton, NJ: Princeton University Press, 2018), 6.
9. Mango, *Atatürk*, 68.
10. Lt. E. S. Dunn, 'Interview with Mustapha Kemal Pasha and Submission of Formal Questions', 1 July 1921, USNA RG 84, Turkey (Constantinople), vol. 440, quoted in Morris and Ze'evi, *Thirty Year Genocide*, 276.
11. Kemal was the 232nd person to join the with the membership number 233, from Erik J. Zürcher, *The Young Turk Legacy and Nation Building: From the Ottoman Empire to Atatürk's Turkey* (London: I.B. Tauris, 2010), 124–5.
12. Dikran Mesrob Kaligian, *Armenian Organization and Ideology under Ottoman Rule: 1908–1914* (New Brunswick, NJ: Transaction Publishers, 2009), 2. The Second Congress sees an irreconcilable split between the CPU and the Liberals.
13. A. L. Macfie, *The End of the Ottoman Empire: 1908–1923* (Harlow: Addison Wesley Longman, 1998), 24–5.
14. Macfie, *The End of the Ottoman Empire*, 20–7.
15. Eugene Rogan, *The Fall of the Ottomans: The Great War in the Middle East 1914–1920* (London: Penguin Books, 2016), 3–4.
16. Varandian, *History of the ARF*, I, 427, quoted in Raymond Kévorkian, *The Armenian Genocide: A Complete History* (London: I.B. Tauris, 2011), 53.
17. Aydemir, *Makedonya'dan Ortaasya'ya Enver Paşa*, I, 561–2, quoted in Mango, *Ataturk*, 80.

18 Sharurian, *Grigor Zohrapi Kianki*, 155–6, quoted in Suny, *They Can Live in the Desert*, 157.
19 Inflation rose to 20 per cent within two months, and in the six months after July, there were over 100 strike actions. Laws passed suppressing organized labour altogether.
20 Zurcher, *The Young Turk Legacy*, 75; Matossian, *Shattered Dreams*, 98.
21 Bahaeddin Şakir, in *Şûra-yı Ümnet*, quoted in Hanioğlu, *Preparation for a Revolution*, 288.
22 Demir, *Osmanlı Devleti'nde II*, 160–1, quoted in Matossian, *Shattered Dreams*, 121.
23 Mihrdat Noradoungian, "'Azatut'ian ginĕ'" (The Price of Freedom), *Puzantion* 3617, 1 September 1908, 1, quoted in Bedross Der Matossian, 'From Bloodless Revolution to Bloody Counterrevolution: The Adana Massacres of 1909', Faculty Publications, Department of History, University of Nebraska Lincoln, Summer 2011, 124
24 *Puzantion*, 28 July 1908, no. 3589, 1, quoted in Matossian, *Shattered Dreams*, 52.
25 'Interestingly, even though the Revolution attempted to create the modern secular Ottoman citizen whose loyalty was going to be to the state, it nevertheless strengthened the ethno-religious political centers of the ethnic groups,' from Matossian, *Shattered Dreams*, 94.
26 Macfie, *The End of the Ottoman Empire*, 44–5.
27 Hrach Papazian's eyewitness account in *Azadamard*, no. 66, 9 September 1909, p. 1, quoted in Kevorkian, *The Armenian Genocide*, 73.
28 Shaw and Shaw, *History of the Ottoman Empire and Modern Turkey: Volume II*, 280–1.
29 Kaligian, *Armenian Organization*, 34–5.
30 Suny, *They Can Live in the Desert*, 168–72.
31 Matossian, 'From Bloodless Revolution to Bloody Counterrevolution', 160.
32 Rigal (P.), 'Adana. Les Massacres d'Adana', *Lettres d'Ore, relations d'Orient* [Confidential Review of the Jesuit Missions Edited in the Order in Lyons and Published in Brussels], November 1909, pp. 359–91, quoted in Kevorkian, *The Armenian Genocide*, 84.
33 Facsimile reproduction from Terzian, *The Catastrophe of Cilicia*, 64–8, quoted in Kevorkian, *The Armenian Genocide*, 87–8.
34 From a French priest, Father Rigal, quoted in Kevorkian, *The Armenian Genocide*, 91–2.
35 Zabel Yessayan, *In the Ruins: The 1909 Massacres of Armenians in* Adana, trans. G. M. Goshgarian, ed. Judith Saryan, Danila Jebejian Terpanjian, and Joy Renjilian-Burgy (Turkey, Boston, MA: AIWA Press, 2016), 12.
36 Yessayan, *In the Ruins*, 13.
37 Yessayan, *In the Ruins*, 25–6.
38 Yessayan, *In the Ruins*, 3.

39 *Azatamart*, no. 156 (9 July 1909): 3, in Suny, *They Can Live in the Desert*, 172.
40 *Azadamard*, no. 9, 2 July 1909, p. 2, records of the 104th Session, quoted in Kevorkian, *The Armenian Genocide*, 109.
41 Yessayan, *In the Ruins*, 5.
42 Sean McMeekin, *The Ottoman Endgame: War, Revolution and the Making of the Modern Middle East, 1908-1923* (London: Penguin Books, 2016), 63-5.
43 Vahan Papazian, *Im Housheruh* [My Memoirs], vol. II. (Beirut: Hamazkain Press, 1952), 159-60, quoted in Kaligian, *Armenian Organization*, 85-6.
44 Yücel Yiğit, 'The *Teşkilat-ı Mahsusa* and World War I', *Middle East Critique* 23:2, 157-74.
45 Kaligian, *Armenian Organization*, 136-8.
46 Kansu, 399-400, quoted in Kiligian, *Armenian Organization*, 137.
47 McMeekin, *The Ottoman Endgame*, 65-71.
48 Sükuti Tükel, Tatlı ve Acı Hatıralar (Izmir: Piyasa, 1952), 4-6, quoted in Suny, *They Can Live in the Desert*, 186.
49 Hüsamettin Ertürk, *Iki Devrin Perde Arkası*, ed. Samih N. Tansu (Istanbul: Batur, 1964), 121, quoted in Uğur Ümit Ungor, *Making of Modern Turkey: Nation and State in Eastern Anatolia, 1913-1950* (Oxford: Oxford University Press, 2012), 45.
50 Arif Cemil Denker, Sürgün Hayatlar (Istanbul: Emre, 2005), 201, quoted in Suny, *They Can Live in the Desert*, 187.
51 *Kievskaya Mysl*, Kiev, no. 355, 23 December 1912. Printed in *Balkany ibalkanskaya voyna*, in *Leo Trotsky, Sočinenia*, vol. 6 (Moscow and Leningrad, 1926), reprinted in German in Leo Trotzki, *Die Balkankriege 1912-13* (Essen: Arbeiterpresse, 1996), 297-303. Translated by Robert Elsie.
52 Toynbee argues that around 177,000 Muslims escape the Balkans in 1912-13. See Arnold Toynbee, *The Western Question in Greece and Turkey: A Study in the Contact of Civilization* (New York: Howard Fertig, 1970), 138.
53 M. Bilal, 'Pagavan E (Enough!): Zabel Yessayan'ın Barış Çağrısını Duyabilmek' (Being Able to Hear Zabel Yessayan's Call for Peace), *Kültür ve Siyasette Feminist Yaklaşımlar (Feminist Approaches in Culture and Politics)*, 2009:7.
54 Aydemir, *Makedonya'da Ortaasya'ya Enver Paşa*, II, 381, quoted in Mango, *Atatürk*, 117.
55 Türkgeldi, 77, quoted in Mango, *Atatürk*, 117.
56 Türkgeldi, 78-9, quoted in Mango, *Atatürk*, 117.
57 Balakian, *The Burning Tigris*, 161.
58 Italics added. *Bahaeddin Şakir Bey'in buraktığı vesikalara göre*, 350, and Hanioğlu, *Preparation for a Revolution*, 260, 297, quoted in Kieser, *Talaat Pasha*, 58.
59 Lewis, *The Emergence*, 218, quoted in Üngör, *Making of Modern Turkey*, 32.
60 Quoted in Üngör, *Making of Modern Turkey*, 32-3.
61 Kieser, *Talaat Pasha*, 98.

62 'During the CUP crisis starting in 1910, both Talaat and Gökalp turned away from the 1908 democratic utopia. They departed toward a right-wing revolutionism that was henceforth fed by a compelling Islamic pan-Turkism: one as its spiritual father, the other its executor', Kieser, *Talaat Pasha*, 105.
63 Ülken, *Türkiye'de Çağdaş*, 310, quoted in Taner Akçam, *A Shameful Act: The Armenian Genocide and the Question of Turkish Responsibility* (New York: Metropolitan Books, 2006), 88.
64 Italics added. Ziya Gokalp, 'Millet Nedir?', *Küçük Mecmua* 28 (25 December 1922), 1–6, quoted in Üngör, *Making of Modern Turkey*, 36.
65 Gökalp, Türkleşmek, 63, quoted in Akçam, *A Shameful Act*, 92.
66 Üngör, *Making of Modern Turkey*, 30–1.
67 'At issue was no longer constitutional rule but the countrywide implementation of a single-party regime, along with a new agenda ... A resentful kind of Turkish nationalism spread', Kieser, *Talaat Pasha*, 155; see also chapter 4: 'Destruction as Self-Construction: Ideology in Command' in Kevorkian, *Armenian Genocide*, 189–206.
68 Zürcher, *The Young Turk Legacy*, 99.
69 Birdoğan, *Ittihat*, 7, quoted in Zürcher, *The Young Turk Legacy*, 120.
70 For the influence of Positivism and Sociology on Gökalp and Turkish Nationalism see M. Sait Özervarlı, 'Positivism in the Late Ottoman Empire: The "Young Turks" as Mediators and Multipliers', in *The Worlds of Positivism* (London: Palgrave Macmillan, 2018), 87–92.
71 Üngör, *Making of Modern Turkey*, 36–42.
72 The phrase is Hannah Arendt's.
73 Ziya Gökalp, *Kızılelma*, ed. Hikmet Tanyu (Ankara: Kültür Bakanlığı Yayınları, 1976 [1914]), quoted in Üngör, *Making of Modern Turkey*, 35.
74 'A Way of Liberation for Muslims', quoted in Ayhan Aktar, 'Economic Nationalism in Turkey: The Formative Years, 1912–1925', *Boğaziçi Journal, Review of Social, Economic and Administrative Studies* 10:1–2 (1996), 263–90.
75 Malcolm Ross and Noel Ross, *Light and Shade in War* (London: Edward Arnold, 1916), 61–5.
76 Akçam, *Young Turks' Crime Against Humanity*, 67–70, BOA/DH.ŞFR, no. 40/11, Coded telegram from interior minister Talat to the Provincial District of Tekfurdağı, dated 14 April 1915 – through this date in Akçam's text is presumably a mistake, and should read '1914'.
77 İAMM: *İskân-ı Aşâir ve Muhâcirîn Müdirîyeti*.
78 Bjørnlund, 'The 1914 Cleansing of Aegean Greeks as a Case of Violent Turkification', in *Late Ottoman Genocides: The Dissolution of the Ottoman Empire and Young Turkish Population and Extermination Policies*, ed. Dominik J. Schaller and Jurgen Zimmerer (New York: Routledge, 2009), 34–55.

79 Papazian, *Housheruh*, 126, quoted in Kaligian, *Armenian Organization*, 44.
80 For the context and negotiating process behind the plan, see Akçam, *The Young Turks', Crime Against Humanity*, 129–35; Kaligian, *Armenian Organization*, 163–80.
81 Zohrab, *Complete Works*, IV, 344–5, 379, quoted in Kevorkian, *Armenian Genocide*, 162.

Chapter 3

1 *Tanin*, 14 November 1914, quoted in Üngör, *Making of Modern Turkey*, 56.
2 Diary 3/16 November 1914, in Zohrab, *Complete Works*, IV … p. 411, quoted in Kevorkian, *Armenian Genocide*, 172.
3 Quoted in Kevorkian, *Armenian Genocide*, 171.
4 Papazian, *Housheruh*, 276–9, quoted in Kaligian, *Armenian Organization*, 222.
5 Vahan Papazian, *Memoirs*, I (Boston, 1950), 280–1, quoted in Kevorkian, *Armenian Genocide*, 176.
6 'Prime Minister's Speech', *Auckland Star* (NZ), 6 August 1914, 5.
7 'Patriotic Scenes', *Evening Post* (NZ), 6 August 1914, 4.
8 'Prevalent in Auckland', *Auckland Star* (NZ), 6 August 1914, 6.
9 'War News Relieves', *The Argus* (AU), 6 August 1914, 6; 'News in Melbourne', *The Age* (AU), 6 August 1914, 6.
10 'Larrikins Run Riot', *The Argus* (AU), 6 August 1914, 6.
11 'Famous Speech', *Canberra Times* (AU), 25 October 1928, 1.
12 O. E. Burton, *The Silent Division: New Zealanders at the Front: 1914–1919* (Sydney: Angus & Robertson, 1935), 1, quoted in Gavin McLean, Ian McGibbon, and Kynan Gentry (eds.), *The Penguin Book of New Zealanders at War* (Auckland: Penguin Books, 2009), 89.
13 See the section 'A Separate Declaration of War?' in Jonathan Curtis, '"To the Last Man" – Australia's Entry to War in 1914', Parliament of Australia, parliamentary research paper, 31 July 2014.
14 BOA/DH.ŞFR, no 44/224, quoted in Akçam, *The Young Turks' Crime against Humanity*, 418–19. Emphasis added.
15 Adamov report on leaving Erzerum, 19 October/1 November 1914, in RGVIA, fond 2000, opis' 1, del' 3860, list' 613–14, quoted in McMeekin, *The Ottoman Endgame*, 147–8, 230.
16 Johannes Lepsius, *Rapport secret sur les massacres d'Armenie* (Paris, 1919), 90, quoted in Kévorkian, *The Armenian Genocide*, 220.
17 Liman von Sanders, *Cinq ans de Turquie* (Paris, 1923), 48, quoted in Kevorkian, *The Armenian Genocide*, 220.
18 McMeekin, *The Ottoman Endgame*, 163–4.

19 For a detailed account of the Battle of Sarıkamış, see McMeekin, *The Ottoman Endgame*, 147–9 and 152–4.
20 Ali Rıza Eti, *Dairy of a Corporal on the Eastern Front* [Bir Onbaşinin doğu cephesi günlügü], 1914–1915 (Istanbul: Türkiye İş Bankasi Kültür Yayınları, 2009), quoted in Rogan, *The Fall of the Ottomans*, 108.
21 Erik J. Zürcher, 'Between Death and Desertion: The Experience of the Ottoman Soldier in World War I', *Turcica*, 28 (1996).
22 Ozan Arslan, 'The "Bon Pour L'Orient" Front: Analysis of Russia's Anticipated Victory over the Ottoman Empire in World War I', *Middle East Critique*, 23:2 (2014), 175–88.
23 Akçam, *A Shameful Act*, 125.
24 Akçam, *The Young Turks' Crime against Humanity*, 175; Kevorkian, *The Armenian Genocide*, 223, cites Arif Cemil, *The Special Organisation in the General War* [*Umumi Harpte Teşkilat-ı Mahsusa*], Vakit/Haratch, no. 88, as saying 'The result of their collaboration was the deportation law'.
25 Taner Akçam, 'When Was the Decision to Annihilate the Armenians Taken?', Journal of Genocide Research, published online 17 July 2019.
26 BOA/DH.ŞFR 44/200, Talat to provinces, 6 September 1914, quoted in Üngör, *Making of Modern Turkey*, 56–7.
27 BOA/DH.ŞFR 48/166, Talat to the provinces of Erzerum, Bitlis, and Van, 26 December 1914, quoted in Üngör, *Making of Modern Turkey*, 59.
28 Akçam, *A Shameful Act*, 144.
29 The liquidation of the labour battalions did not immediately follow the order to disarm them, but rather followed over several months. Often commanders or officers decided whether they lived or died. Thus, some Armenians were serving in the army until very late in the war.
30 S. Zurlinden, *Der Weltkrieg*, vol. 2 (Zürich: Art. Institut O. Füssli, 1918), 639–40, quoted in Vahakan N. Dadrian, 'The Secret Young Turk Ittihadist Conference and the Decision for the World War I Genocide of the Armenians', *Journal of Political and Military Sociology*, 22:1 (1994), 173–202.
31 Halil Paşa, *İttihat ve Terakki'den Cumhuriyet'e Bitmeyen Savaş*, ed. M. Taylan Sorgun (Istanbul, 1972), 241, quoted in Akçam, *A Shameful Act*, 173.
32 McMeekin, *The Ottoman Endgame*, 171–3; Suny, *They Can Live in the Desert*, 252.
33 BOA/DH.ŞFR, no. 50/141, Coded telegram from Interior Minister Talat to the province of Adana, dated 2 March 1915, quoted in Akçam, *The Young Turks' Crime against Humanity*, 176.
34 Suny, *They Can Live in the Desert*, 252.
35 Suny, *They Can Live in the Desert*, 252–3.
36 Suny, *They Can Live in the Desert*, 252–3.

37 1915-14-12-DE-001, quoted in Wolfgang Gust, *The Armenian Genocide: Evidence from the German Foreign Office Archives* (New York: Berghahn Books, 2014), 60.
38 See excerpts from Ward's letters in 'An Ancient Land' (I & II), *Colonist* (NZ), 27 May 1915, 7; 1 June 1915, 2; Ward survived the war: Personnel File, AABK, 18805, W5557, 46/0119005.
39 Message recorded by Second Lieutenant Henry Miller Lanser, 1st Battalion, Mena Camp, Cairo, Egypt, First World War for his family in Australia, AWM, S00104.
40 'Life in Egypt', *Mataura Ensign* (NZ), 17 March 1915, 5; Cullen was killed just two weeks into the Gallipoli campaign: Personnel File, AABK, 18805, W5537, 3/0030707.
41 Suny, *They Can Live in the Desert*, 254; Balakian, *The Burning Tigris*, 197–202.
42 APC/APJ, PCI Bureau, Ձ 58, Memorandum from Vramian, representative for Van, to Talât Bey, Minister of the Interior, March 1915, quoted in Kevorkian, *Armenian Genocide*, 229–31.
43 McMeekin, *The Ottoman Endgame*, 231.
44 Clarence D. Ussher, *An American Physician in Turkey: A Narrative of Adventures in Peace and in War* (Boston, MA: Houghton Mifflin, 1917), 219–20.
45 Henry Morgenthau, *Ambassador Morgenthau's Story* (Doubleday, NY: Page & Company, 1918), 140–1.
46 Ussher, *An American Physician in Turkey*, 237–8.
47 Donald E. Miller and Lorna Touryan Miller, *Survivors: An Oral History of the Armenian Genocide* (Berkley: University of California Press, 1999), 72–3.
48 Miller and Miller, *Survivors*, 72–3.
49 Miller and Miller, *Survivors*, 72–3.
50 Kévorkian, *Armenian Genocide*, 234.
51 Rafael de Nogales, *Four Years beneath the Crescent* (New York: Charles Scribner's Sons, 1926), 170–1.
52 Kévorkian, *Armenian Genocide*, 329–30.
53 Kévorkian, *Armenian Genocide*, 333.
54 Morgenthau, *Ambassador Morgenthau's Story*, 236, quoted in Suny, *They Can Live in the Desert*, 303.
55 Cemal Pasha, *Memories of a Turkish Statesman, 1913–1919* (London: Hutchinson) 1922), 299.
56 HHStA III 171, Yeniköy, 26 August 1914. Telegram no. 494, in Ohandjanian, *Armenien*, vol. 6, 4402, quoted in Akçam, *A Shameful Act*, 126–7.
57 From Taner Akçam, *From Empire to Republic: Turkish Nationalism & the Armenian Genocide* (London: Zed Books, 2004), 55–6. See also Trudinger, 'The View from Constantinople, 1915', 726–43.
58 Akçam, *A Shameful Act*, 126.
59 Akçam, *From Empire to Republic*, 107.

60 See Point C under the heading 'Was the Final Decision for Annihilation Taken at the End of March 1915?' in Akçam, 'When Was the Decision to Annihilate the Armenians Taken?': 'On this date the Special Organization came under the control of the Union and Progress Party. At the head of the organization was Bahaettin Şakir.'
61 John Masefield, *Gallipoli* (New York: Macmillan, 1916), 44–5.

Chapter 4

1 Peter Liddle, *Men of Gallipoli: The Dardanelles and Gallipoli Experience August 1914 to January 1916* (Wiltshire: David & Charles, 1998), 91–3.
2 Kévorkian, *The Armenian Genocide*, 254.
3 Grigoris Balakian, *Armenian Golgotha: A Memoir of the Armenian Genocide, 1915–1918*, trans. Peter Balakian with Aris Sevag (New York: Vintage Books, 2010), 56.
4 Balakian, *Armenian Golgotha*, 56.
5 quoted in Liddle, *Men of Gallipoli*, 100.
6 Aspinall-Oglander, I, 296, n.4, quoted in Mango, *Atatürk*, 146–7. 'I don't order you to attack. I order you to die' – this infamous instruction was never issued on the battlefield. It appears much later from Kemal's own hand.
7 Balakian, *Armenian Golgotha*, 59.
8 Balakian, *Armenian Golgotha*, 66.
9 Balakian, *Armenian Golgotha*, 61.
10 BOA/DH.ŞFR, no. 52/95, Coded telegram from Interior Minister Talat to the Provinces dated 24 April 1915, quoted in Akçam, *The Young Turks' Crime against Humanity*, 185.
11 BOA/DH.ŞFR, no. 52/96-97-98, Coded telegram from Interior Minister Talat to the Provinces, quoted in Akçam, *The Young Turks' Crime against Humanity*, 186.
12 BOA/DH.ŞFR, no. 52/93, Coded telegram from the Interior Ministry's General Directorate of Security to Fourth Army commander Cemal Pasha, dated 24 April 1915.
13 Yeghiayan, *My Patriarchal Memoirs*, 64, quoted in Suny, *They Can Live in the Desert*, 276.
14 Quoted in Kévorkian, *The Armenian Genocide*, 253.
15 Kévorkian, *The Armenian Genocide*, 253.
16 Quoted by Krikor Zohrab, *Voice of Conscience: The Stories of Krikor Zohrab*, trans. Jack Antreassian (New York: St. Vartan Press, 1983), viii.
17 Quoted by Michael Kermian, Introduction to Voice of Conscience, viii–ix.
18 Quoted by Hrant Dink in Çandar, *Hrant Dink*, 319.
19 Balakian, *Armenian Golgotha*, 104–5.

Chapter 5

1. Balakian, *The Burning Tigris*, 185–6.
2. Üngör, *The Making of Modern Turkey*, 70: 'The single instance in which the empire-wide nature of the deportations are reflected in one order at the most central level.'
3. *NARA*, RG 59, 867.4016/67, 28 May 1915.
4. *Ati*, 24 February 1920, quoted in Akçam, *The Young Turks' Crime against Humanity*, 133.
5. Akçam, *The Young Turks' Crime against Humanity*, 235.
6. For a full overview of the apparatus, see Akçam, *A Shameful Act*, 161–8.
7. For a full account of the evidence of this double entendre, see Akçam, *The Young Turks' Crime against Humanity*, 198–202.
8. Akçam, *The Young Turks' Crime against Humanity*, 399–400. Although the majority of Istanbul's Armenians weren't deported, around 30,000 were expelled throughout 1915–16.
9. Suny, *They Can Live in the Desert*, 289.
10. Leslie Davis, *The Slaughterhouse Province: An American Diplomat's Report on the Armenian Genocide, 1915–1917*, ed. Susan K. Blair (New York: Aristide D. Caratazas, 1989), 38.
11. Kévorkian, *The Armenian Genocide*, 382.
12. Davis, *The Slaughterhouse Province*, 62–3.
13. Davis, *The Slaughterhouse Province*, 66–7.
14. Davis, *The Slaughterhouse Province*, 74.
15. Davis, *The Slaughterhouse Province*, 75–6.
16. Kieser, 'Dr Mehmed Reshid (1873–1919): A Political Doctor', in *Der Völkermord an den Armeniern und die Shoah/The Armenian Genocide and the Shoah*, ed. H. Kieser & D. Schaller (Zurich: Chronos, 2002), 245–80.
17. Suny, *They Can Live in the Desert*, 291.
18. De Nogales, *Four Years beneath the Crescent*, 147.
19. Mugerditchian, 'The Dyarbekir Massacres and Kurdish Atrocities', 35–6, quoted in Suny, *They Can Live In the Desert*, 292.
20. Üngör, *Making of Modern Turkey*, 76.
21. H. L. Gates (ed.), *Ravished Armenia: The Story of Aurora Mardiganian* (New York: Kingfield Press, 1918), 178–9.
22. Mardiganian, *Ravished Armenia*, 182.
23. Üngör, *The Making of Modern Turkey*, 98.
24. Üngör, *The Making of Modern Turkey*, 93.
25. Hans-Lukas Keiser, 'From Patriotism to Murder' in Suny, Göçek and Naimark, 137, quoted in Geoffrey Robertson Q. C., *An Inconvenient Genocide* (Sydney: Vintage, 2014), 64.

26 Balakian, *Armenian Golgotha*, 109. Arthur Balfour, British Foreign Secretary, echoes Balakian in February 1917: 'Those massacred died in abominable tortures, but they escaped the longer agonies of the deported'; see Balfour's letter, excerpted in *Christchurch Star* (NZ), 'Armenia's Fate', 27 February 1917, 1.
27 Osmanlı Belgeler, 44, Interior Ministry to Erzerum, 14 June 1915, quoted in Bloxham, *The Great Game of Genocide*, 86.
28 Aghavni's story comes from Miller and Miller's *Survivors*, 94–7, while other events in Sivas are from Kévorkian, *The Armenian Genocide*, 428–44.
29 Matthais Bjørnlund, '"A Fate Worse than Dying": Sexual Violence during the Armenian Genocide', in *Brutality and Desire*, ed. D. Herzog (London: Palgrave Macmillan).
30 Bjørnlund, 'A Fate Worse than Dying'.
31 Akçam, *The Young Turks' Crime against Humanity*, 315.
32 Miller and Miller, *Survivors*, 79.
33 Emphasis added. Morgenthau, *Ambassador Morgenthau's Story*, 336.
34 BOA/DH.ŞFR 54/100, 22 June 1915, quoted in Kurt, 'Cultural Erasure'.
35 DE/PA-AA/Bo.Kons./Band 170, Report by Wedel-Jarlsberg, in which he recounts his observations, dated 28 July 1915, quoted in Akçam, *The Young Turks' Crime against Humanity*, 297–8.
36 BOA.DH.ŞFR 54/254, Coded telegram from the Ministry of Interior's General Security Directorate to the Provinces and Provincial Districts of Erzurum, Adana, Bitlis, Aleppo, Diyarbakır, Trebizond, Mamuretülaziz, Mosul, Van, Urfa, Kütahya, Maraş, İçel and Eskişehir, dated 1 July 1915; F. Dündar, 2008, p. 301, quoted in Kurt, 'Cultural Erasure'.
37 DE/PA-AA/Bo.Kons./Band 101, Mordtmann's notes in the margin of the report of Aleppo consul, Rössler, to the German Embassy, dated 20 April 1917, quoted in Akçam, *The Young Turks' Crime against Humanity*, 307.
38 Bjørnlund, 'A Fate Worse than Dying', 16–58.
39 Akçam, *The Young Turks' Crime against Humanity*, 291.
40 BOA.DH.ŞFR 63/142, 30 April 1916, quoted in Kurt, 'Cultural Erasure'; Akçam, *The Young Turks' Crime against Humanity*, 322–3.
41 Kaiser, 'Armenian Property, Ottoman Law and Nationality Policies during the Armenian Genocide, 1915–1916', in *The First World War as Remembered in the Countries of the Eastern Mediterranean*, ed. O. Farschid, M. Kropp and S. Dähne (Beirut: Orient-Institut, 2006), 49–71.
42 Üngör and Polatel, *Confiscation and Destruction*, 69; Bedross Der Matossian, 'The Taboo within the Taboo: The Fate of "Armenian Capital" at the End of the Ottoman Empire', *European Journal of Turkish Studies*, 1–23.
43 Akçam, *The Young Turks' Crime against Humanity*, 343–5.

44　Balakian, 'Raphael Lemkin, Cultural Destruction, and the Armenian Genocide'.
45　BOA/DH.ŞFR, no. 54/122, Coded telegram from the Interior Ministry's IAMM to the Province of Mosul and the Provincial District of (Der) Zor, dated 23 June 1915, quoted in Akçam, *The Young Turks' Crime against Humanity*, 302.
46　Akçam, *The Young Turks' Crime against Humanity*, 264–7.
47　Kévorkian, *The Armenian Genocide*, 663.
48　Report by Martin Niepage, sent to the German embassy in Constantinople by way of the consul Rössler, on 15 October 1915, published by J. Lepsius (*Deutschland und Armenien*, 165–7, doc. 182), quoted in Kévorkian, *The Armenian Genocide*, 640.
49　Jesse B. Jackson, formerly at Aleppo Syria, now in Washington, to Secretary of State, 4 March 1918, 'Report Entitled "Armenian Atrocities,"' to The Honourable Secretary of State, U.S. State Department Record Group 59, 867.4016/373, 8, quoted in Balakian, *The Burning Tigris*, 254.
50　*Armin T. Wegner and the Armenians in Anatolia, 1915* (Milan: Guerini e Associati, 1996), 61–3, quoted in Balakian, *The Burning Tigris*, 258.
51　Kévorkian, *The Armenian Genocide*, 631–7.
52　Communication from Interior Minister Talat to the Command of the Ottoman Army, dated 25 March 1916, cited in Genelkurmay Başkanlığı, *Arşiv Belgeleriyle Ermeni Faaliyeteri*, vol. 2, 5, quoted in Akçam, *The Young Turks' Crime against Humanity*, 277–8.
53　Kévorkian has speculated that, due to the symmetry between the actions of the Sub-Directorate and the Special Organization, this department was 'merely an extension' of the Special Organization.
54　Auguste Bernau to Jesse B. Jackson, Aleppo, 10 September 1916, U.S. State Department Record Group 59, 867.4016/302, 3–4, quoted in Balakian, *The Burning Tigris*, 262.
55　Kévorkian, *The Armenian Genocide*, 664.
56　Varujan Vosganian, *The Book of Whispers*, trans. Alistair Ian Blyth (London: Yale University Press) 2017), 210.
57　Report by A. Bernau, an employee of the American Vacuum Oil Company, enclosed in a report from the consul in Aleppo (Rössler) to the Imperial chancellor (Bethmann Hollweg), Aleppo, 20 September 1916; PA-AA/; R14094; A 28162; pr. 17.10.1916 p.m.; Gust (ed.), quoted in Suny, *They Can Live in the Desert*, 315.
58　Kévorkian, *The Armenian Genocide*, 664.
59　Kévorkian, *The Armenian Genocide*, 665–6.
60　Kévorkian, *The Armenian Genocide*, 668.
61　Thomas Hugh Greenshields, 'The Settlement of Armenian Refugees in Syria and Lebanon, 1915–1939', Durham theses, Durham University, 1978, 56.
62　'Halep Valisi Celal'in Anıları', *Vakit*, 12 December 1918, quoted in Suny, *They Can Live in the Desert*, 320.

63 Suny, *They Can Live in the Desert*, 319.
64 Akçam, *A Shameful Act*, 166–7.
65 These examples have been taken from Miller and Miller's *Survivors*, and Richard G. Hovannisian's 'Intervention and Shades of Altriusm during the Armenian Genocide' in *The Armenian Genocide: History, Politics, Ethics*.

Chapter 6

1 Masefield, *Gallipoli*, 5–7.
2 Pye, *Bedros Sharian*, 88, quoted in Babkenian and Stanley, *Armenia, Australia & the Great War*, 71–2.
3 Babkenian and Stanley, *Armenia, Australia & the Great War*, 73. Aram Okosdinossian's grandson moved to Australia in the 1990s.
4 'Financial Barometer', Evening Star (NZ), 1 September 1915, 6.
5 *Evening Star* (NZ), 'South Africa', 13 July 1915, 3.
6 Letter from an anonymous colonel on leave in Cairo to 'Major G. Read, transport medical officer', reprinted in 'The Turk', Wanganui Herald (NZ), 23 September 1915, 6.
7 Extracts from Luxford's letter home: 'Cheery and Resourceful', *The Press* (NZ), 3 September 1915, 3.
8 Malcolm Ross, 'Turkish Warfare', *Nelson Evening Mail* (NZ), 11 December 1915, 2; for Charles Bean's version of this same account, see 'Germany's Ally', *Otago Witness* (NZ), 5 January 1916, 30.
9 quoted in Liddle, *Men of Gallipoli*, 214.
10 *Glenn Innes Examiner*, 23 June 1934, 4; AWM 3DRL/6753.
11 Two studies of Australians held prisoner in the Ottoman Empire exist in Ariotti, *Captive Anzacs*, and Lawless, *Kismet: The Story of the Gallipoli Prisoners of War*. A study of New Zealand PoWs by Desmond Hurley remains to be published but is consulted here.
12 Hurley, unpublished manuscript, chapter 3; see also A. J. Shoebridge Postwar Statement. Wellington Infantry Brigade. Director Medical Services: 28 February 1918. From NA File WA ser. 1 File 10/.75 Repatriation Prisoners of War (Pt I).
13 Lushington, referring to Afion camp commandant: 'The Armenian graveyard at Afion contains dozens of bodies of men who died under his neglect and ill treatment,' from *A Prisoner with the Turks*, 63; Ismidt: 'Here we suffered great hardship and it was here that we buried 15 of our lads in an Armenian cemetery', 65.
14 R. F. Lushington, *A Prisoner with the Turks 1915–1918* (London: Simpkin, Marshall, Hamilton, Kent, 1923), 7.
15 Lushington, *A Prisoner with the Turks*, 11.

16 Lushington, *A Prisoner with the Turks*, 11.
17 *Glenn Innes Examiner*, 30 June 1934, 6; AWM 3DRL/6753.
18 Luscombe, *The Story of Harold Earl*, 48–9.
19 George Gunn personnel file, AABK, W5562, Box 125, no. 0131476.
20 'Prisoner of the Turks', *The Press*, 3 February 1919, 7.
21 Lushington, *A Prisoner with the Turks*, 34.
22 Luscombe, *The Story of Harold Earl,* 53.
23 McMeekin, *The Ottoman Endgame*, 28–9.
24 Papers of John Harrison Wheat, diary, 2.
25 Kévorkian, *The Armenian Genocide*, 577–8.
26 Greg Kerr, *Lost Anzacs: The Story of Two Brothers* (Melbourne: Oxford University Press Australia, 1998), 151.
27 L. H. Luscombe, *The Story of Harold Earl – Australian* (Brisbane: W.R. Smith & Paterson, 1970), 52–3.
28 see Kévorkian, *The Armenian Genocide*, 565–6, and Table 1 'Number of Deported Armenians' found in Akçam, *The Young Turks' Crime against Humanity*, 259.
29 Papers of John Harrison Wheat, 26.
30 This is borne out in every Anzac PoW account. See also Luscombe, *The Story of Harold Earl*, 63: 'During the whole of the time we spent in Angora and Afion-kara-hissar we always occupied houses or other buildings that had been taken over from their former owners by the Turks.'
31 Typescript copy of Captain Thomas Walter White's diary, November 1915 – December 1918, AWM 2DRL/0766, 30.
32 White, diary transcript, 33–4. Privates John Coulter, from Wanganui, and John McLennan, from Waipu, will spend time at Nusaybin late in the war.
33 White, diary transcript, 35.
34 White, diary transcript, 35.
35 Luscombe, *The Story of Harold Earl*, 68–9; see also White, diary transcript, 48.
36 *Glenn Innes Examiner*, 28 July 1934, 6; AWM 3DRL/6753.
37 *Glenn Innes Examiner*, 18 August 1934, 6; AWM 3DRL/6753.
38 Frank Allsopp personnel file, AABK, W5614, Box 68, D. 2/5559.
39 White, diary transcript, 76.
40 Desmond Hurley, 'Edward Opotiki Mousley: Author, Lawyer, Soldier, Prisoner of War', New Zealand Studies, November 1996, 10–17.
41 Halil Paşa, *İttihat ve Terakki'den Cumhuriyet'e Bitmeyen Savaş*, ed. M. Taylan Sorgun (Istanbul, 1972), 241, quoted in Akçam, *A Shameful Act*, 173.
42 Report on the treatment of British PoWs in Turkey, miscellaneous no. 24, British white paper, November 1918, 873.
43 Edward Opotiki Mousley, *The Secrets of a Kuttite: An Authentic Story of Kut, Adventures in Captivity and Stamboul Intrigue* (London: John Lane, 1922), 180.

44 Balakian, *Armenian Golgotha*, 294–8.
45 Mousley, *The Secrets of a Kuttite*, 215–16.
46 Mousley, *The Secrets of a Kuttite*, 283.
47 Mousley, *The Secrets of a Kuttite*, 215.
48 Bishop, *A Kut Prisoner*, 63. Italics added.
49 Mousley, *The Secrets of a Kuttite*, 188–9.
50 Mousley, *The Secrets of a Kuttite*, 189.
51 Mousley, *The Secrets of a Kuttite, 193*.
52 Mousley, *The Secrets of a Kuttite*, 285.
53 Lushington, *A Prisoner with the Turks*, 54–5.
54 Repatriation statements are an exception, as these tend to be brief and focus more circumstances of capture and Ottoman treatment of Allied prisoners.
55 George Kerr's diary of his time at Belemedik is filled with near-constant drinking and fighting: the torpor of bored men.
56 *Glenn Innes Examiner*, 18 August 1934, 6; AWM 3DRL/6753. Leslie Luscombe corroborates Davie's account.
57 Copy of diary written by D.B. Creedon …, SQL, OM90-138, 17.

Chapter 7

1 See Diana Preston, *A Higher Form of Killing: Six Weeks in World War I That Forever Changed the Nature of Warfare* (New York: Bloomsbury Press, 2015).
2 'Massacre of Christians by the Turks', *New Zealand Herald* (NZ), 30 July 1915, 7, widely reprinted. For the original statements see House of Lords Debate, Hansard, 28 July 1915, vol. 19, 774–8.
3 This discussion of Australasian newspaper coverage of the Armenian Genocide comes from two principal sources. For Australia, Vahe Kateb's 'Australian Press Coverage of the Armenian Genocide 1915–1923'. For New Zealand, this author's own study and compilation of a dataset, dating from 1913 to 1919. Further close study of NZ coverage is still required.
4 'British Submarine Sunk', *Dominion* (NZ), 18 September 1915, 5.
5 'The Unspeakable Turk', *Christchurch Star* (NZ), 23 September 1915, 1, widely reprinted.
6 'Unhappy Armenia', *Waikato Times* (NZ), 30 September 1915, 4.
7 'The Turk Amok', *Adelaide Advertiser* (AU), 13 November 1915, 14.
8 'News and Notes', *Evening Post* (NZ), 20 November 1915, 10; 'From All Quarters', *Newcastle Morning Herald* (AU), 20 November 1915, 12.
9 'The Martyrdom of a Nation', *Evening Star* (NZ), 4 December 1915, 4.
10 Henry Morgenthau to Secretary of State, 3 September 1915 (telegram) Dept. of State Record Group 59 867.4016/117, quoted in Balakian, *The Burning Tigris*, 278.

11 'Thousands Protest Armenian Murders', *New York Times* (US), 18 October 1915, 3.
12 From 1915 until 1929, when it wound down, Near East Relief managed to raise (in money and goods) $116,000,000 for the victims and survivors of the Armenian Genocide – around a billion US dollars in today's currency.
13 The *New York Times* published an article on average every two and a half days throughout 1915, using terms like 'atrocities', 'massacre', 'deportation' and 'race extermination'.
14 Balakian, *The Burning Tigris*, 288–9.
15 Balakian, *The Burning* Tigris, 289, 291.
16 'Armenia's Martyrdom', *The Argus* (AU), 9 December 1915, 5.
17 L. O. H. Tripp, Chapter XI, 'War Relief and Patriotic Societies', in *The War Effort of New Zealand*, 176–96.
18 'Armenia', *Spectator and Methodist Chronicle* (AU), 28 July 1915, 966–7.
19 M. F. Lloyd Pritchard, *An Economic History of New Zealand to 1939* (Auckland: Collins, 1970), 235; Erik Olssen, 'Negotiating Conditions and Commitment: The Union Movement and the First World War' in *New Zealand Society at War*.
20 *The Press* (NZ), 15 January 1915, 6.
21 'War Relief Funds', *Evening Post* (NZ), 17 October 1916; see also 'Patriotic Funds', *Dominion* (NZ), 18 October 1916, 6.
22 This is the first appeal of its kind published in New Zealand. 'Many Appeals', *Dominion* (NZ), 19 August 1916; 'Aid for Armenians', *Evening Post* (NZ), 21 August 1916, 5; 'News of the Day', *New Zealand Times* (NZ), 16 August 1916, 4; see also *The Sun* (NZ), 17 August 1916, 6.
23 'Roll of Honour', *Dominion* (NZ), 1 June 1917; see also 'War Relief Funds', *New Zealand Times* (NZ), 1 June 1917, 6, 'Patriotic Funds', *Evening Post* (NZ), 1 June 1917, 7.
24 'The Russian Move', *Auckland Star* (NZ), 6 June 1916; 'Diocesan High School', *New Zealand Herald* (NZ), 9 June 1916, 5.
25 Jessie Mackay, 'How Armenia Fares', *Otago Witness* (NZ), 5 December 1917, 57.
26 Balakian travelled to and gave interviews in Auckland: 'Tortured by Turks', *Auckland Star* (NZ), 14 April 1915; and Wellington: 'Why Italy Will Fight', *Dominion* (NZ), 20 May 1915.
27 'The Remnant of Armenia', *The Argus* (AU), 21 February 1917, 9.
28 'Help for Armenia', *The Age* (AU), 5 December 1917, 9.
29 'Armenian relief fund – requesting inauguration of', City of Sydney Archives, Town Clerk's Department Correspondence Files, Item Number 3460/16, quoted in Riccardo Armillei, Nikki Marczak, and Panayiotis Diamadis 'Forgotten and Concealed: The Emblematic Cases of the Assyrian and Romani Genocides', *Genocide Studies and Prevention: An International Journal*, 10:2 (2016), 98–120.
30 Nick Pezikian, 'Tinnies in a Time of Need', *Antiques and Collectables for Pleasure & Profit* (September 2016), 44–6.

31. 'Armenia's Needs', *The Methodist* (AU), 20 January 1917, 6.
32. 'And a Protest', *Evening Post* (NZ), 27 April 1916, 8.
33. Emphasis added. 'Mr. Massey's Answer', *Evening Post* (NZ), 27 April 1916, 8. Also reprinted in 'Against Compulsion', *Dominion* (NZ), 28 April 1916, 6; 'Conscription', *New Zealand Times* (NZ), 28 April 1916, 7; 'Compulsion', *The Sun* (NZ), 28 April 1916, 11; 'Mr Massey and the Pacifists', *Evening Star* (NZ), 1 May 1916, 8. As it stands, Massey's letter is the only evidence so far found of a New Zealand prime minister actively acknowledging that what happened to Armenians during the First World War was a crime, and thus could be considered as an implicit 'recognition' of that event.
34. 'WAKE UP! Australia's Day of Duty', *Sydney Morning Herald* (AU), 22 October 1915, 7.
35. 'More Men', *New Zealand Times* (NZ), 3 March 1916, 6; 'Recruiting Rally', *Evening Post* (NZ), 3 March 1916, 4.
36. 'Recruiting', *New Zealand Times* (NZ), 8 March 1916, 6.
37. Thomas Mason Wilford, *NZPD*, HOR, vol. 175 (9 June 1916), 716–17.
38. William Earnshaw, *NZPD*, LC, vol. 176 (30 June 1916), 360.
39. 'In Egypt', *New Zealand Times* (NZ), 11 May 1916, 2.
40. Richard McCallum, *NZPD*, HOR, vol. 176 (30 June 1916), 370–1. The Auckland War Memorial Museum holds a number of postcards and images of the Armenian refugee camp in Egypt.
41. Richard McCallum, *NZPD*, HOR, vol. 176 (30 June 1916), 371.
42. Emphasis added. 'War Anniversary', *Nelson Evening Mail* (NZ), 5 August 1918, 4.
43. 'At the Dardanelles', *Akaroa Mail and Banks Peninsula Advertiser* (NZ), 22 February 1916, 2.
44. 'Turkish Atrocities', *Patea Mail* (NZ), 19 November 1915, 1.
45. Italics added. 'The Two Turks', *Free Lance* (NZ), 1 October 1915, 6.
46. *The Press* (NZ), 24 November 1915, 6.
47. Emphasis added. 'Topics on the War', *Pelorus Guardian and Miners' Advocate* (NZ), 11 February 1916, 4; see also 'The Turk as Gentleman', *Auckland Star* (NZ), 22 May 1916, 4.
48. 'Turkey – A Past and a Future', *Evening Post* (NZ), 11 August 1917, 6; see also 'War Notes', *Oamaru Mail* (NZ), 9 September 1916, 4 and 'The Unspeakable Turk', *Hawera & Normanby Star* (NZ), 1 November 1917, 4.
49. Bean, *Anzac Book*, quoted in Robert Manne, 'A Turkish Tale: Gallipoli and the Armenian Genocide', *The Monthly* (AU), February 2007

Chapter 8

1. Roosevelt to Dodge, 11 May 1918, *Letters of Theodore Roosevelt*, vol. 8 1316–18, quoted in Balakian, *The Burning Tigris*, 307–8.

2   Kévorkian, *The Armenian Genocide*, 704.
3   A.A., P. A. Türkei (Bonn), 183/54, A44066, Report by Count Lüttichau, dated 18 October 1918, quoted in Akçam, *A Shameful Act*, 173.
4   Akçam, *A Shameful Act*, 324–5.
5   Walker, *Armenia*, 243–58; Bournoutian, *A Concise History*, 293–9; Kevorkian, *The Armenian Genocide*, 702–6.
6   Thomas De Waal, *Great Catastrophe: Armenians and Turks in the Shadow of Genocide* (Oxford: Oxford University Press, 2015), 70.
7   Mary Lewis Shedd, *The Measure of a Man: The Life of William Ambrose Shedd, Missionary to Persia* (New York: George H. Doran Company, 1922), 241.
8   Shedd, *The Measure of a Man*, 242.
9   Lt.-Col. W. Austin, *The Official History of the New Zealand Rifle Brigade* (Wellington: L.T. Watkins, 1924), 536; Stone, *Secret Army*, x.
10 Robert Kenneth Nicol personnel file, AABK, W5549, box 81/, record no. 0086565.
11 Cunningham, Treadwell and Hanna, *The Wellington Regiment (NZEF) 1914–1919*, 199.
12 '100 Kiwi Stories: Kiwi Part of "Hush-Hush Brigade"', *New Zealand Herald* (NZ), 22 January 2015.
13 Captain Stanley Savige, *Stalky's Forlorn Hope* (Melbourne: McCubbin, 1920), 24.
14 Austin, *The Official History of the New Zealand Rifle Brigade*, 537.
15 Savige, *Stalky's Forlorn Hope*, 111; Alexander Nimmo personnel file, AABK, series 18805, box 82/, record no. 0086699; Stone, *Secret Army*, 143–4.
16 Shedd, *The Measure of a Man*, 257.
17 Shedd, *The Measure of a Man*, 258.
18 Shedd, *The Measure of a Man*, 261–2.
19 Shedd, *The Measure of a Man*, 264.
20 Yohannan's testimony in Youel A. Baaba, *An Assyrian Odyssey: Covering the Journey of Kasha Yacoub Yauvre and His Wife Mourassa from Urmia to the Court of Queen Victoria 1879–1881 and the Exodus of the Assyrians from Their Ancestral Home 1918* (Alamo: Youel A Baaba Library, 1998), 99.
21 Yohannan, *Exodus*, 101.
22 Savige, *Stalky's Forlorn Hope*, 130.
23 Savige, *Stalky's Forlorn Hope*, 135.
24 Shedd, *The Measure of a Man*, 268.
25 This village is either Aydisheh or Chalkanian.
26 Savige, *Stalky's Forlorn Hope*, 140.
27 Because of the secret nature of the Dunsterforce mission, Nimmo's diary of this period remains empty.
28 Savige, *Stalky's Forlorn Hope*, 135–46.
29 Savige, *Stalky's Forlorn Hope*, 154.
30 Yohannan, *Exodus*, 102.

31 Letter from Lt. A. Sawyer to his sister, 'Impressions in Persia', *Manawatu Standard* (NZ), 26 December 1918, 6 (widely reprinted). See also Michael O'Hagan from Pukerau, part of Wireless Corps in Iraq, 'Life in the East', *Mataura Ensign* (NZ), 20 December 1918.
32 With the Dunster Force, Persia and Baku, AWM, F00051.
33 Brig.-Gen. H. H. Austin, *The Baqubah Refugee Camp: An Account of Work on behalf of the Persecuted Assyrian Christians* (London: The Faith Press, 1920).
34 *Mémoires*, 92, quoted in Kévorkian, *The Armenian Genocide*, 710.
35 *Mémoires*, footnote 43, quoted in Kévorkian, *The Armenian Genocide*, 710.
36 E. J. Lemon, 'Dunsterforce or Dunsterfarce? Re-evaluating the British Mission to Baku, 1918', *First World War Studies* 6:2 (2015), 133–49.
37 Babkenian and Stanley, *Armenia, Australia, & the Great War*, 135.
38 See David Gaunt, 'The Ottoman Treatment of the Assyrians', in *A Question of Genocide*; Armillei, Marczak, and Diamadis, 'Forgotten and Concealed: The Emblematic Cases of the Assyrian and Romani Genocides'.

Chapter 9

1 'At the Town Hall', *New Zealand Times* (NZ), 2 November 1918, 8.
2 'At the Town Hall', *New Zealand Times* (NZ), 2 November 1918, 8; For reactions in other places see 'Turkey's Surrender', *Greymouth Evening Star* (NZ), 2 November 1918, 'Celebrations in Eltham', *Hawera & Normanby Star* (NZ), 2 November 1918, 'Surrender of Turkey', *Oamaru Mail* (NZ), 2 November 1918, 'Turkey's Surrender', *Otago Daily Times* (NZ), 2 November 1918.
3 *The Age* (AU), 2 November 1918, 13; *Brisbane Courier* (AU), 2 November 1918, 5; *Sydney Morning Herald* (AU), 2 November 1918, 13–14.
4 Balakian, *Armenian Golgotha*, 410–11.
5 Balakian, *Armenian Golgotha*, 414.
6 Balakian, *Armenian Golgotha*, 415.
7 Balakian, *Armenian Golgotha*, 415.
8 *News Bulletin*, American Committee for Armenian and Syrian Relief, vol 2, issue 7, December 1918; 'Relief Mission on Way to Near East', *Christian Science Monitor* (US), 18 February 1919, 5.
9 Teal, 'Public Health Nursing in the Near East', 791, quoted in in Babkenian and Stanley, *Armenia, Australia & the Great War*, 139.
10 Teal, 'Public Health Nursing in the Near East', 791, quoted in in Babkenian and Stanley, *Armenia, Australia & the Great War*, 139.
11 Isobel Hutton, 'A Nation of Martyrs', *Red Cross Record*, 10 October 1922, 16–18.
12 *The Age* (AU), 30 April 1919, 11.

13 Babkenian and Stanley, *Armenia, Australia & the Great War*, 169–70.
14 Department of Internal Affairs War Funds Office memo dated 26 March 1926, ACGO, Series 8333, IA1, Box 3013/, no. 158/208, parts 1 & 2.
15 Greenshields, 'The Settlement of Armenian Refugees in Syria and Lebanon', 56; James G. Harbord, 'Investigating Turkey and Trans-Caucasia', *World's Work* 40 (May 1920), 36.
16 Morris & Ze'evi, *The Thirty Year Genocide*, 315–16.
17 Babkenian & Stanley, *Armenia, Australia & the Great War*, 181–2
18 K. Jeppe, Armeniervennen, VI, nos 7–8 (July–August 1926), 28, quoted in Bjornlund, 'A Fate Worse than Dying'.
19 '1924 Letter from Emily Robinson, Secretary of the Armenian Red Cross and Refugee Fund (Great Britain)', ALON-UNOG 638 12/4631/647, quoted in, Keith David Watenpaugh, *Bread from Stones: The Middle East and the Making of Modern Humanitarianism* (Oakland: University of California Press, 2015), 134.
20 Around three-quarters of those Armenian women and children who entered the rescue home in Syria eventually rediscovered living relatives by 1928.
21 'Registers of Inmates of the Armenian Orphanage in Aleppo', 1922–1930, 4 vols., Records of the Nansen International Refugee Office, 1920–1947, ALON-UNOG, no. 961, 25 March 1926 quoted in Watenpaugh, *Bread from Stones*, 131–2.
22 Kerr, *The Lions of Marash*, 47, quoted in Watenpaugh, *Bread from Stones*, 102–3.
23 Watenpaugh, *Bread from Stones*, 117.
24 Tunaya, *Türkiye'de Siyasi Partiler*, vol. 2, 27, quoted in Akçam, *A Shameful Act*, 216.
25 FO 371/4173/53351, Dossier no. 19293.
26 Akçam, *A Shameful Act*, 221–3.
27 Akçam, *A Shameful Act*, 236, 239.
28 *Alemdar* (12 Mart/March, 4 Nisan/April 1919), quoted in Akçam, *A Shameful Act*, 247.
29 M.M.Z.C., 12 Kânunuevvel 1334 (12 December 1918), 25, İnikad, 316–17, quoted in Akçam, *A Shameful Act*, 259–60.
30 Kevorkian, *The Armenian Genocide*, 735.
31 SHAT, SHM, S. R. Marine, Turquie, 1BB7 236, doc. no. 1805 B-9, Constantinople, 26 February 1920, L. Feuillet, annexe 20, examination of Said Halim, p. 18; *İttihat-Terakki'nin Sorgulanması ve Yargılanması* (1918–19), op. cit., pp. 21–2, quoted in Kevorkian, *The Armenian Genocide*, 727–8.
32 Kevorkian, *The Armenian Genocide*, 736–7.
33 For an overview of the trials, see chapters 6–9 in Dadrian and Akçam, *Judgment at Istanbul*; Akçam, *A Shameful Act*, 283–4.
34 Report by Eugenie Varvarian, 18 years old, … at the first session of the trial of Yozgat, 11 February 1919, quoted in Kevorkian Kévorkian, *The Armenian Genocide*, 511.
35 Kévorkian, *The Armenian Genocide*, 738.

36 'The angle of approach taken by the court-martial … was probably designed to root out the Ittihad's networks and purge the administration and army of their members and sympathizers.' Kévorkian, *The Armenian Genocide*, 785.
37 APC/APJ, PCI Bureau, 662–6, file no. 1, June 1919 letter from Setrag Karageuzian about Trebizond and the investigations conducted there after the armistice, quoted in Kevorkian, *The Armenian Genocide*, 741–2.
38 Geoffrey Robertson QC argues that these trials 'delivered verdicts of guilt for crimes against humanity that would today count as convictions for genocide'. See Robertson, *An Inconvenient Genocide*, 81–5.
39 Paul C. Helmreich, *From Paris to Sèvres: The Partition of the Ottoman Empire at the Peace Conference of 1919–1920* (Columbus: Ohio State University Press, 1974), 110.
40 Rogan, *The Fall of the Ottomans*, 392–3.
41 Kévorkian, *The Armenian Genocide*, 715–16; Erik J. Zürcher, *Turkey: A Modern History* (New York: St Martin's Press, 1994), 141.
42 Kévorkian, *The Armenian Genocide*, 740.

Chapter 10

1 Mango, *Atatürk*, 218–20; Zürcher, *The Young Turk Legacy*, 132–33.
2 *Atatürk'ün Tamim, Telgraf ve Beyannameleri IV*, 49.
3 Shaw and Shaw, *History of the Ottoman Empire and Modern Turkey: Volume II*, 344–9.
4 Crathern, Diary, entry for 4 February 1920, quoted in Morris and Ze'evi, *Thirty Year Genocide*, 339.
5 Morris and Ze'evi, *Thirty Year Genocide*, 334–43.
6 quoted in Mango, *Atatürk*, 272.
7 Babkenian, 'Australian Women and the Armenian Relief Movement'.
8 Babkenian, 'Australian Women and the Armenian Relief Movement'.
9 *Ravished Armenia and the Story of Aurora Mardiganian*, 6, quoted in Balakian, *The Burning Tigris*, 313–15.
10 'Auction of Souls', *Sydney Morning Herald* (AU), 12 January 1920, 5; 'Turkish Horrors Filmed', *Daily Observer* (AU), 1 January 1920, 4.
11 'How Christian Girls Were Massacred in Armenia', *Sunday Times* (AU), 28 December 1919, 13.
12 'Starving Central Europe', *New Zealand Herald* (NZ), 26 March 1920, 4.
13 'Save the Children Fund', *New Zealand Herald* (NZ), 23 June 1920, 6.
14 'Save the Children Fund', *New Zealand Herald* (NZ), 22 September 1920, 7.
15 'The Week of Pity', *Otago Daily Times* (NZ), 17 July 1920, 1.
16 *Otago Daily Times* (NZ), 6 September 1920, 4.
17 'Save the Children Fund', *The Press* (NZ), 18 December 1920, 5.

18 'Save the Children', *Evening Post* (NZ), 16 November 1920, 7; 'Save the Children', *Dominion* (NZ), 12 November 1920, 2; 'Save the Children Fund', *Evening Post* (NZ), 22 January 1921, 2.
19 'Distress in Europe', *New Zealand Herald* (NZ), 26 November 1920, 4.
20 'Save the Children Fund', *Evening Post* (NZ), 6 January 1921, 8.
21 Quoted in Mango, *Atatürk*, 294.
22 Quoted in Balakian, *The Burning Tigris*, 328.
23 Vratsian, *Hayastani Hanrapetutiun*, p. 500, quoted in Walker, *Armenia*, 317.
24 Morris and Ze'evi, *Thirty Year Genocide*, 347–69.
25 Babkenian and Stanley, *Armenian, Australia & the Great War*, 163–6.
26 Babkenian and Stanley, *Armenia, Australia & the Great War*, 195–6.
27 'Meeting with the Clergy', *Mercury* (AU), 6 June 1922, 3.
28 'Distressed Armenia: Support for Relief Work', *The Argus* (AU), 8 July 1922, 20.
29 'The Plight of Armenia', *Auckland Star* (NZ), 18 July 1922, 6; 'Plight of Armenia', *New Zealand Herald* (NZ), 18 July 1922, 7.
30 'Relief for Armenians', *New Zealand Herald* (NZ), 20 July 1922, 8.
31 'Distressed Armenians', *New Zealand Herald* (NZ), 22 July 1922, 10; 'Distress in Armenia', *Auckland Star* (NZ), 22 July 1922, 5.
32 'Local and General', Evening Post (NZ), 27 July 1922, 6.
33 'Help for Armenia', *Evening Post* (NZ), 27 July 1922, 3.
34 'Near East Relief', *Otago Daily Times* (NZ), 29 July 1922, 4; 'Unhappy Armenia', *The Press* (NZ) 2 August 1922, 4.
35 'N.Z. Mercy Ship', *Evening Post* (NZ), 2 August 1922, 6.
36 'Parliament', *New Zealand Herald* (NZ), 3 August 1922, 8; Massey's government also turned down a request from the Armenian National Delegation, via the League of Nations, for funds towards settling refugees in the Caucasus in similar terms, see letter dated 24 July 1926, ACGO, Series 8333, IA1, Box 3013/, no. 158/208, parts 1 & 2, and ACHK, Series 8604, G1 Box 298/, no. 1924/1854.
37 Morris and Ze'evi, *Thirty Year Genocide*, 410–11.
38 Petition signed by fifty-one communities in central Anatolia, attached to de Robeck to Curzon, 8 September 1920, UKNA FO 371/5054, quoted in Morris and Ze'evi, *Thirty Year Genocide*, 405–6.
39 McMeekin, *The Ottoman Endgame*, 451–70.
40 Babkenian and Stanley, *Armenia, Australia & the Great War*, 203–4.
41 Babkenian and Stanley, *Armenia, Australia & the Great War*, 204–6.
42 Charles Dobson 9/633 military personnel file, AABK 18805, 82/03592444.
43 'The Horrors of Smyrna', *The Register* (AU), 11 November 1922, 12.
44 Maynard B. Barnes, Smyrna, 'Evacuation of Christian Population of Western Anatolia', 12 October 1922, USNA RG 84, Turkey (Constantinople), vol. 646, quoted in Morris and Ze'evi, *Thirty Year Genocide*, 441.
45 Morris and Ze'evi, *Thirty Year Genocide*, 452.

46 All quotes and details taken from Joanna Hyslop (2013–14) 'A brief and personal account': the evidence of Charles Dobson on the destruction of the city of Smyrna in September 1922, *Crisis, Criticism and Critique in Contemporary Greek Studies*, vol. 16–17.
47 Charles Dobson, *The Smyrna Holocaust*, 21–9, appendix to Lysimachos Oeconomos, *The Tragedy of the Christian Near East* (London: Anglo-Hellenic League, 1923), 27.
48 The burning of Izmir prompted the various relief committees in Victoria, Western Australia, South Australia and Queensland to consolidate under the umbrella of Save the Children, forming a cooperative association called the Save the Children Fund and Armenian Relief Fund. The New South Wales branch maintained its connection to Near East Relief.
49 Wirt, *The World Is My Parish*, 29, quoted in Babkenian and Stanley, *Armenia, Australia & the Great War*, 206–7.
50 Nureddin, 'Proclamation', 23 September 1922, UKNA FO 371/7898, quoted in Morris and Ze'evi, *Thirty Year Genocide*, 452–3.
51 G.S. Hatton, 'French Troops of Occupation in the Gallipoli Peninsula', 30 November 1922, UKNA FO 371/7964, quoted in Morris and Ze'evi, *Thirty Year Genocide*, 288.
52 Ernest Hemingway, *Toronto Daily Star* (CA), 22 October 1922.
53 quoted in McMeekin, *The Ottoman Endgame*, 478–9.
54 McMeekin, *The Ottoman Endgame*, 479.
55 Zürcher, *Turkey*, 169–74.
56 Mann, *The Dark Side of Democracy*, 140.
57 'The Armenian Remnant', *New Zealand Herald* (NZ), 30 May 1916, 6.

Chapter 11

1 John Knudsen military personnel file, AABK, series 18805, box 110, record number 0065484.
2 'Hobart Hospital', *The Press* (NZ), 21 May 1932, 6.
3 *Acorne*, News Bulletin, 29 May 1920.
4 It remains a mystery how John and Lydia met, but there is some evidence to suggest Lydia was a nurse, perhaps attached to a military force, or in a humanitarian outfit, like John's mother.
5 'Near East Tragedy', *The Register* (AU), 18 December 1922, 8.
6 Vicken Babkenian, 'A Humanitarian Journey: The Reverend James Edwin Cresswell and the Armenian Relief Fund', *Journal of the Historical Society of South Australia* 37 (2009), 61–75.
7 Letter from Hilda King, *Sydney Morning Herald* (AU), Thursday, 15 February 1923, 5.

8   Watenpaugh, *Bread from Stones*, 114–15.
9   Watenpaugh, *Bread from Stones*, 115–16.
10 Charles V. Vickrey, 'Preliminary Report: Observations in Central Europe and the Near East', July/September 1920, p. 12. RAC, NEF, Box 1, Minutes 1920–1.
11 Letter from Hilda King, *Sydney Morning Herald* (AU), Thursday, 15 February 1923, 5.
12 Letter from Hilda King, *Sydney Morning Herald* (AU), Thursday, 15 February 1923, 5.
13 Asdghig Avakian, *Stranger among Friends* (Beirut, 1960), 25
14 Avakian, *Stranger among Friends*, 28.
15 Avakian, *Stranger among Friends*, 34–8.
16 Avakian, *Stranger among Friends*, 77.
17 Avakian, *Stranger among Friends*, 77.
18 Babkenian and Stanley, *Armenia, Australia & the Great War*, 269–71.
19 Avakian, *Stranger among Friends*, 78.
20 Interview with survivor Souren Antoyan in Lebanon, aged 93. 'Souren's Story: A Voice Recovered from Armenia's Bitter Past', ABC Hindsight, 25 October 2009.
21 Babkenian and Stanley, *Armenia, Australia & the Great War*, 210–11.
22 quoted in Babkenian, 'A Humanitarian Journey'.
23 Australasian Relief Fund Committee, South Australian Auxiliary, *The Armenian*, 1, quoted in Babkenian & Stanley, *Armenia, Australia & the Great War*, 212
24 *The New Near East*, July 1923, 15.
25 Transcript of James Cresswell's diary dated 21 February 1923, courtesy of Vicken Babkenian.
26 Babkenian and Stanley, *Armenia, Australia & the Great War*, 220.
27 'Plight of Armenia', *Manawatu Standard* (NZ), 5 September 1922; 'Armenians' Appeal', *Manawatu Times* (NZ), 5 September 1922, 5.
28 'Armenian Relief', *Manawatu Times* (NZ), 17 November 1922.
29 *Otago Daily Times* (NZ), 1 November 1922, 1.
30 'Armenian Relief Fund', *Otago Daily Times* (NZ), 4 November 1922, 5.
31 *Otago Daily Times* (NZ), 18 January 1923, 6.
32 'Armenian Relief Fund', *Evening Post* (NZ), 2 September 1922.
33 *Evening Post* (NZ), 17 October 1922, 8, column 2.
34 Armenian Relief Fund – Cash book, 1922–3, ATL, MS Papers 2626-2/9/9.
35 Surprisingly, the cause in Auckland went nowhere. The committee resolved to leave any appeals to the churches. See 'Near East Appeal', *Auckland Star* (NZ), 28 July 1922, 7.
36 'Women in Print', *Evening Post* (NZ), 7 May 1923; see also 'Women in Print', *Evening Post* (NZ), 1 September 1923; Minute book 1921–3, New Zealand Red Cross Society, Wellington centre, ATL, MS-Group 1896, Qms-1535.
37 'Armenian Relief', *Evening Post* (NZ), 21 September 1923.
38 'Peace-Time Work', *Evening Post* (NZ), 20 December 1923.

39   'Armenian Relief', *New Zealand Herald* (NZ), 23 July 1923, 10; 'Near East Report', *Evening Post* (NZ), 21 July 1923, 8.
40   Interview with Dr Armstrong Smith of Save the Children, *The Press* (NZ), 21 April 1923, 13.
41   'Save the Children', *Manawatu Times* (NZ), 16 April 1923, 4.
42   The Auckland YWCA held annual jumble sales and lectures as late as 1927: see *New Zealand Herald* (NZ), 10 December 1926, 24, column 6; *New Zealand Herald* (NZ), 29 July 1927, 22, column 6. The Canterbury fund is something of an anomaly, because of its connections to Save the Children rather than NER, and doesn't hold a major appeal for 'stricken Greece and Armenia, Homeless, Destitute, Starving', until 1924: see *The Press* (NZ), 29 May 1924, 11, column 1.
43   Babkenian, 'Australian Women and the Armenian Relief Movement'; Babkenian and Stanley, *Armenia, Australia & the Great War*, 225–6.
44   'Armenia's Children', *Manchester Guardian* (UK), 4 October 1926, 6.
45   'Armenian Children', *New Zealand Herald* (NZ), 22 September 1923, 9.
46   'Hobart Hospital', *The Press* (NZ), 21 May 1932, 6. John Knudsen died a day after his sixtieth birthday in NSW in 1950. Lydia died in NSW in 1971.
47   'Near East Relief', *The Argus* (AU), 20 February 1925, 14.

Chapter 12

1   Arsan (ed.), *Atatürk'ün Söylev ve Demeçleri*, vol. III, 50–1, quoted in Üngör, *The Making of Modern Turkey*, 224.
2   Fatma Müge Göçek, *Denial of Violence: Ottoman Past, Turkish Present, and Collective Violence against the Armenians 1789–2009* (Oxford: Oxford University Press, 2015), 263.
3   Zürcher, *Turkey*, chapters 10 & 11, 173–215.
4   Zürcher, *Turkey*, 184–90.
5   FO371/6504/E10319; FO371/6509, folio 159, quoted in Dadrian, 'Ottoman Archives and Denial of the Armenian Genocide', in *The Armenian Genocide*, ed. Hovannisian, 280–310; For analysis of the Malta Exiles' Republican status see Sait Çetinoğlu, Malta Documents – Continuity of CUP and Turkish Republic, 15 July 2009; See also Zürcher, 'Renewal and Silence'.
6   Vahagn Avedian, 'State Identity, Continuity, and Responsibility: The Ottoman Empire, the Republic of Turkey and the Armenian Genocide', *The European Journal of International Law* 23:3 (2012), 810–11.
7   See Üngör, *The Making of Modern Turkey*, chapter 3, 107–70.
8   İsmet İnönü, *Hatıralar* (Ankara: Bilgi, 1987), vol. 2, 272, quoted in Üngör, *The Making of Modern* Turkey, 229.

9   *Türkiye Büyük Millet Meclisi Zabıt Ceridesi*, vol. 16, period V, meeting 2 (1937), 59, quoted in Üngör, *The Making of Modern Turkey*, 229.
10 Üngör, *The Making of Modern Turkey*, 225.
11 Göçek, *Denial of Violence*, 288.
12 Nimet Unan (ed.), *Atatürk'ün Söylev ve Demeçleri, vol. 2 (1906-1938)* (Ankara: Türk Tarih Kurumu, 1959), 12, quoted in Zurcher, 'Renewal and Silence: Postwar Unionist and Kemalist Rhetoric on the Armenian Genocide', in *A Question of Genocide: Armenians and Turks at the End of the Ottoman Empire*, ed. Ronald Grigory Suny, Fatma Müge Göçek, and Norman M. Naimark (New York: Oxford University Press, 2011), 6.
13 Öztürk, Atatürk'ün TBMM Açık ve Gizli Oturumlarındaki Konuşmaları, 59-61, quoted in Fatma Ulgen, 'Reading Mustafa Kemal Atatürk on the Armenian Genocide of 1915', *Patterns of Prejudice* 44:4, 369-91. Italics own.
14 Öztürk, Atatürk'ün TBMM Açık ve Gizli Oturumlarındaki Konuşmaları, 84, quoted in Ulgen, 'Reading Mustafa Kemal Atatürk on the Armenian Genocide of 1915'.
15 Öztürk, Atatürk'ün TBMM Açık ve Gizli Oturumlarındaki Konuşmaları, 142, quoted in Ulgen, 'Reading Mustafa Kemal Atatürk on the Armenian Genocide of 1915'.
16 Atatürk'ün Söylev ve Demeçleri II, 9, quoted in Ulgen, 'Reading Mustafa Kemal Atatürk on the Armenian Genocide of 1915'.
17 Atatürk, *A Speech Delivered by Mustafa Kemal*, quoted in Ulgen, 'Reading Mustafa Kemal Atatürk on the Armenian Genocide of 1915'.
18 quoted in Philippe Sands, *East West Street: On the Origins of Genocide and Crimes against Humanity* (London: Weidenfeld & Nicolson, 2016), 143.
19 Peter Bogosian, *Operation Nemesis: The Assassination Plot That Avenged the Armenian Genocide* (New York: Little, Brown and Company, 2015), 9-11.
20 Sands, *East West Street*, 148.
21 See chapters 3-5 in Stefan Ihrig, *Atatürk in the Nazi Imagination* (Cambridge: Belknap Press, 2014).
22 Johann von Leers, *Adolf Hitler* (Berlin: R. Kittler, 1934 [1932]), 5, quoted in Ihrig, *Atatürk in the Nazi Imagination*, 114.
23 'Der Führer über das Verhältnis Deutschlands zur Türkei', *Völkischer Beobachter*, 21 July 1933, quoted in Ihrig, *Atatürk in the Nazi Imagination*, 115.
24 Ihrig, *Atatürk in the Nazi Imagination*, 224.
25 Sands, *East West Street*, 157.
26 Peter Balakian, 'Raphael Lemkin, Cultural Destruction, and the Armenian Genocide', *Holocaust and Genocide Studies* 27:1 (2013), 57-89.
27 Perry Anderson, 'Kemalism', *London Review of Books*, 11 September 2008.
28 From the Convention on the Prevention and Punishment of the Crime of Genocide. Adopted by the General Assembly of the United Nations on 9 December 1948.

29 Balakian, 'Raphael Lemkin, Cultural Destruction, and the Armenian Genocide'.
30 Communism by jackboot. The phrase is Ernst Fischer's.
31 Balakian, *The Burning Tigris*, 377; Suny, *They Can Live in the Desert*, 369; De Waal, *Great Catastrophe*, 142.
32 This was the prevailing view, until scholars of genocide recognized the German destruction of the Herero and Nama people in Namibia between 1904 and 1908.
33 Balakian, *The Burning Tigris*, 377–8.
34 Bedross Der Matossian, 'Explaining the Unexplainable: Recent Trends in the Armenian Genocide Historiography', *Journal of Levantine Studies* 5:2 (2015), 143–66.
35 Dugan, Huang, LaFree and McCauley (2008) 'Sudden Desistance from Terrorism'.
36 For a meditation on the Australian bombings and shootings, see the essay 'Writing Violence, Arousing Curiosity', in Kaligian Blunt's *My Name Is Revenge*.
37 The terror campaign 'provided the "rationalizing event"' for an 'emerging Turkish official narrative that attempted to explain this recent Armenian violence' Göçek, *Denial of Violence*, 391, 428–55.
38 The substance of this official narrative hasn't changed much in the last thirty years. The modern version now helpfully appears on the Turkish Ministry of Foreign Affairs' website. See 'An Overview': http://www.mfa.gov.tr/the-events-of-1915-and-the-turkish-armenian-controversy-over-history_-an-overview.en.mfa, and 'The Armenian Allegation of Genocide: The Issue and the Facts': http://www.mfa.gov.tr/the-armenian-allegation-of-genocide-the-issue-and-the-facts.en.mfa
39 Jennifer M. Dixon, 'Defending the Nation? Maintaining Turkey's Narrative of the Armenian Genocide', *South European Society and Politics* 15:3 (2010), 467–85. See also Gürpınar (2016) 'The Manufacturing of Denial', 217–40.
40 A rebuttal to modern denial, and a mock prosecution for the crime of genocide can be found in Robertson, *An Inconvenient Genocide*, 91–124; For a rebuttal of a Western author's representative equivocations, see Taner Akçam, 'Guenter Lewy's *The Armenian Massacres in Ottoman Turkey*', *Genocide Studies and Prevention* 3:1 (2008), 111–45.
41 Nazan Maksudyan, 'Walls of Silence: Translating the Armenian Genocide into Turkish and Self-Censorship', *Critique* 37:4 (2009), 635–49.
42 Göçek, *Denial of Violence*, 465.
43 Dixon, 'Defending the Nation'.
44 Göçek, *Denial of Violence*, 447–8.
45 Balakian, *The Burning Tigris*, 384.
46 Roger W. Smith, Eric Markusen, and Robert Jay Lifton, 'Professional Ethics and the Denial of the Armenian Genocide', *Holocaust and Genocide Studies* 9:1 (1995).
47 Balakian, *The Burning Tigris*, 384–5.
48 Marc A. Mamigonian, 'Academic Denial of the Armenian Genocide in American Scholarship: Denialism as Manufactured Controversy', *Genocide Studies International* 9:1 (2015), 61–82; Vicken Cheterian, 'Censorship, Indifference,

Oblivion: The Armenian Genocide and Its Denial', in Russell, *Truth, Silence and Violence*, 188–214.

49 Ergun Kirlikovali, 'Genocide Crowds Are the New KKK', Turkish Forum, 15 November 2008, quoted in Mamigonian, 'Academic Denial of the Armenian Genocide', 76.

50 Balakian, *The Burning Tigris*, 386–9.

51 Adam Gabbatt, 'Turkish PM Threatens to Expel 100,000 Armenians over Genocide Vote', *The Guardian* (UK), 19 March 2010: https://www.theguardian.com/world/2010/mar/18/turkey-threatens-expel-armenians-genocide

52 Elise Harris, 'Pope Recalls Slaughter of Armenians in "First Genocide of the 20th Century"', Catholic News Agency, 12 April 2015: http://www.catholicnewsagency.com/news/pope-recalls-slaughter-of-armenians-in-first-genocide-of-the-20th-century-92710/

53 Jim Yardley, 'Pope Calls Killings of Armenians "Genocide," Provoking Turkish Anger', *New York Times* (US), 12 April 2015: https://www.nytimes.com/2015/04/13/world/europe/pope-calls-killings-of-armenians-genocide-provoking-turkish-anger.html

54 Unofficial translation of the message of the prime minister of The Republic of Turkey, Recep Tayyip Erdoğan, on the events of 1915, Republic of Turkey Ministry of Foreign Affairs, 23 April 2014: http://www.mfa.gov.tr/turkish-prime-minister-mr_-recep-tayyip-erdo%C4%9Fan-published-a-message-on-the-events-of-1915_-23-april-2014.en.mfa

55 Letter from Turkish Prime Minister Recep Tayyip Erdoğan to Armenian President Robert Koçaryan, 10 April 2005, retrieved from Republic of Turkey Ministry of Foreign Affairs website: http://www.mfa.gov.tr/data/DISPOLITIKA/text-of-the-letter-of-h_e_-prime-minister-recep-tayyip-erdogan-addressed-to-h_e_-robert-kocharian.pdf

56 Alison Smale and Melissa Eddy, 'German Parliament Recognizes Armenian Genocide, Angering Turkey', *New York Times* (US), 2 June 2016: https://www.nytimes.com/2016/06/03/world/europe/armenian-genocide-germany-turkey.html

57 Philip Oltermann and Constanze Letsch, 'Turkey Recalls Ambassador after German MPs' Armenian Genocide Vote', *The Guardian* (UK), 2 June 2016: https://www.theguardian.com/world/2016/jun/02/germany-braces-for-turkish-backlash-as-it-votes-to-recognise-armenian-genocide

58 Harat Sassounian, 'Cem Ozdemir: "Young Turks Are Traitors; Talat and Enver Criminals"', The Armenian Weekly, 13 July 2016: http://armenianweekly.com/2016/07/13/sassounian-ozdemir/

59 De Waal, *Great Catastrophe*, 185–92.

60 Hrant Dink (trans. Nazım Hikmet and Richard Dikbaş), *Two Close Peoples, Two Distant Neighbours* (Istanbul: Hrant Dink Foundation Publications, 2014), 36.

61 Dink, *Two Close Peoples*, 72.

62 Dink, *Two Close Peoples*, 71–2.
63 Hrant Dink's final article, BBC (UK), 20 January 2007.

A conclusion: Lying side by side

1   Sigmund Freud, *Psychopathology of Everyday Life* (New York: Macmillan, 1914.
2   See Anna Haebich, *Spinning the Dream: Assimilation in Australia 1950–1970* (Fremantle: Fremantle Press, 2008); Vincent O'Malley, *The New Zealand Wars/Ngā Pakanga o Aotearoa* (Wellington: BWB, 2019).
3   'New Zealanders' Fight at Gaba Tepe', *New Zealand Herald* (NZ), 8 May 1915, 9: widely reprinted.
4   New Zealand *Free Lance*, vol. XV, no. 813, 28 January 1916, 16; no. 823, 7 April 1916, 10; no. 824, 14 April 1916, 6, 10.
5   Emphasis added. 'The Salonica Expedition', *The Sun* (NZ), 24 April 1916, 6.
6   Bill Gammage, *The Broken Years: Australian Soldiers in the Great War* (Canberra: Australian National University Press, 1974), 115.
7   For criticism of the 'born in war' belief, see Henry Reynolds, 'Are Nations Really Made in War?', in *What's Wrong with Anzac?*
8   For general overviews, see Jenny Macleod, 'The Fall and Rise of Anzac Day: 1965–1990', 2002; Martin Crotty and Christina Spittel, 'The One Day of the Year and All That: Anzac between History and Memory', *Australian Journal of Politics and History* 58:1 (2012), 123–31; George Frederick Davis (2008), 'Anzac Day Meanings and Memories: New Zealand, Australian and Turkish Perspectives on a Day of Commemoration in the Twentieth Century', PhD thesis, University of Otago; Stephen J. Clarke (1994), 'The One Day of the Year: Anzac Day in Aotearoa/New Zealand 1946–1990', MA thesis, University of Otago.
9   Maureen Sharpe, 'Anzac Day in New Zealand: 1916–1939', *NZ Journal of History* 15:2 (1981), 99.
10 See Chapter Five in Davis, 'Anzac Meanings and Memories'.
11 Ayhan Aktar, 'Rewriting the History of Gallipoli: A Turkish Perspective', Honest History, 25 July 2017.
12 'Visit to New Zealand by Hon. Vahit Halefoglu, Minister of Foreign Affairs, Republic of Turkey, 28–30 April 1985' in Turkey: Political Affairs – General [06/82-12/85], ABHS, W4627, Box 4121, no. 274/4/1.
13 Memo from New Zealand Embassy, Tehran, to Secretary of Foreign Affairs, 'Possible Cross-accreditation to Turkey', dated 12 June 1985, in Turkey: Political Affairs – General [06/82-12/85], ABHS, W4627, Box 4121, no. 274/4/1.
14 Şimşir, p. 649, quoted in David Stephens, 'Turks Did the Heavy Lifting: A Longer Look at the Story of the Atatürk Memorial, Canberra, 1984–85: Part I', Honest History, 11 October 2016.

15 David Stephens, 'Turks Did the Heavy Lifting: A Longer Look at the Building of the Atatürk Memorial in Anzac Parade, Canberra, 1984–85: Part II', *Honest History* 25 October 2016.
16 Ministry for Culture and Heritage, 'Atatürk Memorial', updated 30 November 2017, available at: mch.govt.nz/nz-identity-heritage/national-monuments-war-graves/atat%C3%BCrk-memorial. The Declaration that 675 square metres of land of the 'Atatürk Historic Reserve' is a Reserve under the 1977 Reserves Act was Gazetted by the delegation of the Minister of Conservation on 27 August 1991. New Zealand Government, Department of Internal Affairs, *New Zealand Gazette*, Issue 133 (Wellington: Government Printer, 5 September 1991), 2871; New Zealand Government, Department of Internal Affairs, *New Zealand Gazette*, Issue 76 (Wellington: Government Printer, 23 May 1991), 1684.
17 Memorandum dated 21 November 1988 from Rosalind Hickey to Deputy Secretary 1 said, 'The Pa belonged to the Ngai Tara people whose Maori "rights" had been negated by the conquest of the area by the Te Ati Awa people' (SDC16014).
18 9 December 1988 memorandum between D. G. Weir from the Constitutional and Ministerial Services Department and the Minister of Internal Affairs (SDC16001).
19 'Security Tight for Minister's Visit', *Canberra Times* (AU), 24 April 1985, 1.
20 Photographs of the memorial can be viewed at: Ministry for Culture and Heritage, 'Atatürk Memorial', updated 30 November 2017: mch.govt.nz/nz-identity-heritage/national-monuments-war-graves/atat%C3%BCrk-memorial. The monument itself was dedicated in 1990 by Lutfullah Kayalar, see Memorandum to Minister of Foreign Affairs dated 19 April 1985, in Turkey: Political Affairs – General [06/82-12/85], ABHS, W4627, Box 4121, no. 274/4/1 and Craig Foss, *NZPD*, vol. 724 (15 August 2017).
21 quoted in Robert Manne, 'A Turkish Tale: Gallipoli and the Armenian Genocide', *The Monthly*, February 2007.
22 Foreign Affairs Minister Winston Peters, Speech at Anzac Cove, Gallipoli, 25 April 2007.
23 '2015 Year of Turkey in Australia', *Sydney Morning Herald* (AU), 27 April 2012.
24 Phone interview with Matt Gauldie, conducted early March 2018. See also James Robins, 'Immortal Wartime Words a Fiction', Newsroom (NZ), 25 April 2018.
25 Ministry for Culture and Heritage, 'Memorial Unveiling Strengthens New Zealand-Turkish Ties', 13 April 2017: mch.govt.nz/memorial-unveiling-strengthens-new-zealand-turkish-ties
26 see Stanton Hope, 'ANZAC To-day', *Sydney Morning Herald* (AU), 7 July 1934, 11; 'Gallipoli Pilgrims', *Sydney Morning Herald* (AU), 5 May 1934, 13.
27 Davis, 'Anzac Day Meanings and Memories', 213.
28 quoted in Paul Daley, 'Ataturk's "Johnnies and Mehmets" Words about the Anzacs Are Shrouded in Doubt', *The Guardian* (UK), 20 April 2015.
29 'Heroism at Anzac', *New Zealand Herald* (NZ), 2 May 1934, 15.

30 quoted in Daley, 'Ataturk's "Johnnies and Mehmets" Words about the Anzacs Are Shrouded in Doubt'; see also Ulug Igdemir, *Ataturk ve Anzaklar (Atatürk and the Anzacs)* (Ankara: Türk Tarih Kurumu Basımevi, 1978).
31 Kaya did once give a speech at Gallipoli, but in 1931, not 1934: *Hakimiyet-i Milliye*, 26 August 1931, translated by Cengiz Özakıncı in 'The Words "There Is No Difference between the Mehmets and the Johnnies" engraved on the 1915 Gallipoli Monuments Do Not Belong to Ataturk. Part I', *Bütün Dünya*, March 2015, 23–9.
32 It is not clear either where the ellipses in the quote come from. Kaya's 1953 version does not contain them.
33 Memorandum from Bob Cater to Dr Jock Phillips dated 29 March 1990. On being approached by this author for a story about the Tarakena Bay monument, Phillips denied any memory of being asked to check the quote's veracity.
34 Trudinger, 'The View From Constantinople', 727.
35 Emphasis added. Robert Manne, 'A Turkish Tale: Gallipoli and the Armenian Genocide', *The Monthly* (AU), February 2007. This goes for historians of Anzac – historians of the genocide including Jay Winter and Taner Akçam, cited in Chapter 5, have been more diligent.
36 Babkenian and Stanley, *Armenia, Australia & the Great War*, 50.
37 'Armenian, Assyrian and Greek Genocides', Motion agreed by the Legislative Council of the New South Wales parliament, 1 May 2013. It reaffirmed a memo passed in 1998.
38 No: 133, Press Release Regarding the Motion Passed by the Legislative Council of the Parliament of the State of New South Wales in Australia, Republic of Turkey Ministry of Foreign Affairs, 7 May 2013.
39 Michel Brissenden, 'Turkey Threatens to Ban MPs from Gallipoli Centenary over Genocide Vote', ABC News, 21 August 2013.
40 Julia Hollingsworth, 'NZ Armenians Call for Genocide to Be Recognised', Newshub (via New Zealand Newswire) (NZ), 14 April 2015.
41 Most of the documents are heavily redacted 'to avoid prejudicing the international relations of the New Zealand Government' and 'to protect the free and frank expression of opinions by departments'.
42 An MFA position file on the question of genocide from the early 1980s can be found at ABHS, 6958, Box 230/, no. NYP 3/70/2 part 1.
43 Briefing paper titled 'Turkey/Armenia', Internal correspondence from Ministry of Foreign Affairs and Trade and the Minister of Foreign Affairs' Office, released under the Official Information Act.
44 Jenny Macleod and Gizem Tongo, 'Between Memory and History: Remembering Johnnies, Mehmets, and the Armenians', Beyond Gallipoli: New Perspectives on Anzac.

45 Constanze Letsch, 'Commemorations for Armenian Genocide Victims Held in Turkey', *The Guardian* (UK), 24 April 2015.
46 This author spoke alongside Professor Akçam at the New Zealand Parliament and in meetings with MPs of three political parties.
47 Emily Cooper, 'Greens Call on Parliament to Recognise WWI Deaths of Armenians in Turkey as Genocide', *1 News*, 6 August 2018, found at https://www.tvnz.co.nz/one-news/new-zealand/greens-call-parliament-recognise-wwi-deaths-armenians-in-turkey-genocide?variant=tb_v_1; Armenian National Committee of New Zealand press release, 'New Zealand Prime Minister Jacinda Ardern Called to Correct Appeasement of Armenian Genocide Denial by Turkey', 7 August 2018, found at http://www.anc.org.au/news/Media-Releases/New-Zealand-Prime-Minister-Jacinda-Ardern-called-to-correct-appeasement-of-Armenian-Genocide-denial-by-Turkey
48 Australian Department of Foreign Affairs and Trade FOI Disclosure Log, reference 15/25024, 14 August 2015, 2,3.
49 Australian Department of Foreign Affairs and Trade FOI Disclosure Log, reference 15/25024, 14 August 2015, 1. See also The Hon Julie Bishop MP, Minister for Foreign Affairs, letter to Mr Ertund Ozen, Australian Turkish Advocacy Alliance, 4 June 2014.
50 See Macleod and Tongo, 'Between Memory and History: Johnnies, Mehmets, and the Armenians'.
51 Although he campaigned on the fraught question of Armenian Genocide recognition, and presumably intended his remark as all-encompassing, Wiesel always insisted on the primacy and uniqueness of the Holocaust.
52 quoted in De Waal, *Great Catastrophe*, 192–4.
53 See section VI. 'Neglect and Cultural Destruction of Armenian Cultural Heritage', in Tessa Hoffman, 'Armenians in Turkey Today: A Critical Assessment of the Armenian Minority in the Turkish Republic', report prepared for the Forum of Armenian Associations in Europe, 2002.
54 'Minorities in Turkey Tagged by "Race Codes," Official Document Reveals', *Hürriyet Daily News* (Turkey), 1 August 2013: http://www.hurriyetdailynews.com/minorities-in-turkey-tagged-by-race-codes-official-document-reveals-51849; 'Türkiye soy kodunu tartışıyor', *Agos* (Turkey), 2 August 2013: http://www.agos.com.tr/tr/yazi/5390/turkiye-soy-kodunu-tartisiyor
55 Fehim Tastekin, 'Turkish Genealogy Database Fascinates, frightens Turks', *Al-Monitor* (US), 21 February 2018: https://www.al-monitor.com/pulse/originals/2018/02/turkey-turks-become-obsessed-with-genealogy.html
56 Avedis Hadjian, *Secret Nation: The Hidden Armenians of Turkey* (London: I.B. Tauris, 2018), 152.
57 Primo Levi, *If This Is a Man/The Truce*, trans. Stuart Woolf (London: Sphere Books, 1987), 17.

Bibliography

ARCHIVE SOURCES

Alexander Turnbull Library

MS-Group 1896, Qms-1535 Minute book 1921–1923, New Zealand Red Cross Society, Wellington centre
MS Papers 2626-2/9/9 Armenian Relief Fund – Cash book, 1922–1923

National Archives New Zealand

AABK W5562, Box 125, no. 0131476 George Gunn personnel file
AABK W5614, Box 68, D. 2/5559 Frank Allsopp personnel file
AABK 18805, Box 82, no. 03592444 Charles Dobson 9/633 military personnel file
AABK 18805, Box 110, no. 0065484 John Knudsen military personnel file
AAEG W3240 950 Box 40, A, 201/4/4, 1, Countries – United Kingdom – External Relations – Turkey, 1926–1931
AAEG W3240 950 Box 89, A, 201/4/4, 2A, Countries – United Kingdom – External Relations – Turkey, 1931–1939
AAEG W3240 950 Box 8, B, 378/1/1, 1A, Countries – Armenia – General, 1920–1922
AAEG W3240 950 Box 333, B, 378/1/1, 1B, Countries – Armenian – General, 1945–1948
ABHS, 6958, Box 230/, no. NYP 3/70/2 part 1 Political Affairs – Turkey – Question of Armenian Genocide [04/1980–12/1983]
ABHS W4627 950 Box 4121, no. 274/4/1, Turkey: Political Affairs – General [01/71–03/79]
ABHS W4627, Box 4121, no. 274/4/1 Turkey: Political Affairs – General [06/82–12/85],
ACGO 8333, IA1, Box 3013/, no. 158/208, parts 1 & 2 Miscellaneous – Armenian and Russian Refugees Relief Fund – Appeal for
ACHK, Series 8604, G1 Box 298/, no. 1924/1854 Appeal for financial assistance in establishing Armenian Refugees in Transcaucasia or elsewhere
WA ser. 1 File 10/.75 Repatriation Prisoners of War (Pt I)

Australian War Memorial

2DRL/0766 Typescript copy of Captain Thomas Walter White's diary, November 1915–December 1918

3DRL/2965 Papers of Able Seaman John Harrison Wheat
3DRL/6753 Davie, Reginald John (Private, Wellington Infantry Battalion, NZEF and POW, Turkey)
F00051 With the Dunster Force, Persia and Baku [film]
S00104 Message recorded by Second Lieutenant Henry Miller Lanser, 1st Battalion, Mena Camp, Cairo, Egypt, First World War for his family in Australia

State Library of Queensland

OM90-138 D.B. Creedon Diary, 1915

UNPUBLISHED SOURCES

Desmond Hurley's manuscript on New Zealand Prisoners of War, courtesy Hurley family
Typescript of Rev. James E. Cresswell's Diary, courtesy Vicken Babkenian

PUBLISHED SOURCES

Taner Akçam, *From Empire to Republic: Turkish Nationalism & the Armenian Genocide*, London: Zed Books, 2004.
Taner Akçam, *A Shameful Act: The Armenian Genocide and the Question of Turkish Responsibility*, New York: Metropolitan Books, 2006.
Taner Akçam, *The Young Turks' Crime against Humanity: The Armenian Genocide and Ethnic Cleansing in the Ottoman Empire*, Princeton, NJ: Princeton University Press, 2012.
Kate Ariotti, *Captive Anzacs: Australian POWs of the Ottomans during the First World War*, Sydney: Cambridge University Press, 2018.
Brig.-Gen. H. H. Austin, *The Baqubah Refugee Camp: An Account of Work on behalf of the Persecuted Assyrian Christians*, London: The Faith Press, 1920.
Lt.-Col. W. Austin, *The Official History of the New Zealand Rifle Brigade*, Wellington: L.T. Watkins, 1924.
Asdghig Avakian, *Stranger among Friends*, Beirut, 1960. Youel A. Baaba, *An Assyrian Odyssey: Covering the Journey of Kasha Yacoub Yauvre and His Wife Mourassa from Urmia to the Court of Queen Victoria 1879–1881 and the Exodus of the Assyrians from Their Ancestral Home 1918*, Alamo: Youel A Baaba Library, 1998.
Vicken Babkenian and Peter Stanley, *Armenian, Australia & the Great War*, Sydney: New South Publishing, 2016.
Grigoris Balakian, *Armenian Golgotha: A Memoir of the Armenian Genocide, 1915–1918*, trans. Peter Balakian with Aris Sevag, New York: Vintage Books, 2010.

Peter Balakian, *The Burning Tigris: The Armenian Genocide and America's Response*, New York: HarperCollins, 2003.

Donald Bloxham, T*he Great Game of Genocide: Imperialism, Nationalism, and the Destruction of the Ottoman Armenians*, Oxford: Oxford University Press, 2005.

Ashley Kaligian Blunt, *My Name Is Revenge: A Novella and Collected Essays*, Sydney: New South, 2019.

Peter Bogosian, *Operation Nemesis: The Assassination Plot That Avenged the Armenian Genocide*, New York: Little, Brown and Company, 2015.

George A. Bournoutian, *A Concise History of the Armenian People* (Second Edition), Costa Mesa: Mazda, 2003.

Ian Buruma, *The Wages of Guilt: Memories of War in Germany and Japan*, New York: Meridian, 1995.

Tuba Çandar, *Hrant Dink: An Armenian Voice of the Voiceless in Turkey*, New Brunswick, NJ: Transaction Publishers, 2016.

William Henry Cunningham, Charles Archibald Lawrence Treadwell, James Sugden Hanna, *The Wellington Regiment (NZEF) 1914 – 1919*, Wellington: Ferguson & Osborn, 1928.

Vahakn N. Dadrian and Taner Akçam, *Judgment at Istanbul: The Armenian Genocide Trials*, New York: Bergbahn Books, 2011.

Leslie Davis, *The Slaughterhouse Province: An American Diplomat's Report on the Armenian Genocide, 1915 – 1917*, ed. Susan K. Blair, New York: Aristide D. Caratazas, 1989.

Hrant Dink (trans. Nazım Hikmet and Richard Dikbaş), *Two Close Peoples, Two Distant Neighbours*, Istanbul: Hrant Dink Foundation Publications, 2014.

Lt. H. T. B. Drew, *The War Effort of New Zealand*, Auckland: Whitcombe and Tombs, 1923.

Lewis Einstein, *Inside Constantinople: A Diplomatist's Diary during the Dardanelles Expedition, April – September, 1915*, New York: E. P. Dutton, 1918.

Edward J. Erickson, *Ordered to Die: A History of the Ottoman Army in the First World War*, Westport, CT: Greenwood Press, 2001.

Olaf Farschid, Manfred Kropp and Stephan Dahne (eds.), *The First World War as Remembered in the Countries of the Eastern Mediterranean*, Beirut: Orient-Institut, 2006.

Johannes Feichtinger, Franz L. Fillafer and Jan Surman (eds.), *The Worlds of Positivism: A Global Intellectual History, 1770 – 1930*, London: Palgrave Macmillan, 2018.

Charles Ferrall and Harry Ricketts (eds.), *How We Remember: New Zealanders and the First World War*, Wellington: Victoria University Press, 2014.

Raelene Frances and Bruce Scates (eds.), *Beyond Gallipoli: New Perspectives on Anzac*, Melbourne: Monash University Publishing, 2016.

Bill Gammage, *The Broken Years: Australian Soldiers in the Great War*, Canberra: Australian National University Press, 1974.

H. L. Gates (ed.), *Ravished Armenia: The Story of Aurora Mardiganian*, New York: Kingfield Press, 1918.

Ryan Gingeras, *The Fall of the Sultanate: The Great War and the End of the Ottoman Empire 1908–1922*, Oxford: Oxford University Press, 2016.

Ryan Gingeras, *Sorrowful Shores: Violence, Ethnicity, and the End of the Ottoman Empire, 1912–1923*, Oxford: Oxford University Press, 2009.

Fatma Müge Göçek, *Denial of Violence: Ottoman Past, Turkish Present, and Collective Violence against the Armenians 1789 – 2009*, Oxford: Oxford University Press, 2015.

Wolfgang Gust, *The Armenian Genocide: Evidence from the German Foreign Office Archives*, New York: Berghahn Books, 2014.

Avedis Hadjian, *Secret Nation: The Hidden Armenians of Turkey*, London: I.B. Tauris, 2018.

Şükrü Hanioğlu, *Preparation for a Revolution: The Young Turks 1902 – 1908*, Oxford: Oxford University Press, 2001.

Dagmar Herzog (ed.), *Brutality and Desire: War and Sexuality in Europe's Twentieth Century*, New York: Palgrave Macmillan, 2009.

Marjorie Housepian, *Smyrna 1922: The Destruction of a City*, London: Faber & Faber, 1974.

Richard G. Hovannisian (ed.), *The Armenian Genocide: History, Politics Ethics*, Hampshire: Macmillan 1992.

Stefan Ihrig, *Atatürk in the Nazi Imagination*, Cambridge: Belknap Press, 2014.

Dikran Mesrob Kaligian, *Armenian Organization and Ideology under Ottoman Rule: 1908 – 1914*, New Brunswick, NJ: Transaction Publishers, 2009.

Greg Kerr, *Lost Anzacs: The Story of Two Brothers*, Melbourne: Oxford University Press Australia, 1998.

Raymond Kévorkian, *The Armenian Genocide: A Complete History*, London: I.B. Tauris, 2011.

Hans-Lukas Kieser, *Talaat Pasha: A Father of Modern Turkey, Architect of Genocide*, Princeton, NJ: Princeton University Press, 2018.

Hans-Lukas Kieser and Dominik J. Schaller (eds.), *Der Völkermord an den Armeniern und die Shoah*, Zurich: Chronos, 2002.

Marilyn Lake and Henry Reynolds with Mark McKenna and Joy Damousi, *What's Wrong with Anzac? The Militarisation of Australian History*, Sydney: New South, 2010.

Jennifer Lawless, *Kismet: The Story of the Gallipoli Prisoners of War*, Melbourne: Australian Scholarly, 2015.

Johannes Lepsius, *Armenia and Europe: An Indictment*, London: Hodder & Stoughton, 1897.

Primo Levi, *If This Is a Man/The Truce*, trans. Stuart Woolf, London: Sphere Books, 1987.

Peter Liddle, *Men of Gallipoli: The Dardanelles and Gallipoli Experience August 1914 to January 1916*, Wiltshire: David & Charles, 1998.

Patrick Lindsay, *The Spirit of Gallipoli: The Birth of the Anzac Legend*, Victoria: Hardie Grant Books, 2006.
Deborah Lipstadt, *Denying the Holocaust: The Growing Assault on Truth and Memory*, London: Penguin Books, 2016.
Steven Loveridge (ed.), *New Zealand Society at War 1914 – 1918*, Wellington: Victoria University Press, 2016.
Leslie Henry Luscombe, *The Story of Harold Earl – Australian*, Brisbane: W.R. Smith & Paterson, 1970.
R. F. Lushington, *A Prisoner with the Turks 1915 – 1918*, London: Simpkin, Marshall, Hamilton, Kent, 1923.
A. L. Macfie, *The End of the Ottoman Empire: 1908 – 1923*, Harlow: Addison Wesley Longman, 1998.
Andrew Mango, *Atatürk: The Biography of the Founder of Modern Turkey*, New York: The Overlook Press, 2000.
Michael Mann, *The Dark Side of Democracy: Explaining Ethnic Cleansing*, Cambridge: Cambridge University Press, 2011.
John Masefield, *Gallipoli*, New York: Macmillan, 1916.
Bedross Der Matossian, *Shattered Dreams of Revolution: From Liberty to Violence in the Late Ottoman Empire*, Stanford, CA: Stanford University Press, 2014.
Gavin McLean, Ian McGibbon and Kynan Gentry (eds.), *The Penguin Book of New Zealanders at War*, Auckland: Penguin Books, 2009.
Sean McMeekin, *The Ottoman Endgame: War, Revolution and the Making of the Modern Middle East, 1908 – 1923*, London: Penguin Books, 2016.
Donald E. Miller and Lorna Touryan Miller, *Survivors: An Oral History of the Armenian Genocide*, Berkeley: University of California Press, 1999.
Henry Morgenthau, *Ambassador Morgenthau's Story*, Doubleday, NY: Page & Company, 1918.
Edward Opotiki Mousley, *The Secrets of a Kuttite: An Authentic Story of Kut, Adventures in Captivity and Stamboul Intrigue*, London: John Lane, 1922.
Louise Nalbandian, *The Armenian Revolutionary Movement: The Development of Armenian Political Parties through the Nineteenth Century*, Berkeley: University of California Press, 1963.
Rafael de Nogales, *Four Years beneath the Crescent*, New York: Charles Scribner's Sons, 1926.
Diana Preston, *A Higher Form of Killing: Six Weeks in World War I That Forever Changed the Nature of Warfare*, New York: Bloomsbury Press, 2015.
M. F. Lloyd Pritchard, *An Economic History of New Zealand to 1939*, Auckland: Collins, 1970.
Christopher Pugsley, *Gallipoli: The New Zealand Story*, Auckland: Oratia Books, 2016.
Donald Quataert, *The Ottoman Empire: 1700 – 1922* (Second Edition), Cambridge: Cambridge University Press, 2005.
Raffi (trans. Jane S. Wingate), *The Fool*, Los Angeles, CA: IndoEuropean Publishing, 2009.

Geoffrey Robertson Q. C., *An Inconvenient Genocide*, Sydney: Vintage, 2014.
Eugene Rogan, *The Fall of the Ottomans: The Great War in the Middle East 1914 – 1920*, London: Penguin Books, 2016.
Malcolm Ross and Noel Ross, *Light and Shade in War*, London: Edward Arnold, 1916.
Victoria Rowe, *A History of Armenian Women's Writing: 1880 – 1922*, London: Cambridge Scholars Press, 2003.
Aidan Russell (ed.), *Truth, Silence and Violence in Emerging States: Histories of the Unspoken*, London: Routledge, 2018.
Philippe Sands, *East West Street: On the Origins of Genocide and Crimes against Humanity*, London: Weidenfeld & Nicolson, 2016.
Jean Paul Sartre, *On Genocide*, Boston, MA: Beacon Press, 1968.
Cap. S. Savige, *Stalky's Forlorn Hope*, Melbourne: McCubbin, 1920.
Dominik J. Schaller and Jurgen Zimmerer (eds.), *Late Ottoman Genocides: The Dissolution of the Ottoman Empire and Young Turkish Population and Extermination Policies*, New York: Routledge, 2009.
Stanford J. Shaw and Ezel Kural Shaw, *History of the Ottoman Empire and Modern Turkey, Volume II: Reform, Revolution, and Republic: The Rise of Modern Turkey 1808-1975*, Cambridge: Cambridge University Press, 1977.
Mary Lewis Shedd, *The Measure of a Man: The Life of William Ambrose Shedd, Missionary to Persia*, New York: George H. Doran Company, 1922.
Barry Stone, *Secret Army: An Elite Force, a Secret Mission, a Fleet of Model-T Fords, a Far-Flung Corner of WWI*, Crows Nest: Allen & Unwin, 2017.
Ronald Grigory Suny, Fatma Müge Göçek, and Norman M. Naimark (eds.), *A Question of Genocide: Armenians and Turks at the End of the Ottoman Empire*, New York: Oxford University Press, 2011.
Ronald Grigor Suny, *'They Can Live in the Desert but Nowhere Else': A History of the Armenian Genocide*, Princeton, NJ: Princeton University Press, 2015.
Colin Tatz (ed.), *Genocide Perspectives IV: Essays on Holocaust and Genocide*, The Australian Institute for Holocaust & Genocide Studies, 2012.
Alistair Thomson, *Anzac Memories: Living with the Legend*, Melbourne: Oxford University Press Australia, 1995.
Arnold Toynbee, *The Western Question in Greece and Turkey: A Study in the Contact of Civilization*, New York: Howard Fertig, 1970.
Uğur Ümit Üngör, *The Making of Modern Turkey: Nation and State in Eastern Anatolia, 1913 – 1950*, Oxford: Oxford University Press, 2012.
Uğur Ümit Üngör and Mehmet Polatel, *Confiscation and Destruction: The Young Turk Seizure of Armenian Property*, London: Bloomsbury, 2011.
Clarence D. Ussher, *An American Physician in Turkey: A Narrative of Adventures in Peace and in War*, Boston, MA: Houghton Mifflin, 1917.
Thomas De Waal, *Great Catastrophe: Armenians and Turks in the Shadow of Genocide*, Oxford: Oxford University Press, 2015.
Christopher J. Walker, *Armenia: The Survival of a Nation* (Second Edition), London: Routledge, 1990.

Keith David Watenpaugh, *Bread from Stones: The Middle East and the Making of Modern Humanitarianism*, Oakland: University of California Press, 2015.

Alyson Wharton, *The Architects of Ottoman Constantinople: The Balyan Family and the History of Ottoman Architecture*, London: I.B. Tauris, 2015.

Zabel Yessayan (trans. G. M. Goshgarian, eds. Judith Saryan, Danila Jebejian Terpanjian, and Joy Renjilian-Burgy), *In the Ruins: The 1909 Massacres of Armenians in Adana, Turkey*, Boston, MA: AIWA Press, 2016.

Krikor Zohrab (trans. Jack Antreassian), *Voice of Conscience: The Stories of Krikor Zohrab*, New York: St. Vartan Press, 1983.

Erik J. Zürcher, *Turkey: A Modern History*, New York: St Martin's Press, 1994.

Erik J. Zürcher, *The Young Turk Legacy and Nation Building: From the Ottoman Empire to Atatürk's Turkey*, London: I.B. Tauris, 2010.

ARTICLES & THESES

Idad Ben Aharon (2015) 'A Unique Denial: Israel's Foreign Policy and the Armenian Genocide', *British Journal of Middle Eastern Studies*, 42:4, 638–54.

Taner Akçam (2005) 'Anatomy of a Crime: The Turkish Historical Society's Manipulation of Archival Documents', *Journal of Genocide Research*, 7:2, 255–77.

Taner Akçam (2008) 'Guenter Lewy's *The Armenian Massacres in Ottoman Turkey*', *Genocide Studies and Prevention*, 3:1, 111–45.

Taner Akçam (2019) 'When Was the Decision to Annihilate the Armenians Taken?', *Journal of Genocide Research*, published online 17 July 2019.

Ayhan Aktar (1996) 'Economic Nationalism in Turkey: The Formative Years, 1912 – 1925', *Boğaziçi Journal, Review of Social, Economic and Administrative Studies*, 10:1 – 2, 263–90.

Riccardo Armillei, Nikki Marczak, and Panayiotis Diamadis (2016) 'Forgotten and Concealed: The Emblematic Cases of the Assyrian and Romani Genocides', *Genocide Studies and Prevention: An International Journal*, 10:2, 98–120.

Ozan Arslan (2014) 'The "Bon Pour L'Orient" Front: Analysis of Russia's Anticipated Victory over the Ottoman Empire in World War I', *Middle East Critique*, 23:2, 175–88.

Arlene Avakian and Hourig Attarian (2015) 'Imagining Our Foremothers: Memory and Evidence of Women Victims and Survivors of the Armenian Genocide: A Dialogue', *European Journal of Women's Studies*, 22:4, 476–83.

Vahagn Avedian (2012) 'State Identity, Continuity, and Responsibility: The Ottoman Empire, the Republic of Turkey and the Armenian Genocide', *The European Journal of International Law*, 23:3, 797–820.

Vicken Babkenian (2009) 'A Humanitarian Journey: The Reverend James Edwin Cresswell and the Armenian Relief Fund', *Journal of the Historical Society of South Australia*, 37, 61–75.

Vicken Babkenian (2010) '"An SOS from beyond Gallipoli": Victoria and the Armenian Relief Movement', *Victorian Historical Journal*, 81:2, 250–76.

Vicken Babkenian (2015) 'Australian Women and the Armenian Relief Movement', *Journal of the Royal Australian Historical Society*, 101:2, 111–33.

Peter Balakian (2013) 'Raphael Lemkin, Cultural Destruction, and the Armenian Genocide', *Holocaust and Genocide Studies*, 27:1, 57–89.

Myriam Bienenstock (October 2010) 'Is There a Duty of Memory? Reflections on a French Debate', *Modern Judaism: A Journal of Jewish Ideas & Experience*, 30:3, 332–47.

Donald Bloxham (2002) 'Three Imperialisms and a Turkish Nationalism: International Stresses, Imperial Disintegration and the Armenian Genocide', *Patterns of Prejudice*, 36:4, 37–58.

Donald Bloxham (2003) 'The Armenian Genocide of 1915 – 1916: Cumulative Radicalization and the Development of a Destruction Policy', *Past & Present*, 181, 141–91.

Donald Bloxham (2006) 'The Roots of American Genocide Denial: Near Eastern Geopolitics and the Interwar Armenian Question', *Journal of Genocide Research*, 8:1, 27–49.

Donald Bloxham (2007) 'Terrorism and Imperial Decline: The Ottoman-Armenian Case', *European Review of History*, 14:3, 301–24.

Stephen J. Clarke (1994) 'The One Day of the Year: Anzac Day in Aotearoa/New Zealand 1946 – 1990', MA thesis, University of Otago.

Vahakan N. Dadrian (1994) 'The Secret Young Turk Ittihadist Conference and the Decision for the World War I Genocide of the Armenians', *Journal of Political and Military Sociology*, 22:1, 173–202.

George Frederick Davis (2008) 'Anzac Day Meanings and Memories: New Zealand, Australian and Turkish Perspectives on a Day of Commemoration in the Twentieth Century', PhD thesis, University of Otago.

Jennifer M. Dixon (2010) 'Defending the Nation? Maintaining Turkey's Narrative of the Armenian Genocide', *South European Society and Politics*, 15:3, 467–85.

Laura Dugan, Julie Y. Huang, Gary LaFree and Clark McCauley (2008) 'Sudden Desistance from Terrorism: The Armenian Secret Army for the Liberation of Armenia and the Justice Commandos of the Armenian Genocide', *Dynamics of Asymmetric Conflict*, 1:3, 231–49.

Patrick Dumberry (2014) 'The Consequences of Turkey Being the "Continuing" State of the Ottoman Empire in Terms of International Responsibility for Internationally Wrongful Acts', *International Criminal Law Review* 14, 261–73.

Thomas Hugh Greenshields (1978) 'The Settlement of Armenian Refugees in Syria and Lebanon, 1915 – 1939', Durham theses, Durham University.

Doğan Gürpınar (2016) 'The Manufacturing of Denial: The Making of the Turkish "Official Thesis" on the Armenian Genocide between 1974 and 1990', *Journal of Balkan and Near Eastern Studies*, 18:3, 217–40.

Wolfgang Gust (2012) 'The Question of an Armenian Revolution and the Radicalization of the Committee of Union and Progress toward the Armenian Genocide', *Genocide Studies and Prevention: An International Journal*, 7:2, 251–64.

Joanna Hyslop (2013) '"A Brief and Personal Account": The Evidence of Charles Dobson on the Destruction of the City of Smyrna in September 1922', *Crisis, Criticism and Critique in Contemporary Greek Studies*, 16:17, 69–89.

Susan L. Karamanian (2014) 'Economic-Legal Perspectives on the Armenian Genocide', *International Criminal Law Review*, 14, 242–60.

Vahe G. Kateb (2003) 'Australian Press Coverage of the Armenian Genocide 1915 – 1923', MA thesis, Graduate School of Journalism, University of Wollongong Thesis Collection.

Murat Kaya (2014) 'Western Interventions and Formation of the Young Turks' Siege Mentality', *Middle East Critique*, 23:2, 127–45.

Ümit Kurt (2015) 'Legal and Official Plunder of Armenian and Jewish Properties in Comparative Perspective: The Armenian Genocide and the Holocaust', *Journal of Genocide Research*, 17:3, 305–26.

Ümit Kurt (2016) 'Cultural Erasure: The Absorption and Forced Conversion of Armenian Women and Children, 1915-1916', Études arméniennes contemporaines, 7 | 2016, Online since 30 May 2017.

Jo Laycock (2015) 'Beyond National Narratives? Centenary Histories, the First World War and the Armenian Genocide', *Revolutionary Russia*, 28:2, 93–117.

E. J. Lemon (2015) 'Dunsterforce or Dunsterfarce? Re-evaluating the British Mission to Baku, 1918', *First World War Studies*, 6:2, 133–49.

Jenny Macleod and Gizem Tongo (2016) 'Between Memory and History: Remembering Johnnies, Mehmets, and the Armenians', *Beyond Gallipoli: New Perspectives on Anzac* ed. Raelene Frances and Bruce Scates (Melbourne: Monash University Publishing).

Nazan Maksudyan (2009) 'Walls of Silence: Translating the Armenian Genocide into Turkish and Self-Censorship', *Critique*, 37:4, 635–49.

Marc A. Mamigonian (2015) 'Academic Denial of the Armenian Genocide in American Scholarship: Denialism as Manufactured Controversy', *Genocide Studies International*, 9:1, 61–82.

Selina L. Mangassarian (2016) '100 Years of Trauma: The Armenian Genocide and Intergenerational Cultural Trauma', *Journal of Aggression, Maltreatment & Trauma*, 25:4, 371–81.

Bedross Der Matossian (2011) 'From Bloodless Revolution to Bloody Counterrevolution: The Adana Massacres of 1909', Faculty Publications, Department of History, University of Nebraska Lincoln, Summer 2011.

Bedross Der Matossian (2011) 'The Taboo within the Taboo: The Fate of "Armenian Capital" at the End of the Ottoman Empire', *European Journal of Turkish Studies* [Online], 1–23.

Bedross Der Matossian (2015) 'Explaining the Unexplainable: Recent Trends in the Armenian Genocide Historiography', *Journal of Levantine Studies*, 5:2, 143–66.

Daniel Marc Segesser (2008) 'Dissolve or Punish? The International Debate amongst Jurists and Publicists on the Consequences of the Armenian Genocide for the Ottoman Empire, 1915-23', *Journal of Genocide Research*, 10:1, 95-110.

Maureen Sharpe (1981), 'Anzac Day in New Zealand: 1916 - 1939', *NZ Journal of History*, 15:2, 97-114.

Gabrielle Simm (2016) 'The Paris People's Tribunal and the Istanbul Trials: Archives of the Armenian Genocide', *Leiden Journal of International Law*, 29, 245-68.

Roger W. Smith, Eric Markusen and Robert Jay Lifton (1995) 'Professional Ethics and the Denial of the Armenian Genocide', *Holocaust and Genocide Studies*, 9:1, 1-22.

Henry C. Theriault (2012) 'The Armenian Genocide's Outstanding Damage and the Complexities of Repair', *Armenian Review* 53:1-4, 121-66.

David Trudinger (2018) 'The View from Constantinople, 1915: The Australian, the Ambassador and the Agent on Gallipoli and the Armenian Genocide', *History Australia*, 15:4, 725-43.

Michelle Tusan (2014) '"Crimes against Humanity": Human Rights, the British Empire, and the Origins of Response to the Armenian Genocide', *American Historical Review*, 119:1, 47-77.

Fatma Ulgen (2010) 'Reading Mustafa Kemal Atatürk on the Armenian Genocide of 1915', *Patterns of Prejudice*, 44:4, 369-91.

Uğur Ümit Üngör (2012) 'Orphans, Converts, and Prostitutes: Social Consequences of War and Persecution in the Ottoman Empire, 1914-1923', *War in History*, 19:2, 173-92.

Uğur Ümit Üngör (2014) 'Lost in Commemoration: The Armenian Genocide in Memory and Identity', *Patterns of Prejudice*, 48:2, 147-66.

David Welky (2006) 'Global Hollywood versus National Pride: The Battle to Film the Forty Days of Musa Dagh', *Film Quarterly Spring*, 59:3, 35-43.

Yücel Yiğit (2014) 'The *Teşkilat-ı Mahsusa* and World War I', *Middle East Critique*, 23:2, 157-74.

Erik J. Zürcher (1996) 'Between Death and Desertion: The Experience of the Ottoman Soldier in World War I', *Turcica*, 28, 235-58.

Index

Abdülhamid II 14, 15–16, 17–18, 25, 29, 35; attempted assassination of 26;
Abdülmecid 10
Action Army 35, 36–7
Adana, pogrom of 1909 36–9
Adelaide *Advertiser* 106
Adelaide Register 106
Afionkarahissar 95–6, 98
Agamemnon 59, 131, 133
The Age 51, 106, 132
Agos 193–4
Akçam, Taner 193, 206, 209
Albania, Albanians 39, 40
Aleppo 19, 97, 99, 133, 135, 136, 150, 163, 167, 169, 170
Alice in Hungerland 152
Allen, James 113–14, 131
Allsopp, Frank 99
Anatolia 3, 6, 7, 11, 17, 20, 23, 32, 41, 45, 49, 52, 56, 68, 70, 72, 75, 82, 83, 84, 94, 95, 108, 118, 131, 141, 143, 149, 154, 158, 160, 161, 167, 172, 173, 209
Ankara 60, 69, 70, 93, 97, 103, 131, 139, 145, 146, 150, 154, 181, 190, 198
Antoyan, Souren 171
Anzac Book 116
Anzac Day 1, 66, 96; origins of 196–7
Anzacs (Australia New Zealand Army Corps) 57, 64, 65–70, 131; encounters with Armenians 56–8, 89–104; mythology 195–7, 203–4
Arabs 6, 23, 31, 33, 45, 56, 57, 69, 84, 87, 90, 97, 100, 104, 112, 118, 119, 136, 143, 149, 170
Ardern, Jacinda 206–7
The Argus 51, 106, 108
Armenakans 16
Armenian Genocide Memorial Day 2, 186–187
Armenian Genocide, aftermath 133–7; architecture of 71–2; arrest of the elite, *see* Red Sunday; cultural destruction 82–3; death camps 69, 83–6; death toll 2, 162; denial of 3, 187–94; deportations 56–7, 69, 76–80; 'dual mechanism' 72; early planning 54–5; expropriation and destruction of property 82–3; final triggers 62–4; forced assimilation 81; forced religious conversion 81; killing fields 72–4; mercy during the 79–80; purging army of Armenians 55–6; sexual violence 80
Armenian Golgotha 132
Armenian Question 14, 20, 47–8
Armenian relief movement 3, 107–11, 133–7, 146–8, 151–4, 155–6
Armenian Revolutionary Federation (ARF) 16–17, 22, 26–7, 28, 31, 33, 35, 39–40, 47, 50, 66, 119
Armenians, Armenian Soviet Socialist Republic 182–3; class composition 7–9; feminism 11; First Republic of 119, 148–9; First World War and 50–2, 54; origins of 5–6; post-Soviet independence 191; self-defence 17, 50, 86–7; Tanzimât and 11; terrorism 187; under Russian rule 10–11
Ashmead-Bartlett, Ellis 196
Assembly of Turkish American Associations (ATAA) 189
Assyria, Assyrian Genocide, Assyrians 2, 7, 8, 11, 14, 45, 119–30, 135, 137, 138, 145, 167, 180, 181, 188, 195, 203, 204, 205, 207, 209
The Auction of Souls 147
Auckland 51, 99, 100, 106, 107, 109, 148, 152, 153, 175
Auckland Star 106, 152
Australasian Orphanage 163–77
Australia, Australians, Armenian relief efforts 108–11, 134, 146–8, 151–4, 155–6; denial of Armenian Genocide 204–8; end of First World War 131–2; entry into First World War 51–2; newspaper coverage of Armenian

Genocide 105–16; relationship with Turkey, *see* Special Relationship
Australian War Memorial (AWM) 198, 204
Avakian, Asdghig 168–71
Axis Rule in Occupied Europe 184
Azerbaijan, Azeris 119, 191

Baghdad 84, 97, 100, 101, 122, 128, 131
Baghdadbahn 49, 94–5, 103
Baku 120, 121, 122, 129, 148
Balakian, Haroutiun 110
Balakian, Krikoris 65–7, 76, 102, 132–3
Balkan Wars, First and Second 40–2, 45
Balkans 6, 14, 27, 29, 40, 42, 45, 47
Barrell, Raymond 123
Barry, Maggie 199–200
Barton, Clara 20
Barton, James L. 107
Bayar, Celal 180
Bean, Charles 90–1, 116
Beirut 2, 159, 164, 169, 171, 176
Belgium, Belgians 109, 111, 112, 113, 152, 162
Berlin 11, 49, 110, 131, 183
Bernau, Auguste 85
Beylerian, Marie 18, 23, 68
Bishop, Julie 207
Black Sea 5, 52, 143
Boer War 52
Boghosian, Dr. 65–6
Britain, British Empire 47, 71, 135, liberal interventionism 10
Brophy, Frank 123
Bryce, Earnest and Mary 156, 176
Bryce, James 105–6, 108
Bulgaria, Bulgarians 7, 13, 14, 15, 16, 18, 19, 27, 33, 39, 40, 41, 42, 131
Bulgarian Horrors 13–14, 18, 19

Cabot, Dolce 21–2
Campbell, Alan 202–3
Canbolat, İsmail 140
Carruthers, Joseph 112
Carter, Jimmy 191
Caspian Sea 5, 52
Caucasus 6, 10, 11, 12, 14, 44, 52, 53, 54, 90, 117, 118, 119, 143, 149, 183
Caucasus Committee 119
Çavuşoğlu, Mevlüt 191
Çelik, Gülseren 205

Cemal Paşa 63
Çetin, Fethiye 209
Cevdet Bey 58–9, 60–2
Christchurch *Press* 109, 115
Chunuk Bair 1, 91–2, 98, 121, 143, 208
Churchill, Winston 57, 59
Cilicia 6, 36, 133, 141, 145, 149, 150, 154, 164
Clinton, Bill 191
Committee on Armenian Atrocities, *see* Near East Relief
Committee of Union and Progress 2, 28, 29, 33–4, 39, 55, 56; founding of 26; coup of 1913 42; siege mentality of 62–4
The Communist Manifesto (Marx & Engels) 16
Comte, Auguste 26
Convention on the Prevention and Punishment of the Crime of Genocide 185
Counterrevolution of 1909 35–6, 39
Creedon, Daniel 104
Cresswell, James 171–4
Cullen, Blair 57–8

Dadrian, Vahakn 187
Daghalian, Levon 164
Daily Chronicle 162
Dardanelles 40, 49, 63, 96, 103, 132, 154; naval battle (1915) 59–60
David, Lady Cara 146, 152
Davie, Reginald 91–3, 98–9, 104
Davis, Leslie 72–4, 107
Davutoğlu, Ahmet 205–6
de Nogales, Rafael 61–2, 97
Der Zor, *see* Armenian Genocide, death camps
Dilanian, Haroutiun 170
Dink, Hrant 192–4, 208–9
Directorate for the Settlement of Tribes and Immigrants (İAMM) 47–8, 71, 72, 180
Diyarbakır 7, 19, 44, 70, 72, 73, 74, 75, 79, 142, 147, 210
Dobson, Charles 156–9
Dodge, Cleveland 107
Dominion 106
Dörtyol 56
Dunstan Times 106
Dunsterforce 120–30
Dunsterville, Lionel 120, 129

Earnshaw, William 113
Egypt 56-8
Elias, Sian 109
Enver, Ismail 27, 29, 31, 39, 49, 52, 53-4, 55, 59, 62, 71, 93, 100, 118, 131, 140
Erdoğan, Recep Tayyip 191-2
Erzerum 33, 47, 52, 53, 72, 73, 87, 119, 145
Ethnic 'cleansing' 42-3
Eti, Ali Rıza 54
Evening Post 21, 107, 115-16, 153
Evening Star 107
Evren, Kenan 198

Fielding 91, 104, 174
Fifth Commission 139
First Congress of Ottoman Opposition 25, 33
Fisher, Andrew 51
Free Lance 115
Freud, Sigmund 195

Gallipoli 1, 2, 3, 46, 56, 63-4, 97, 115, 117, 121, 131, 143, 154, 202, 205; Campaign 65-70, 89-92, 100
Gallipoli (Moorehead) 188
Gallipoli (Weir) 199
Garo, Armen 22, 33
Genocide, creation of word 3, 184
George, David Lloyd 137, 141, 154
Georgia, Georgians 53, 119
Germans, Germany 3, 11, 19, 27, 44, 47, 49, 50, 53, 56, 59, 61, 63, 65, 94, 104, 105, 111, 112, 113, 114, 115, 116, 117, 118, 121, 129, 131, 132, 137, 141, 170, 183, 184, 192
Gillard, Julia 199
Gladstone, William 14, 20
Glanville, Edith 176
Gökalp, Ziyâ 44-5, 81, 140, 180
Goldstein, Vida 146
Greece, Greeks 2, 5, 6, 7, 8, 10, 15, 18, 31, 33, 34, 39, 40, 42, 45, 46-7, 52, 57, 59, 72, 90, 92, 94, 95, 103, 133, 137, 138, 141, 142, 143, 145, 154-9, 160-1, 164, 167, 172, 173-4, 180, 188, 198, 203, 204, 205, 207, 209
Grey River Argus 20-1
The Guardian, Manchester Guardian 107
Gunn, George 93
Gunson, James 153

Hague Conventions 137-8
Hakobian, Hakob (Raffi) 12-13
Halajian, Bedros 35
Halefoğlu, Vahit 198-9
Halil Paşa 55, 118, 142
Hamidian Terror 17-23, 53, 108, 109
Hamilton, Ian 91
Harney, Jeffrey 93
Harput 7, 72, 75, 77, 107, 167, 168, 171
Havard, Jonas 104
Hawke, Bob 198
Hidden Nation (Hadjian) 209
Hitler, Adolf 184
Hobson's Bay 156, 159-60, 165, 171
Hoff, Nicolai 47, 50
Holocaust 184-5, 187
Hovannisian, Richard 187
Hutton, Isobel 133-4

İnönü, İsmet 180
Institute of Turkish Studies (ITS) 189
Iran 118, 119, 126, 127
Iraq, Mesopotamia 94, 95, 97, 100, 121, 128, 141, 167, 191
İskenderun 55-6
Istanbul 6, 8, 18, 19, 22, 31, 35, 37, 41, 48
Italy 121, 133, 141, 179
Ittidal 36
İzmir, burning of 156-9

Jackson, Jesse B. 84-5
Jebb, Eglantyne 146
Jeppe, Karen 135, 136
John, Cecilia 146
July Crisis 49

Kâmil Paşa 34
Karabekir, Kâzım 118-19, 143, 148-9, 180
Karageuzian, Setrag 140-1
Karakol 142
Kars 53, 118, 119, 149
Kaya, Şükrü 71, 82, 180, 200-3
Kemal, Mustafa (Atatürk) 3, 27-8, 39, 67, 91-2, 143-6, 149-50, 154-5, 157-9, 160-2, 179-82, 195, 200-3
Kerensky, Alexander 118
Kerkyasharian, Bedros 89

Kerr, George 95
Kerr, Stanley 136
Khrimian, Mkrtich 11–12, 14–15, 16, 23, 31
King, Hilda 156, 165, 167, 176–7
Kipling, Rudyard 44
Kitchener, Herbert 57
Knudsen, John and Lydia 163–7
Komitas 23, 32, 65–7
Kurds 6, 8, 15, 17, 33, 44, 50, 52, 53, 62, 77, 78, 117, 120 124, 136, 141, 180, 210
Kut el-Amara 100–1

Lake Urmia 5, 119, 123
Lanser, Henry 57
The Last Post 1, 197
League of Nations 125
Lemkin, Raphael 3, 183–6
Lenin, Vladimir 118
Lepsius, Johannes 19
Levi, Primo 210
Libya 39, 40, 43
Lifton, Robert Jay 187, 189–90
Lipstadt, Deborah 208
Lone Pine 1
Lord Mayor's Fund (LMF) 108, 109, 124–33, 148, 150
Lowry, Heath 189–90
Luke, JP 109
Luscombe, Leslie 93, 95, 98
Lushington, Reginald Frances 92, 93, 103–4
Lusitania 105
Luxford, John 90

Mackay, Jessie 22, 109–10
MacKinnon, Eleanor 146, 152
Mahmud II 10
Manukian, Aram 58, 60–2, 119
Maraş 145–6, 170
Marashlian, Levon 187
Mardiganian, Aurora 75, 147
Marxism 44
Masefield, John 64
Massey, William 51, 111–12, 131, 153–4, 174, 175, 205, 206
Mazhar Commission 139–40
Mazmanian, Aghavni 77–8
McCallum, Richard 113–14
Mechian, Setrag 57
Mehmed V 35

Mehmed VI 179
Melbourne 51, 93, 110, 111, 132, 134, 146, 147, 152, 156, 165, 187
The Mercury 106
Metternich, Paul Wolff 81
Michanian, Vahan 57–8
Ministry of Foreign Affairs and Trade (NZ – MFAT) 206
Moorehead, Alan 188
Morgenthau, Henry 59, 62, 107–8, 186
Mousley, Edward Opotiki 100–3
Mt Ararat 5, 149
Muhtar, Ahmed 40, 41
Murphy, Bernard 123
Musa Dağ 86, 113

Nalbandian, Mattheos 138–9
Nash, James 174
National Council of Women 146
Nationalism 9–10, 15, 42–5
Nazım Paşa 42
Nâzım, Dr. 26, 28, 33, 35, 39, 43, 131, 140, 180
Near East Relief (NER) 107–8, 133–7, 150, 155–6, 159–60, 166–7, 171–3
The Nek 91
Nelson Evening Mail 114
New South Wales 112, 133, 146, 147, 176, 204, 205, 206
New Zealand, New Zealanders, Armenian relief efforts 108–11, 134, 146–8, 151–4, 155–6, 174–6; denial of Armenian Genocide 204–8; end of First World War 131–2; entry into First World War 51–2; newspaper coverage of Armenian Genocide 105–16; relationship with Turkey, see Special Relationship
New Zealand Herald 106, 201
New Zealand Times 112
Nicholas, Grand Duke 54, 56
Nicol, Robert Kenneth 120–3, 125–8, 167
Niepage, Dr. Martin 83–4
Nietzsche 44
Nile, Fred 204
Nimmo, Alexander 123, 126–8
Niyazi, Ahmed 29
Northern Miner 106
Nuri Paşa 118

Ohannesian, Ashkhen 60–1
Okosdinossian, Aram 89
Once on Chunuk Bair (Shadbolt) 199
Orr, S. Robertson 174
Otago Daily Times 148, 174
Ottoman Bank raid 22, 33
Ottoman Empire, constitution 14, 25, 29; decline 9–10, 15, 17, 25–6, 40–2; elections 33, 40; entry into First World War 49–50; fall of 179; founding of 6; genocide trials 137–41; millet system 6–7; nationalism and 11, 12–13; occupation of 133; parliament 33–4, 71, 138–9; partition of 137; surrender 131
Ottoman Liberty Society 27–8
Ottomanism 10, 26
Özdemir, Cem 192

Palmerston North 174, 175
Pamuk, Orhan 194
Pankhurst, Adela 146
Pan-Islamism 16
Pan-Turanism 44, 118
Pan-Turkism, *see* pan-Turanism
Papazian, Hrach 85
Papazian, Vahan 33, 50, 58
Passchendaele 121
Pelorus Guardian 115
Perth 156
Peters, Winston 199
Petros, Agha 122–3, 125
Poland 109, 111, 112, 183, 184
Pope France 191
Pope, Ley 89
Prahran 108
Prince Sabaheddin 25, 28, 33
Prisoners of War 3, 89–104
Pukeahu National War Memorial Park 199

Reagan, Ronald 191
Red Sunday 2, 65–70, 110, 143, 146, 199, 206
Reform Plan (1914) 47–8
Reilly, Hugh 97–100, 101
Renda, Abdülhalik 180
Reşid, Dr. Mehmed 74–5, 142
Revolution of 1908 28–34
Rıza, Ahmed 26, 28, 33

Robertson, William 121
Robinson, Emily 135–6
Roosevelt, Theodore 117
Ross, Malcolm 46, 90–1
Rössler, Walter 56
Russia 16, 22, 27, 29, 40, 47, 49, 50, 52–4, 118; irredentism 10, 14
Russian Revolution 118

Sâbis, Ali Ihsan 118, 120, 129, 180
Said Halim Paşa 42, 69, 72, 139, 140
Şakir, Bahaeddin 26, 33, 39–40, 43, 52, 54–5, 64, 71–2, 131, 140
Samsun 143, 155
Sarıkamış, battle of 53–4
Sason 17, 18
Save the Children Fund (SCF) 146–8
Savige, Stanley 122–3, 125–8
Searle, Edith 108–9
Second Congress of Ottoman Opposition 28
Serbia, Serbs 7, 10, 18, 33, 39, 40, 42, 109, 111, 112, 113, 162
Seringiulian, Vartkes 33, 39, 40, 50, 69–70
Sharpe, Maureen 197
Shedd, Dr. William 119–20, 123–4, 127
Shedd, Mary Lewis 120, 123–4, 126, 130
Shoebridge, Albert 91–2
Sivas 7, 72, 77, 90
Smith, Armstrong 175–6
Social Democrats 16–17, 18–19, 22, 23, 26, 66
South Canterbury Times 21
Special Organization (*Teşkîlât-ı Mahsûsa*) 46, 52, 54, 139, 142, 155; creation of 40; as killing squads 72
Special Relationship 3, 203, 208; creation of 197–200
Spooner, Gee 114
Starnes, Fred 128
Stranger among Friends 171
Sub-Directorate for Deportees 85
Sullivan, JR 114–15
The Sun 196
Sunday Times 147
Surgenor, William 91–2
Sydney 1, 57, 90, 111, 132, 134, 146, 147, 150, 152, 153, 156, 175, 187, 205
Sydney Morning Herald 106, 167

Taksim Square 31
Talât, Mehmed 27, 31, 33, 35, 39, 42, 43–5, 50, 52–3, 55, 64, 68–70, 71–2, 75, 80, 81, 93, 131, 140
Tanzimât reforms 10–13
Tarakena Bay 1, 199
Te Papa 204
Ternon, Yves 187
Tollan, Henry 123
Townshend, Charles 97, 100
Toynbee, Arnold 187
Trabzon 19, 140
Treaty of Berlin 14–15, 18
Treaty of Brest-Litovsk 118
Treaty of Lausanne 161
Treaty of Sèvres 141, 149
Treaty of Versailles 141
Trentham 121, 130
Trotsky, Leon 41
Tsitsernakaberd, Armenian Genocide Memorial 2, 186
Turkish nationalism, demography and 45; Grand National Assembly 146; National Pact 145; origins of 43–5; resistance to Allied occupation 141–2, 143–6, 149–50
Turkish Republic, Turks, continuity with CUP 180; denial of genocide 181–94; founding of 179; ideology 179–80; relationship with Australia and New Zealand, *see* Special Relationship

United Nations 185, 186
United States of America (US) 11, 20, 105, 108, 117, 150, 184, 186, 189, 191, 205
Urmia 119–20, 123–6, 129, 167, 180
Ussher, Clarence D. 59, 60–2

Van 5, 11, 16, 31, 33, 50, 58–9, 119, 129 siege of 60–2
Varoujan, Daniel 70
Varvarian, Eugenie 140–1
Victoria 95, 96, 108, 110, 111, 122
Victorian Friends of Armenia (VFA) 110
von Lossow, Otto 118–19

von Sanders, Otto Liman 49, 53, 92
von Wangeheim, Hans 63
Vramian, Arshak 33, 58–9, 60–2

Waikato Times 106
War of Independence 154–5, 157–9, 160–2
Ward, Joseph 131
Ward, Raymond 57
Webb, Richard 137
Wegner, Armin T. 84, 186
Wellington 51, 91, 107, 109, 112, 114, 121, 130, 131, 148, 153, 163, 175, 198, 199
Wellington Māori Council 198
Westenenk, Louis Constant 47
Wheat, John Harrison 96
White, Thomas Walter 97–100, 101, 152
Wiesel, Elie 208
Wilford, Thomas Mason 113, 131–2
Wilhelm II 49
Williams, Harold 162
Wilson, Woodrow 108, 117, 141
Wirt, Loyal Lincoln 150–4, 155–6, 159–60, 165
Women's Christian Temperance Union (WCTU) 21–2, 148
Words to the Anzac Mothers 1, 205; origins of 200–3
Wright, Robert Alexander 112–13, 153

Yalçin, Hüseyin Cahit 49
Yeghiayan, Zaven Der 59
Yerevan 2, 118, 119, 148, 186, 206
Yessayan, Zabel 23, 32, 37–9, 41, 68–9, 135, 186
Yıldırım, Binali 192
Yılmaz, Mesut 188
Yohannan, Miriam 124, 128

Zeitun 56
Zeki Bey 85, 131
Zohrab, Krikor 23, 31, 33, 39, 47–8, 50–1; death of 69–70